Social Engineering
Advanced Topics in Computer Security

Contents

Chapter 1

Social engineering (security)

This article is about the information security concept. For influencing society on a large scale, see Social engineering (political science).

Social engineering, in the context of information secu-

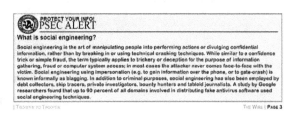

OPSEC alert

rity, refers to psychological manipulation of people into performing actions or divulging confidential information. A type of confidence trick for the purpose of information gathering, fraud, or system access, it differs from a traditional "con" in that it is often one of many steps in a more complex fraud scheme.

The term "social engineering" as an act of psychological manipulation is also associated with the social sciences, but its usage has caught on among computer and information security professionals.[1]

1.1 Techniques and terms

All social engineering techniques are based on specific attributes of human decision-making known as cognitive biases.[2] These biases, sometimes called "bugs in the human hardware", are exploited in various combinations to create attack techniques, some of which are listed. The attacks used in social engineering can be used to steal employees' confidential information. The most common type of social engineering happens over the phone. Other examples of social engineering attacks are criminals posing as exterminators, fire marshals and technicians to go unnoticed as they steal company secrets.

One example of social engineering is an individual who walks into a building and posts an official-looking announcement to the company bulletin that says the number for the help desk has changed. So, when employees call for help the individual asks them for their passwords and IDs thereby gaining the ability to access the company's private information. Another example of social engineering would be that the hacker contacts the target on a social networking site and starts a conversation with the target. Slowly and gradually, the hacker gains trust of the target and then uses it to get access to sensitive information like password or bank account details.[3]

1.1.1 Pretexting

Pretexting (adj. **pretextual**), also known in the UK as *blagging* or *bohoing*, is the act of creating and using an invented scenario (the pretext) to engage a targeted victim in a manner that increases the chance the victim will divulge information or perform actions that would be unlikely in ordinary circumstances.[4] An elaborate lie, it most often involves some prior research or setup and the use of this information for impersonation (*e.g.*, date of birth, Social Security number, last bill amount) to establish legitimacy in the mind of the target.[5]

This technique can be used to fool a business into disclosing customer information as well as by private investigators to obtain telephone records, utility records, banking records and other information directly from company service representatives.[6] The information can then be used to establish even greater legitimacy under tougher questioning with a manager, *e.g.*, to make account changes, get specific balances, etc.

Pretexting can also be used to impersonate co-workers, police, bank, tax authorities, clergy, insurance investigators — or any other individual who could have perceived authority or right-to-know in the mind of the targeted victim. The pretexter must simply prepare answers to questions that might be asked by the victim. In some cases, all that is needed is a voice that sounds authoritative, an earnest tone, and an ability to think on one's feet to create a pretextual scenario.

1.1.2   Diversion theft

Diversion theft, also known as the "Corner Game"[7] or "Round the Corner Game", originated in the East End of London.

In summary, diversion theft is a "con" exercised by professional thieves, normally against a transport or courier company. The objective is to persuade the persons responsible for a legitimate delivery that the consignment is requested elsewhere — hence, "round the corner".

1.1.3   Phishing

Main article: Phishing

Phishing is a technique of fraudulently obtaining private information. Typically, the phisher sends an e-mail that appears to come from a legitimate business—a bank, or credit card company—requesting "verification" of information and warning of some dire consequence if it is not provided. The e-mail usually contains a link to a fraudulent web page that seems legitimate—with company logos and content—and has a form requesting everything from a home address to an ATM card's PIN.

For example, 2003 saw the proliferation of a phishing scam in which users received e-mails supposedly from eBay claiming that the user's account was about to be suspended unless a link provided was clicked to update a credit card (information that the genuine eBay already had). Because it is relatively simple to make a Web site resemble a legitimate organization's site by mimicking the HTML code, the scam counted on people being tricked into thinking they were being contacted by eBay and subsequently, were going to eBay's site to update their account information. By spamming large groups of people, the "phisher" counted on the e-mail being read by a percentage of people who already had listed credit card numbers with eBay legitimately, who might respond.

IVR or phone phishing

Main article: Vishing

Phone phishing (or "vishing") uses a rogue interactive voice response (IVR) system to recreate a legitimate-sounding copy of a bank or other institution's IVR system. The vic-

tim is prompted (typically via a phishing e-mail) to call in to the "bank" via a (ideally toll free) number provided in order to "verify" information. A typical "vishing" system will reject log-ins continually, ensuring the victim enters PINs or passwords multiple times, often disclosing several different passwords. More advanced systems transfer the victim to the attacker, posing as a customer service agent for further questioning.

1.1.4   Baiting

Baiting is like the real-world Trojan Horse that uses physical media and relies on the curiosity or greed of the victim.[8]

In this attack, the attacker leaves a malware infected floppy disk, CD-ROM, or USB flash drive in a location sure to be found (bathroom, elevator, sidewalk, parking lot), gives it a legitimate looking and curiosity-piquing label, and simply waits for the victim to use the device.

For example, an attacker might create a disk featuring a corporate logo, readily available from the target's web site, and write "Executive Salary Summary Q2 2012" on the front. The attacker would then leave the disk on the floor of an elevator or somewhere in the lobby of the targeted company. An unknowing employee might find it and subsequently insert the disk into a computer to satisfy their curiosity, or a good samaritan might find it and turn it in to the company.

In either case, as a consequence of merely inserting the disk into a computer to see the contents, the user would unknowingly install malware on it, likely giving an attacker unfettered access to the victim's PC and, perhaps, the targeted company's internal computer network.

Unless computer controls block the infection, PCs set to "auto-run" inserted media may be compromised as soon as a rogue disk is inserted.

Hostile devices, more attractive than simple memory, can also be used.[9] For instance, a "lucky winner" is sent a free digital audio player that actually compromises any computer it is plugged to.

1.1.5   Quid pro quo

Quid pro quo means *something for something*:

- An attacker calls random numbers at a company, claiming to be calling back from technical support. Eventually this person will hit someone with a legitimate problem, grateful that someone is calling back to help them. The attacker will "help" solve the problem and, in the process, have the user type commands that give the attacker access or launch malware.

- In a 2003 information security survey, 90% of office workers gave researchers what they claimed was their password in answer to a survey question in exchange for a cheap pen.[10] Similar surveys in later years obtained similar results using chocolates and other cheap lures, although they made no attempt to validate the passwords.[11]

1.1.6 Tailgating

Main article: Piggybacking (security)

An attacker, seeking entry to a restricted area secured by unattended, electronic access control, e.g. by RFID card, simply walks in behind a person who has legitimate access. Following common courtesy, the legitimate person will usually hold the door open for the attacker or the attackers themselves may ask the employee to hold it open for them. The legitimate person may fail to ask for identification for any of several reasons, or may accept an assertion that the attacker has forgotten or lost the appropriate identity token. The attacker may also fake the action of presenting an identity token.

1.1.7 Other types

Common confidence tricksters or fraudsters also could be considered "social engineers" in the wider sense, in that they deliberately deceive and manipulate people, exploiting human weaknesses to obtain personal benefit. They may, for example, use social engineering techniques as part of an IT fraud.

A very recent type of social engineering technique includes spoofing or hacking IDs of people having popular e-mail IDs such as Yahoo!, Gmail, Hotmail, etc. Among the many motivations for deception are:

- Phishing credit-card account numbers and their passwords.

- Cracking private e-mails and chat histories, and manipulating them by using common editing techniques before using them to extort money and creating distrust among individuals.

- Cracking websites of companies or organizations and destroying their reputation.

- Computer virus hoaxes

- Convincing users to run malicious code within the web browser via self-XSS attack to allow access to their web account

1.1.8 Countermeasures

Organizations reduce their security risks by:

- Establishing frameworks of trust on an employee/personnel level (i.e., specify and train personnel when/where/why/how sensitive information should be handled)

- Identifying which information is sensitive and evaluating its exposure to social engineering and breakdowns in security systems (building, computer system, etc.)

- Establishing security protocols, policies, and procedures for handling sensitive information.

- Training employees in security protocols relevant to their position. (e.g., in situations such as tailgating, if a person's identity cannot be verified, then employees must be trained to politely refuse.)

- Performing unannounced, periodic tests of the security framework.

- Reviewing the above steps regularly: no solutions to information integrity are perfect.[12]

- Using a waste management service that has dumpsters with locks on them, with keys to them limited only to the waste management company and the cleaning staff. Locating the dumpster either in view of employees such that trying to access it carries a risk of being seen or caught or behind a locked gate or fence where the person must trespass before they can attempt to access the dumpster.[13]

1.2 Notable social engineers

1.2.1 Kevin Mitnick

Reformed computer criminal and later security consultant Kevin Mitnick points out that it is much easier to trick someone into giving a password for a system than to spend the effort to crack into the system.[14][15]

1.2.2 Christopher Hadnagy

Christopher Hadnagy is the security professional who wrote the first framework defining the physical and psychological principles of social engineering.[16] He is most widely known for his books, podcast and the being the creator of the DEF CON Social Engineer Capture the Flag and the Social Engineer CTF for Kids.[17]

1.2.3 Mike Ridpath

Mike Ridpath Security consultant, published author, and speaker. Emphasizes techniques and tactics for social engineering cold calling. Became notable after his talks where he would play recorded calls and explain his thought process on what he was doing to get passwords through the phone and his live demonstrations.[18][19][20][21][22] As a child Ridpath was connected with Badir Brothers and was widely known within the phreaking and hacking community for his articles with popular underground ezines, such as, Phrack, B4B0 and 9x on modifying Oki 900s, blueboxing, satellite hacking and RCMAC.[23][24]

1.2.4 Badir Brothers

Brothers Ramy, Muzher, and Shadde Badir—all of whom were blind from birth—managed to set up an extensive phone and computer fraud scheme in Israel in the 1990s using social engineering, voice impersonation, and Braille-display computers.[25][26]

1.2.5 Others

Other social engineers include Frank Abagnale, David Bannon, Peter Foster, Steven Jay Russell, Anonymous, SecTec.

1.3 Law

In common law, pretexting is an invasion of privacy tort of appropriation.[27]

1.3.1 Pretexting of telephone records

In December 2006, United States Congress approved a Senate sponsored bill making the pretexting of telephone records a federal felony with fines of up to $250,000 and ten years in prison for individuals (or fines of up to $500,000 for companies). It was signed by President George W. Bush on 12 January 2007.[28]

1.3.2 Federal legislation

The 1999 "GLBA" is a U.S. Federal law that specifically addresses pretexting of banking records as an illegal act punishable under federal statutes. When a business entity such as a private investigator, SIU insurance investigator, or an adjuster conducts any type of deception, it falls under the authority of the Federal Trade Commission (FTC).

This federal agency has the obligation and authority to ensure that consumers are not subjected to any unfair or deceptive business practices. US Federal Trade Commission Act, Section 5 of the FTCA states, in part: "Whenever the Commission shall have reason to believe that any such person, partnership, or corporation has been or is using any unfair method of competition or unfair or deceptive act or practice in or affecting commerce, and if it shall appear to the Commission that a proceeding by it in respect thereof would be to the interest of the public, it shall issue and serve upon such person, partnership, or corporation a complaint stating its charges in that respect."

The statute states that when someone obtains any personal, non-public information from a financial institution or the consumer, their action is subject to the statute. It relates to the consumer's relationship with the financial institution. For example, a pretexter using false pretenses either to get a consumer's address from the consumer's bank, or to get a consumer to disclose the name of his or her bank, would be covered. The determining principle is that pretexting only occurs when information is obtained through false pretenses.

While the sale of cell telephone records has gained significant media attention, and telecommunications records are the focus of the two bills currently before the United States Senate, many other types of private records are being bought and sold in the public market. Alongside many advertisements for cell phone records, wireline records and the records associated with calling cards are advertised. As individuals shift to VoIP telephones, it is safe to assume that those records will be offered for sale as well. Currently, it is legal to sell telephone records, but illegal to obtain them.[29]

1.3.3 1st Source Information Specialists

U.S. Rep. Fred Upton (R-Kalamazoo, Michigan), chairman of the Energy and Commerce Subcommittee on Telecommunications and the Internet, expressed concern over the easy access to personal mobile phone records on the Internet during Wednesday's E&C Committee hearing on "Phone Records For Sale: Why Aren't Phone Records Safe From Pretexting?" Illinois became the first state to sue an online records broker when Attorney General Lisa Madigan sued 1st Source Information Specialists, Inc., on 20 January, a spokeswoman for Madigan's office said. The Florida-based company operates several Web sites that sell mobile telephone records, according to a copy of the suit. The attorneys general of Florida and Missouri quickly followed Madigan's lead, filing suit on 24 and 30 January, respectively, against 1st Source Information Specialists and, in Missouri's case, one other records broker – First Data Solutions, Inc.

Several wireless providers, including T-Mobile, Verizon, and Cingular filed earlier lawsuits against records brokers, with Cingular winning an injunction against First Data Solutions and 1st Source Information Specialists on 13 January. U.S. Senator Charles Schumer (D-New York) introduced legislation in February 2006 aimed at curbing the practice. The Consumer Telephone Records Protection Act of 2006 would create felony criminal penalties for stealing and selling the records of mobile phone, landline, and Voice over Internet Protocol (VoIP) subscribers.

1.3.4 HP

Patricia Dunn, former chairwoman of Hewlett Packard, reported that the HP board hired a private investigation company to delve into who was responsible for leaks within the board. Dunn acknowledged that the company used the practice of pretexting to solicit the telephone records of board members and journalists. Chairman Dunn later apologized for this act and offered to step down from the board if it was desired by board members.[30] Unlike Federal law, California law specifically forbids such pretexting. The four felony charges brought on Dunn were dismissed.[31]

1.4 In popular culture

- In the movie *Identity Thief*, Melissa McCarthy used pretexting to get the name and other identifying information of Jason Bateman enabling her to steal his identity.

- In the film *Hackers*, the protagonist used pretexting when he asked a security guard for the telephone number to a TV station's modem while posing as an important executive.

- In Jeffrey Deaver's book *The Blue Nowhere*, social engineering to obtain confidential information is one of the methods used by the killer, Phate, to get close to his victims.

- In the movie *Die Hard 4.0*, Justin Long is seen pretexting that his father is dying from a heart attack to have an On-Star Assist representative start what will become a stolen car.

- In the movie *Sneakers*, one of the characters poses as a low level security guard's superior in order to convince him that a security breach is just a false alarm.

- In the movie *The Thomas Crown Affair*, one of the characters poses over the telephone as a museum guard's superior in order to move the guard away from his post.

- In the James Bond movie *Diamonds Are Forever*, Bond is seen gaining entry to the Whyte laboratory with a then-state-of-the-art card-access lock system by "tailgating". He merely waits for an employee to come to open the door, then posing himself as a rookie at the lab, fakes inserting a non-existent card while the door is unlocked for him by the employee.

- In the television show Rockford Files, The character Jim Rockford used pretexting often in his private investigation work.

- In the popular TV Show The Mentalist, protagonist Patrick Jane often uses pretexting to trick criminals into confessing to the crimes they committed.

- In the TV show Burn Notice, many characters are seen using social engineering; in Michael Westen's psych profile it is stated that he is very skilled in social engineering.

- In the TV show Psych, protagonist Shawn Spencer often uses pretexting to gain access to locations he would otherwise not be allowed into without police credentials.

- In the videogame Watch Dogs, protagonist Aiden Pearce states that he studied social engineering when growing up into a life of crime and uses social engineering tactics to manipulate other characters throughout the game to get the information he wants.

- In the TV show Mr. Robot, Darlene scatters USB flash drives (containing malware) outside a prison entrance, baiting a curious guard into compromising the prison's internal network when he plugs one of the drives into his computer workstation.

1.5 See also

- Confidence trick

- Countermeasure (computer)

- Certified Social Engineering Prevention Specialist (CSEPS)

- Cyber-HUMINT

- Cyberheist

- Internet Security Awareness Training

- IT risk

- Media pranks, which often use similar tactics (though usually not for criminal purposes)

- Penetration test

- Phishing

- Physical information security

- Piggybacking (security)

- SMiShing

- Threat (computer)

- Vishing

- Vulnerability (computing)

1.6   References

[1] Anderson, Ross J. (2008). *Security engineering: a guide to building dependable distributed systems* (2nd ed.). Indianapolis, IN: Wiley. p. 1040. ISBN 978-0-470-06852-6. Chapter 2, page 17

[2] Jaco, K: "CSEPS Course Workbook" (2004), unit 3, Jaco Security Publishing.

[3] "Hack a Facebook Account with Social Engineering (Easiest Way) ~ Amazing Hacking Tricks". *amazinghackingtricks.com.*

[4] The story of HP pretexting scandal with discussion is available at Davani, Faraz (14 August 2011). "HP Pretexting Scandal by Faraz Davani". Scribd. Retrieved 15 August 2011.

[5] "Pretexting: Your Personal Information Revealed", Federal Trade Commission

[6] Fagone, Jason. "The Serial Swatter". *New York Times.* Retrieved 25 November 2015.

[7] "Train For Life". Web.archive.org. 5 January 2010. Archived from the original on 5 January 2010. Retrieved 9 August 2012.

[8] "Social Engineering, the USB Way". Light Reading Inc. 7 June 2006. Archived from the original on 13 July 2006. Retrieved 23 April 2014.

[9] http://md.hudora.de/presentations/firewire/PacSec2004.pdf

[10] Leyden, John (18 April 2003). "Office workers give away passwords". Theregister.co.uk. Retrieved 11 April 2012.

[11] "Passwords revealed by sweet deal". BBC News. 20 April 2004. Retrieved 11 April 2012.

[12] Mitnick, K., & Simon, W. (2005). "The Art Of Intrusion". Indianapolis, IN: Wiley Publishing.

[13] Allsopp, William. Unauthorised access: Physical penetration testing for it security teams. Hoboken, NJ: Wiley, 2009. 240-241.

[14] Mitnick, K: "CSEPS Course Workbook" (2004), p. 4, Mitnick Security Publishing. A documentary based on Kevin Metnick "Freedom Downtime" was made featuring the real story of Kevin Metnick, featuring some real Hackers.

[15] *Social Hacking* (Thesis). Maxim Maximov, Ruslan Iskhakov. Retrieved 11 Feb 2003.

[16] "Social Engineering Framework". Social-engineer.org. 1 October 2010.

[17] *Social Hacking* (Thesis). Maxim Maximov, Ruslan Iskhakov. Retrieved 11 Feb 2003.

[18] *Social Engineering: Manipulating the human.* Scorpio Net Security Services. Retrieved 11 April 2012.

[19] "Mobile Devices and the Military: useful Tool or Significant Threat". academia.edu. Retrieved 11 May 2013.

[20] "Social Engineering: Manipulating the human". YouTube. Retrieved 11 April 2012.

[21] "BsidesPDX Track 1 10/07/11 02:52PM, BsidesPDX Track 1 10/07/11 02:52PM BsidesPDX on USTREAM. Conference". Ustream.tv. 7 October 2011. Retrieved 11 April 2012.

[22] "Automated Social Engineering". BrightTALK. 29 September 2011. Retrieved 11 April 2012.

[23] "Social Engineering a General Approach" (PDF). Informatica Economica journal. Retrieved 11 Jan 2015.

[24] *Social Hacking* (Thesis). Maxim Maximov, Ruslan Iskhakov. Retrieved 11 Feb 2003.

[25] "Wired 12.02: Three Blind Phreaks". Wired.com. 14 June 1999. Retrieved 11 April 2012.

[26] *Social Hacking* (Thesis). Maxim Maximov, Ruslan Iskhakov. Retrieved 11 Feb 2003.

[27] Restatement 2d of Torts § 652C.

[28] "Congress outlaws pretexting". *Ars Technica.*

[29] Mitnick, K (2002): "The Art of Deception", p. 103 Wiley Publishing Ltd: Indianapolis, Indiana; United States of America. ISBN 0-471-23712-4

[30] HP chairman: Use of pretexting 'embarrassing' Stephen Shankland, 2006-09-08 1:08 PM PDT *CNET News.com*

[31] "Calif. court drops charges against Dunn". News.cnet.com. 14 March 2007. Retrieved 11 April 2012.

1.7 Further reading

- Boyington, Gregory. (1990). 'Baa Baa Black Sheep' Published by Gregory Boyington ISBN 0-553-26350-1

- Harley, David. 1998 *Re-Floating the Titanic: Dealing with Social Engineering Attacks* EICAR Conference.

- Laribee, Lena. June 2006 *Development of methodical social engineering taxonomy project* Master's Thesis, Naval Postgraduate School.

- Leyden, John. 18 April 2003. *Office workers give away passwords for a cheap pen.* The Register. Retrieved 2004-09-09.

- Long, Johnny. (2008). *No Tech Hacking – A Guide to Social Engineering, Dumpster Diving, and Shoulder Surfing* Published by Syngress Publishing Inc. ISBN 978-1-59749-215-7

- Mann, Ian. (2008). *Hacking the Human: Social Engineering Techniques and Security Countermeasures* Published by Gower Publishing Ltd. ISBN 0-566-08773-1 or ISBN 978-0-566-08773-8

- Mitnick, Kevin, Kasperavičius, Alexis. (2004). *CSEPS Course Workbook.* Mitnick Security Publishing.

- Mitnick, Kevin, Simon, William L., Wozniak, Steve,. (2002). *The Art of Deception: Controlling the Human Element of Security* Published by Wiley. ISBN 0-471-23712-4 or ISBN 0-7645-4280-X

- Hadnagy, Christopher, (2011) *Social Engineering: The Art of Human Hacking* Published by Wiley. ISBN 0-470-63953-9

1.8 External links

- Social Engineering Fundamentals – *Securityfocus.com.* Retrieved on 3 August 2009.

- "Social Engineering, the USB Way". Light Reading Inc. 7 June 2006. Archived from the original on 13 July 2006. Retrieved 23 April 2014.

- Should Social Engineering be a part of Penetration Testing? – *Darknet.org.uk.* Retrieved on 3 August 2009.

- "Protecting Consumers' Phone Records", Electronic Privacy Information Center *US Committee on Commerce, Science, and Transportation* . Retrieved on 8 February 2006.

- Plotkin, Hal. Memo to the Press: Pretexting is Already Illegal. Retrieved on 9 September 2006.

- Striptease for passwords – *MSNBC.MSN.com.* Retrieved on 1 November 2007.

- Social-Engineer.org – *social-engineer.org.* Retrieved on 16 September 2009.

Chapter 2

419eater.com

419eater.com is a scam baiting website which focuses on advance-fee fraud. The name 419 comes from "419 fraud", another name for advance fee fraud, and itself derived from the relevant section of the Nigerian criminal code. The website founder, Michael Berry, goes by the alias Shiver Metimbers. As of 2013, the 419 Eater forum had over 55,000 registered accounts. According to one member, "Every minute the scammer I'm communicating with is spending on me is a minute he is not scamming a real potential victim."[1]

2.1 Concept

The website chronicles various reverse scams, known as "baits," with e-mail exchanges between the baiters and the scammers, and commentary by the participants. The site hosts photographs of individuals reported to be scammers in humorous poses, or holding signs such as "I recommend 419eater". These photographs, according to the members who post them, were in most cases obtained during the process of a bait: the baiter, posing as an actual victim, will request the photos from the scammer, who will comply in the belief that the "victim" is about to fall for the scam and send money.

In some cases, the scambaiter claims to have had the scammers send *them* money with a ploy similar to the original flim flam. This is known informally as cash baiting. According to Berry as documented in some of his successful cash baits, the proceeds of such reverse scams were given to a local charity. Now however, cash-baiting is frowned upon and is against 419eater.com rules which are rigorously enforced.

The website also includes a message forum and a bulletin board where scambaiters can post messages to communicate with each other. New scambaiters can request to be assigned a "mentor" to assist them in learning how to bait.

The 419eater community also engages in the activity of identifying and removing fake banks and other websites created by the scammers from the Internet, as well as shutting down bank accounts used by scammers in the process of their illegal scamming activities. It does this in cooperation with Artists Against 419 which host a large, publicly accessible database of fake banks and similar fraudulent websites.

During their baiting activities, experienced members may often gain information on victims of scams. This information is used constructively in the battle against the scammers.

2.2 Notable events in the timeline of the site

Berry was a featured guest on BBC Radio 2's *The Jeremy Vine Show* on 1 November 2006. Berry has also collected some of the scambaits shown on website, to a book *Greetings in Jesus' Name!: The Scambaiter Letters.*[2] In early 2008, Berry retired from active involvement in 419eater.com to concentrate on work and other projects,[3] handing control over to one of the site's long-running system administrators.

Beginning September 6, 2007,[4] the 419eater.com website—among other "scam warning" websites—was subjected to a massive botnet DDoS attack which rendered the site unreachable. However, by September 18, 2007, the site and forums were both back online.

419eater and its operatives was profiled on the September 9th, 2008 episode of Public Radio International's *This American Life*,[5] specifically one particular bait that ran for 100 days starting in April 2008 and involved sending a scammer named Adamu from Lagos, Nigeria to Abéché, Chad, a dangerous and politically unstable region.[6]

In January 2014, members of the scambaiting website 419eater.com appeared in two segments of the Channel 4 show "Secrets of the Scammers". In the first segment scambaiters persuaded a scammer to travel from London to a remote location in Cornwall by train and taxi to meet a victim (played by a baiter) and collect payment for a gold deal. In the second segment a female scammer met with two scambaiters posing as victims in Trafalgar Square to pass them a fake check. This scammer was subsequently questioned by the police.[7]

2.3 See also

- Scam baiting

- Advance fee fraud

2.4 References

[1]

[2] Berry, Mike (2006). *Greetings in Jesus' Name!: The Scambaiter Letters*. Harbour Books Ltd. ISBN 1-905128-08-8.

[3] "View Topic - *** Thanks For All The Fish, Jim Lad! ***". forum.419eater.com. Retrieved 2011-11-29.

[4] spamnation on September 6, 2007 06:43 AM (2007-09-06). "419Eater DDoS'd?". Spamnation.info. Retrieved 2011-11-29.

[5] "Enforcers". This American Life. Retrieved 2011-11-29.

[6] "Travel Warning - Chad". U.S. Department of State Bureau of Consular Affairs. June 2, 2009. Archived from the original on 27 August 2009. Retrieved August 26, 2009.

[7] Secrets of the Scammers on YouTube

2.5 External links

- 419eater.com (Mobile)

- The 419eater forum

- "Turning the tables on Nigeria's e-mail conmen", 13 July 2004, *BBC News*

- Greetings in Jesus Name!: The Scambaiter Letters

- "Pining for the frauds: scammers act up", February 20, 2007, *The Sydney Morning Herald*

- A Web Cadre Turns the Tables on African Scam Artists, *New York Times*

- Scam Baiting Technic

- Baiting Nigerian scammers for fun (not so much for profit)

Chapter 3

Clickjacking

Clickjacking (**User Interface redress attack**, **UI redress attack**, **UI redressing**) is a malicious technique of tricking a Web user into clicking on something different from what the user perceives they are clicking on, thus potentially revealing confidential information or taking control of their computer while clicking on seemingly innocuous web pages.[1][2][3][4] It is a browser security issue that is a vulnerability across a variety of browsers and platforms. A clickjack takes the form of embedded code or a script that can execute without the user's knowledge, such as clicking on a button that appears to perform another function.[5] The term "clickjacking" was coined by Jeremiah Grossman and Robert Hansen in 2008.[6] Clickjacking can be understood as an instance of the confused deputy problem, a term used to describe when a computer is innocently fooled into misusing its authority.[7]

"potential clickjacking" warning from the "NoScript" internet-browser addon

3.1 Description

Clickjacking is possible because seemingly harmless features of HTML web pages can be employed to perform unexpected actions.

A clickjacked page tricks a user into performing undesired actions by clicking on a concealed link. On a clickjacked page, the attackers load another page over it in a transparent layer. The users think that they are clicking visible buttons, while they are actually performing actions on the hidden/invisible page. The hidden page may be an authentic page; therefore, the attackers can trick users into performing actions which the users never intended. There is no way of tracing such actions to the attackers later, as the users would have been genuinely authenticated on the hidden page.

3.2 Examples

A user might receive an email with a link to a video about a news item, but another valid page, say a product page on Amazon.com, can be "hidden" on top or underneath the "PLAY" button of the news video. The user tries to "play" the video but actually "buys" the product from Amazon.

Other known exploits include:

- Tricking users into enabling their webcam and microphone through Flash (though this has since been fixed since originally reported)

- Tricking users into making their social networking profile information public

- Making users follow someone on Twitter[8]

- Sharing links on Facebook[9][10]

- Getting likes on Facebook fan page

- Making illegal revenue from Google Adsense program

While technical implementation of these attacks may be challenging due to cross-browser incompatibilities, a number of tools such as BeEF or Metasploit Project offer almost fully automated exploitation of clients on vulnerable websites. Clickjacking may be facilitated by - or may facilitate - other web attacks, such as XSS.[11][12]

3.2.1 Likejacking

Likejacking is a malicious technique of tricking users of a website into posting a Facebook status update for a site they did not intentionally mean to "like".[13] The term "likejacking" came from a comment posted by Corey Ballou in the article *How to "Like" Anything on the Web (Safely)*,[14] which is one of the first documented postings explaining the possibility of malicious activity regarding Facebook's "like" button.[15]

According to an article in *IEEE Spectrum*, a solution to likejacking was developed at one of Facebook's hackathons.[16] A "Like" bookmarklet is available that avoids the possibility of likejacking present in the Facebook Like Button.[17]

3.2.2 Cursorjacking

Cursorjacking is a UI redressing technique to change the cursor from the location the user perceives, discovered in 2010 by Eddy Bordi, a researcher at Vulnerability.fr, Marcus Niemietz demonstrated this with a custom cursor icon, and in 2012 Mario Heiderich by hiding the cursor.[18][19]

Jordi Chancel, a researcher at Alternativ-Testing.fr, discovered a cursorjacking vulnerability using Flash, HTML and JavaScript code in Mozilla Firefox on Mac OS X systems (fixed in Firefox 30.0) which can lead to arbitrary code execution and webcam spying.[20]

A second CursorJacking vulnerability was again discovered by Jordi Chancel in Mozilla Firefox on Mac OS X systems (fixed in Firefox 37.0) using once again Flash, HTML and JavaScript code which can lead also to the spying of the webcam and the execution of a malicious addon allowing the execution of a malware on the computer of the trapped user.[21]

3.2.3 Password manager attack

A 2014 paper from researcher at the Carnegie Mellon University found that whilst browsers refuse to autofill if the protocol on the current login page is different from the protocol at the time the password was saved, some password managers would insecurely fill in passwords for the http version of https-saved passwords. Most managers did not pro-

tect against iFrame and redirection based attacks and exposed additional passwords where password synchronization had been used between multiple devices.[22]

3.3 Prevention

3.3.1 Client-side

NoScript

Protection against clickjacking (including likejacking) can be added to Mozilla Firefox desktop and mobile[23] versions by installing the NoScript add-on: its ClearClick feature, released on 8 October 2008, prevents users from clicking on invisible or "redressed" page elements of embedded documents or applets.[24] According to Google's "Browser Security Handbook" from year 2008, NoScript's ClearClick is "the only freely available product that offers a reasonable degree of protection" against Clickjacking.[25] Protection from the newer cursorjacking attack was added to NoScript 2.2.8 RC1.[18]

GuardedID

GuardedID (a commercial product) includes client-side clickjack protection for users of Internet Explorer and Firefox[26] without interfering with the operation of legitimate iFrames. GuardedID clickjack protection forces all frames to become visible.

Gazelle

Gazelle is a Microsoft Research project secure web browser based on IE, that uses an OS-like security model, and has its own limited defenses against clickjacking.[27] In Gazelle, a window of different origin may only draw dynamic content over another window's screen space if the content it draws is opaque.

3.3.2 Server-side

Framekiller

Web site owners can protect their users against UI redressing (frame based clickjacking) on the server side by including a framekiller JavaScript snippet in those pages they do not want to be included inside frames from different sources.[25]

Such JavaScript-based protection, unfortunately, is not always reliable. This is especially true on Internet

Explorer,[25] where this kind of countermeasure can be circumvented "by design" by including the targeted page inside an <IFRAME SECURITY=restricted> element.[28]

X-Frame-Options

Introduced in 2009 in Internet Explorer 8 was a new HTTP header X-Frame-Options which offered a partial protection against clickjacking[29][30] and was shortly after adopted by other browsers (Safari,[31] Firefox,[32] Chrome,[33] and Opera[34]). The header, when set by website owner, declares its preferred framing policy: values of DENY, SAMEORIGIN, or ALLOW-FROM *origin* will prevent any framing, framing by external sites, or allow framing only by the specified site, respectively. In addition to that, some advertising sites return a non-standard ALLOWALL value with the intention to allow framing their content on any page (equivalent of not setting X-Frame-Options at all).

In 2013 the X-Frame-Options header has been officially published as RFC 7034,[35] but is not an internet standard. The document is provided for informational purposes only.

Content Security Policy

The frame-ancestors directive of Content Security Policy (introduced in version 1.1) can allow or disallow embedding of content by potentially hostile pages using iframe, object, etc. This directive obsoletes the X-Frame-Options directive. If a page is served with both headers, the frame-ancestors policy should be preferred by the browser.[36]—although some popular browsers disobey this requirement.[37]

Example frame-ancestors policies:

Disallow embedding. All iframes etc. will be blank, or contain a browser specific error page. Content-Security-Policy: frame-ancestors 'none' # Allow embedding of [[same-origin policy|own content]] only. Content-Security-Policy: frame-ancestors 'self' # Allow specific origins to embed this content Content-Security-Policy: frame-ancestors example.com wikipedia.org

3.4   See also

- Browser security

- Internet security

- Internet safety

- Hacker (computer security)

- Cross-site scripting

- Phishing

- Ghostery

- Social jacking

3.5   References

[1] Robert McMillan (17 September 2008). "At Adobe's request, hackers nix 'clickjacking' talk". PC World. Retrieved 2008-10-08.

[2] Megha Dhawan (29 September 2008). "Beware, clickjackers on the prowl". India Times. Retrieved 2008-10-08.

[3] Dan Goodin (7 October 2008). "Net game turns PC into undercover surveillance zombie". *The Register*. Retrieved 2008-10-08.

[4] Fredrick Lane (8 October 2008). "Web Surfers Face Dangerous New Threat: 'Clickjacking'". newsfactor.com. Archived from the original on 13 October 2008. Retrieved 2008-10-08.

[5] Sumner Lemon (30 September 2008). "Business Center: Clickjacking Vulnerability to Be Revealed Next Month". Retrieved 2008-10-08.

[6] You don't know (click)jack Robert Lemos, October 2008

[7] The Confused Deputy rides again!, Tyler Close, October 2008

[8] Daniel Sandler (12 February 2009). "Twitter's "Don't Click" prank, explained (dsandler.org)". Retrieved 2009-12-28.

[9] Krzysztof Kotowicz (21 December 2009). "New Facebook clickjacking attack in the wild". Retrieved 2009-12-29.

[10] BBC (3 June 2010). "Facebook "clickjacking" spreads across site". *BBC News*. Retrieved 2010-06-03.

[11] "The Clickjacking meets XSS: a state of art". Exploit DB. 2008-12-26. Retrieved 2015-03-31.

[12] Krzysztof Kotowicz. "Exploiting the unexploitable XSS with clickjacking". Retrieved 2015-03-31.

[13] Cohen, Richard (31 May 2010). "Facebook Work - "Likejacking"". Sophos. Retrieved 2010-06-05.

[14] Ballou, Corey (2 June 2010). ""Likejacking" Term Catches On". jqueryin.com. Retrieved 2010-06-08.

[15] Perez, Sarah (2 June 2010). ""Likejacking" Takes Off on Facebook". ReadWriteWeb. Retrieved 2010-06-05.

[16] Kushner, David (June 2011). "Facebook Philosophy: Move Fast and Break Things". spectrum.ieee.org. Retrieved 2011-07-15.

[17] Perez, Sarah (23 April 2010). "How to "Like" Anything on the Web (Safely)". *ReadWriteWeb*. Retrieved 24 August 2011.

[18] Krzysztof Kotowicz (18 January 2012). "Cursorjacking Again". Retrieved 2012-01-31.

[19] Aspect Security. "Cursor-jacking attack could result in application security breaches". Retrieved 2012-01-31.

[20] "Mozilla Foundation Security Advisory 2014-50". Mozilla. Retrieved 17 August 2014.

[21] "Mozilla Foundation Security Advisory 2015-35". Mozilla. Retrieved 25 October 2015.

[22] "Password Managers: Attacks and Defenses" (PDF). Retrieved 26 July 2015.

[23] Giorgio Maone (24 June 2011). "NoScript Anywhere". hackademix.net. Retrieved 2011-06-30.

[24] Giorgio Maone (8 October 2008). "Hello ClearClick, Goodbye Clickjacking". hackademix.net. Retrieved 2008-10-27.

[25] Michal Zalevski (10 December 2008). "Browser Security Handbook, Part 2, UI Redressing". Google Inc. Retrieved 2008-10-27.

[26] Robert Hansen (4 February 2009). "Clickjacking and GuardedID ha.ckers.org web application security lab". Retrieved 2011-11-30.

[27] Wang, Helen J.; Grier, Chris; Moschchuk, Alexander; King, Samuel T.; Choudhury, Piali; Venter, Herman (August 2009). "The Multi-Principal OS Construction of the Gazelle Web Browser" (PDF). 18th Usenix Security Symposium, Montreal, Canada. Retrieved 2010-01-26.

[28] Giorgio Maone (27 October 2008). "Hey IE8, I Can Has Some Clickjacking Protection". hackademix.net. Retrieved 2008-10-27.

[29] Eric Lawrence (27 January 2009). "IE8 Security Part VII: ClickJacking Defenses". Retrieved 2010-12-30.

[30] Eric Lawrence (30 March 2010). "Combating ClickJacking With X-Frame-Options". Retrieved 2010-12-30.

[31] Ryan Naraine (8 June 2009). "Apple Safari jumbo patch: 50+ vulnerabilities fixed". Retrieved 2009-06-10.

[32] https://developer.mozilla.org/en/The_ X-FRAME-OPTIONS_response_header The X-Frame-Options response header — MDC

[33] Adam Barth (26 January 2010). "Security in Depth: New Security Features". Retrieved 2010-01-26.

[34] "Web specifications support in Opera Presto 2.6". 12 October 2010. Retrieved 2012-01-22.

[35] "HTTP Header Field X-Frame-Options". IETF. 2013.

[36] "Content Security Policy Level 2". *w3.org*. 2014-07-02. Retrieved 2015-01-29.

[37] "Clickjacking Defense Cheat Sheet". Retrieved 2016-01-15.

3.6 External links

- Original paper on clickjacking

Chapter 4

Cyber spying

Cyber spying, or **cyber espionage**, is the act or practice of obtaining secrets without the permission of the holder of the information (personal, sensitive, proprietary or of classified nature), from individuals, competitors, rivals, groups, governments and enemies for personal, economic, political or military advantage using methods on the Internet, networks or individual computers through the use of cracking techniques and malicious software including Trojan horses and spyware.[1][2] It may wholly be perpetrated online from computer desks of professionals on bases in far away countries or may involve infiltration at home by computer trained conventional spies and moles or in other cases may be the criminal handiwork of amateur malicious hackers and software programmers.[1]

Cyber spying typically involves the use of such access to secrets and classified information or control of individual computers or whole networks for a strategic advantage and for psychological, political and physical subversion activities and sabotage.[3] More recently, cyber spying involves analysis of public activity on social networking sites like Facebook and Twitter.[4]

Such operations, like non-cyber espionage, are typically illegal in the victim country while fully supported by the highest level of government in the aggressor country. The ethical situation likewise depends on one's viewpoint, particularly one's opinion of the governments involved.[3]

In response to reports of cyber spying by China against the United States, Amitai Etzioni of the Institute for Communitarian Policy Studies has suggested that China and the United States should agree to a policy of mutually assured restraint with respect to cyberspace. This would involve allowing both states to take the measures they deem necessary for their self-defense while simultaneously agreeing to refrain from taking offensive steps or engaging in cyber espionage; it would also entail vetting these commitments.[5] In September 2015, the United States and China agreed not to allow parties in their nations to cyberspy on each other for commercial gain, but did not prohibit government spying.[6]

4.1 See also

- Cyber-collection

- Cyberwarfare

- Computer surveillance

- Computer insecurity

- Chinese intelligence operations in the United States

- Cyber-security regulation

- Employee monitoring software

- Industrial espionage

- GhostNet

- Proactive Cyber Defence

- Surveillance

- Chaos Computer Club

- Titan Rain

- the Dukes, a well-resourced, highly dedicated and organized cyberespionage group that F-Secure believe has been working for the Russian Federation since at least 2008.[7][8][9]

4.2 References

[1] "Cyber Espionage". PC Magazine.

[2] "Cyberspying". Techopedia.

[3] Messmer, Ellen. "Cyber Espionage: A Growing Threat to Business". Retrieved Jan 21, 2008.

[4] Five ways the government spies on you

[5] Etzioni, Amitai, "MAR: A Model for US-China Relations," The Diplomat, September 20, 2013, .

[6] Joseph Steinberg (September 27, 2015). "Why the China-US CyberSecurity Agreement Will Fail". *Inc.* Retrieved September 27, 2015.

[7] the Dukes, timeline

[8] The Dukes Whitepaper

[9] 17 September 2015, F-Secure Labs links nearly a decade of state-sponsored cyberattacks to a group of hackers backed by Russia.

4.3 Sources

- Bill Schiller, Asia Bureau (Apr 1, 2009), "Chinese ridicule U of T spy report - But government officials choose words carefully, never denying country engages in cyber-espionage", *Toronto Star (Canada)* (Toronto, Ontario, Canada), retrieved 2009-04-04

- Kelly, Cathal (Mar 31, 2009), "Cyberspies' code a click away - Simple Google search quickly finds link to software for Ghost Rat program used to target governments", *Toronto Star (Canada)* (Toronto, Ontario, Canada), retrieved 2009-04-04

- *All about Chinese cyber spying*, infotech.indiatimes.com (Times of India), March 30, 2009, retrieved 2009-04-01

- Cooper, Alex (March 30, 2009), "We can lead in cyber spy war, sleuth says; Toronto investigator helped expose hacking of embassies, NATO", *Toronto Star (Canada)* (Toronto, Ontario, Canada), retrieved 2009-03-31

- *Chinese-based cyber spy network exposes need for better security: Cdn researchers*, Yahoo News Canada, March 30, 2009, retrieved 2009-03-31

- Steve Herman (30 March 2009), *Exiled Tibetan Government Expresses Concern over Cyber-Spying Traced to China*, New Delhi: GlobalSecurity.org, retrieved 2009-03-31

- "Chinese government accused of cyber spying", *Belfast Telegraph*, 30 March 2009

- Patrick Goodenough, International Editor (March 30, 2009), *China Rejects Cyber Spying Allegations; 'Dalai Lama Propaganda'*, CNSNews.com, retrieved 2009-03-31

- Harvey, Mike (March 29, 2009), "'World's biggest cyber spy network' snoops on classified documents in 103 countries", *The Times* (London), retrieved 2009-03-30

- *Major cyber spy network uncovered*, BBC News, 29 March 2009, retrieved 2009-03-30

- *SciTech Cyber spy network 'smoking gun' for China: expert*, CTV Canada, March 29, 2009, retrieved 2009-03-30

- Kim Covert (March 28, 2009), "Canadian researchers uncover vast Chinese cyber spy network", *National Post, Don Mills, Ontario, Canada* (Canwest News Service)

- *US warned of China 'cyber-spying'*, BBC News, 20 November 2008, retrieved 2009-04-01

- Mark Hosenball (June 2, 2008), "Intelligence - Cyber-Spying for Dummies", *Newsweek*

- Walton, Gregory (April 2008). "Year of the Gh0st RAT". World Association of Newspapers. Retrieved 2009-04-01.

- *German court limits cyber spying*, BBC News, 27 February 2008

- Rowan Callick; Jane Macartney (December 7, 2007), "Chinese fury at cyber spy claims", *The Australian*

4.4 External links

- Congress to Investigate Google Charges Of Chinese Internet Spying (AHN)

- Information Warfare Monitor - Tracking Cyberpower (University of Toronto, Canada/Munk Centre)

Chapter 5

Cyber-collection

Cyber-collection refers to the use of cyber-warfare techniques in order to conduct espionage. Cyber-collection activities typically rely on the insertion of malware into a targeted network or computer in order to scan for, collect and exfiltrate sensitive information.

Cyber-collection started as far back as 1996, when widespread deployment of Internet connectivity to government and corporate systems gained momentum. Since that time, there have been numerous cases of such activity.[1][2][3]

In addition to the state sponsored examples, cyber-collection has also been used by organized crime for identity and e-banking theft and by corporate spies. Operation High Roller used cyber-collection agents in order to collect PC and smart-phone information that was used to electronically raid bank accounts.[4] The Rocra, aka Red October, collection system is an "espionage for hire" operation by organized criminals who sell the collected information to the highest bidder.[5][6]

5.1 Platforms and Functionality

Cyber-collection tools have been developed by governments and private interests for nearly every computer and smart-phone operating system. Tools are known to exist for Microsoft, Apple, and Linux computers and iPhone, Android, Blackberry, and Windows phones.[7] Major manufacturers of Commercial off-the-shelf (COTS) cyber collection technology include Gamma Group from the UK[8] and Hacking Team from Italy.[9] Bespoke cyber-collection tool companies, many offering COTS packages of zero-day exploits, include Endgame, Inc. and Netragard of the United States and Vupen from France.[10] State intelligence agencies often have their own teams to develop cyber-collection tools, such as Stuxnet, but require a constant source of *zero-day exploits* in order to insert their tools into newly targeted systems. Specific technical details of these attack methods often sells for six figure sums.[11]

Common functionality of cyber-collection systems include:

- *Data scan*: local and network storage are scanned to find and copy files of interest, these are often documents, spreadsheets, design files such as Autocad files and system files such as the passwd file.

- *Capture location*: GPS, WiFi, network information and other attached sensors are used to determine the location and movement of the infiltrated device

- *Bug*: the device microphone can be activated in order to record audio. Likewise, audio streams intended for the local speakers can be intercepted at the device level and recorded.

- *Hidden Private Networks* that bypass the corporate network security. A compute that is being spied upon can be plugged into a legitimate corporate network that is heavy monitored for malware activity and at same time belongs to a private wifi network outside of the company network that is leaking confidential information off of an employee's computer. A computer like this is easily set up by a double-agent working in the IT department by install a second Wireless card in a computer and special software to remotely monitor an employee's computer through this second interface card without them being aware of a side-band communication channel pulling information off of his computer.

- *Camera*: the device cameras can be activated in order to covertly capture images or video.

- *Keylogger and Mouse Logger*: the malware agent can capture each keystroke, mouse movement and click that the target user makes. Combined with screen grabs, this can be used to obtain passwords that are entered using a virtual on-screen keyboard.

- *Screen Grabber*: the malware agent can take periodic screen capture images. In addition to showing sensitive information that may not be stored on the machine, such as e-banking balances and encrypted web mail, these can be used in combination with the key and mouse logger data to determine access credentials for other Internet resources.

- *Encryption*: Collected data is usually encrypted at the time of capture and may be transmitted live or stored for later exfiltration. Likewise, it is common practice for each specific operation to use specific encryption and poly-morphic capabilities of the cyber-collection agent in order to ensure that detection in one location will not compromise others.

- *Bypass Encryption*: Because the malware agent operates on the target system with all the access and rights of the user account of the target or system administrator, encryption is bypassed. For example, interception of audio using the microphone and audio output devices enables the malware to capture to both sides of an encrypted Skype call.[12]

- *Exfiltration*: Cyber-collection agents usually exfiltrate the captured data in a discrete manner, often waiting for high web traffic and disguising the transmission as secure web browsing. USB flash drives have been used to exfiltrate information from air gap protected systems. Exfiltration systems often involve the use of reverse proxy systems that anonymize the receiver of the data.[13]

- *Replicate*: Agents may replicate themselves onto other media or systems, for example an agent may infect files on a writable network share or install themselves onto USB drives in order to infect computers protected by an air gap or otherwise not on the same network.

- *Manipulate Files and File Maintenance*: Malware can be used to erase traces of itself from log files. It can also download and install modules or updates as well as data files. This function may also be used to place "evidence" on the target system, e.g. to insert child pornography onto the computer of a politician or to manipulate votes on an electronic vote counting machine.

- *Combination Rules*: Some agents are very complex and are able to combine the above features in order to provide very targeted intelligence collection capabilities. For example, the use of GPS bounding boxes and microphone activity can be used to turn a smart phone into a smart bug that intercepts conversations only within the office of a target.

- *Compromised cellphones*. Since, modern cellphones are increasingly similar to general purpose computer, these cellphones are vulnerable to the same cyber-collect attacks as computer systems, and are vulnerable to leak extremely sensitive conversational and lo-

cation information to an attackers.[14] Leaking of cellphone GPS location and conversational information to an attacker has been reported in a number of recent cyber stalking cases where the attacker was able to use the victim's GPS location to call nearby businesses and police authorities to make false allegations against the victim depending on his location, this can range from telling the restaurant staff information to tease the victim, or making false witness against the victim. For instance if the victim were parked in large parking lot the attackers may call and state that they saw drug or violence activity going on with a description of the victim and directions to their GPS location.

5.2 Infiltration

There are several common ways to infect or access the target:

- An *Injection Proxy* is a system that is placed upstream from the target individual or company, usually at the Internet service provider, that injects malware into the targets system. For example, an innocent download made by the user can be injected with the malware executable on the fly so that the target system then is accessible to the government agents.[15]

- *Spear Phishing*: A carefully crafted e-mail is sent to the target in order to entice them to install the malware via a Trojan document or a drive by attack hosted on a web server compromised or controlled by the malware owner.[16]

- *Surreptitious Entry* may be used to infect a system. In other words, the spies carefully break into the target's residence or office and install the malware on the target's system.[17]

- An *Upstream monitor* or *sniffer* is a device that can intercept and view the data transmitted by a target system. Usually this device is placed at the Internet service provider. The Carnivore system developed by the U.S. FBI is a famous example of this type of system. Based on the same logic as a telephone intercept, this type of system is of limited use today due to the widespread use of encryption during data transmission.

- A *wireless infiltration* system can be used in proximity of the target when the target is using wireless technology. This is usually a laptop based system that impersonates a WiFi or 3G base station to capture the target systems and relay requests upstream to the Internet. Once the target systems are on the network, the system then functions as an *Injection Proxy* or as an *Upstream Monitor* in order to infiltrate or monitor the target system.

- A *USB Key* preloaded with the malware infector may be given to or dropped at the target site.

Cyber-collection agents are usually installed by payload delivery software constructed using zero-day attacks and delivered via infected USB drives, e-mail attachments or malicious web sites.[13][18] State sponsored cyber-collections efforts have used official operating system certificates in place of relying on security vulnerabilities. In the Flame operation, Microsoft states that the Microsoft certificate used to impersonate a Windows Update was forged;[19] however, some experts believe that it may have been acquired through HUMINT efforts.[20]

5.3 Examples of Cyber-Collection Operations

- Stuxnet
- Flame
- Duqu
- Bundestrojaner
- Rocra[21][22]
- Operation High Roller[23]

5.4 References

[1] Pete Warren, *State-sponsored cyber espionage projects now prevalent, say experts,*, The Guardian, August 30, 2012

[2] Nicole Perlroth, *Elusive FinSpy Spyware Pops Up in 10 Countries,*, New York Times, August 13, 2012

[3] Kevin G. Coleman, *Has Stuxnet, Duqu and Flame Ignited a Cyber Arms Race?,*, AOL Government, July 2, 2012

[4] Rachael King, *Operation High Roller Targets Corporate Bank Accounts,*, June 26, 2012

[5] Frederic Lardinois, *Eugene Kaspersky And Mikko Hypponen Talk Red October And The Future Of Cyber Warfare At DLD,*, TechCrunch, January 21, 2013

[6] Mark Prigg, *The hunt for Red October: The astonishing hacking ring that has infiltrated over 1,000 high level government computers around the world,*, Daily Mail, January 16, 2013

[7] Vernon Silver, *Spyware Matching FinFisher Can Take Over IPhones,* , Bloomberg, August 29, 2012

[8] FinFisher IT Intrusion

[9] Hacking Team, Remote Control System

[10] Mathew J. Schwartz, *Weaponized Bugs: Time For Digital Arms Control,* , Information Week, 9 October 2012

[11] Ryan Gallagher, *Cyberwar's Gray Market,* , Slate, 16 Jan 2013

[12] Daniele Milan, The Data Encryption Problem,, Hacking Team

[13] Robert Lemos, *Flame stashes secrets in USB drives,*, InfoWorld, June 13, 2012

[14] how to spy on a cell phone without having access

[15] Pascal Gloor, *(Un)lawful Interception,*, SwiNOG #25, 07 November 2012

[16] Mathew J. Schwartz, *Operation Red October Attackers Wielded Spear Phishing,*, Information Week, January 16, 2013

[17] FBI Records: The Vault, *Surreptitious Entries,*, Federal Bureau of Investigation

[18] Anne Belle de Bruijn, *Cybercriminelen doen poging tot spionage bij DSM,*, Elsevier, July 9, 2012

[19] Mike Lennon, *Microsoft Certificate Was Used to Sign "Flame" Malware,*, June 4, 2012

[20] Paul Wagenseil, *Flame Malware Uses Stolen Microsoft Digital Signature,*, NBC News, June 4, 2012

[21] *"Red October" Diplomatic Cyber Attacks Investigation,*, Securelist, January 14, 2013

[22] *Kapersky Lab Identifieds Operation Red October,*, Kapersky Lab Press Release, January 14, 2013

[23] Dave Marcus & Ryan Cherstobitoff, *Dissecting Operation High Roller,*, McAfee Labs

5.5 See also

- Cyberwarfare
- Computer surveillance
- Computer insecurity
- Chinese intelligence operations in the United States
- Cyber-security regulation
- Industrial espionage
- GhostNet
- Proactive Cyber Defence

- Surveillance
- Chaos Computer Club

Chapter 6

Cyberwarfare

"Cyberwar" redirects here. For the video game, see Cyberwar (video game). For the 2004 movie also known as Cyber Wars, see Avatar (2004 film).

Not to be confused with Electronic warfare or software wars.

Cyberwarfare has been defined as "actions by a nation-state to penetrate another nation's computers or networks for the purposes of causing damage or disruption,"[1]:6 but other definitions also include non-state actors, such as terrorist groups, companies, political or ideological extremist groups, hacktivists, and transnational criminal organizations.[2][3][4][5][6]

Some governments have made it an integral part of their overall military strategy, with some having invested heavily in cyberwarfare capability.[7][8][9][10]

6.1 Types of threat

Cyberattacks, where damage or disruption is caused are the main concern.[11]

Cyber espionage, which can provide the information needed to launch a successful attack.

6.1.1 Espionage

Traditional espionage is not an act of war, nor is cyber-espionage,[12] and both are generally assumed to be ongoing between major powers.

Despite this assumption, some incidents can cause serious tensions between nations, and are often described as "attacks". For example:

- Massive spying by the US on many countries, revealed by Edward Snowden.

- After the NSA's spying on Germany's Chancellor

Angela Merkel was revealed the Chancellor compared the NSA with the Stasi.[13]

- NSA recording nearly every cell phone conversation in the Bahamas without the Bahamian government's permission,[14] and similar programes in Kenya, the Philippines, Mexico and Afghanistan.[15]

- The "Titan Rain" probes of American defence contractors computer systems since 2003.[16]

- The Office of Personnel Management data breach, in the US, widely attributed to China.[17][18]

6.1.2 Sabotage

Computers and satellites that coordinate other activities are vulnerable components of a system and could lead to the disruption of equipment. Compromise of military systems, such as C4ISTAR components that are responsible for orders and communications could lead to their interception or malicious replacement. Power, water, fuel, communications, and transportation infrastructure all may be vulnerable to disruption. According to Clarke, the civilian realm is also at risk, noting that the security breaches have already gone beyond stolen credit card numbers, and that potential targets can also include the electric power grid, trains, or the stock market.[19]

In mid July 2010, security experts discovered a malicious software program called Stuxnet that had infiltrated factory computers and had spread to plants around the world. It is considered "the first attack on critical industrial infrastructure that sits at the foundation of modern economies," notes *The New York Times*.[20]

Denial-of-service attack

Main article: Denial-of-service attack

In computing, a denial-of-service attack (DoS attack) or distributed denial-of-service attack (DDoS attack) is an attempt to make a machine or network resource unavailable to its intended users. Perpetrators of DoS attacks typically target sites or services hosted on high-profile web servers such as banks, credit card payment gateways, and even root nameservers. DoS attacks may not be limited to computer-based methods, as strategic physical attacks against infrastructure can be just as devastating. For example, cutting undersea communication cables may severely cripple some regions and countries with regards to their information warfare ability.

Electrical power grid

The federal government of the United States admits that the electric power grid is susceptible to cyberwarfare.[21][22] The United States Department of Homeland Security works with industry to identify vulnerabilities and to help industry enhance the security of control system networks, the federal government is also working to ensure that security is built in as the next generation of "smart grid" networks are developed.[23] In April 2009, reports surfaced that China and Russia had infiltrated the U.S. electrical grid and left behind software programs that could be used to disrupt the system, according to current and former national security officials.[24] The North American Electric Reliability Corporation (NERC) has issued a public notice that warns that the electrical grid is not adequately protected from cyber attack.[25] China denies intruding into the U.S. electrical grid.[26][27] One countermeasure would be to disconnect the power grid from the Internet and run the net with droop speed control only.[28][29] Massive power outages caused by a cyber attack could disrupt the economy, distract from a simultaneous military attack, or create a national trauma.

Howard Schmidt, former Cyber-Security Coordinator of the US, commented on those possibilities:[30]

> It's possible that hackers have gotten into administrative computer systems of utility companies, but says those aren't linked to the equipment controlling the grid, at least not in developed countries. [Schmidt] has never heard that the grid itself has been hacked.

6.2 Motivations

6.2.1 Military

In the U.S., General Keith B. Alexander, first head of the recently formed USCYBERCOM, told the Senate Armed Services Committee that computer network warfare is evolving so rapidly that there is a "mismatch between our technical capabilities to conduct operations and the governing laws and policies. Cyber Command is the newest global combatant and its sole mission is cyberspace, outside the traditional battlefields of land, sea, air and space." It will attempt to find and, when necessary, neutralize cyberattacks and to defend military computer networks.[31]

Alexander sketched out the broad battlefield envisioned for the computer warfare command, listing the kind of targets that his new headquarters could be ordered to attack, including "traditional battlefield prizes – command-and-control systems at military headquarters, air defense networks and weapons systems that require computers to operate."[31]

One cyber warfare scenario, Cyber ShockWave, which was wargamed on the cabinet level by former administration officials, raised issues ranging from the National Guard to the power grid to the limits of statutory authority.[32][33][34][35]

The distributed nature of internet based attacks means that it is difficult to determine motivation and attacking party, meaning that it is unclear when a specific act should be considered an act of war.[36]

Examples of cyberwarfare driven by political motivations can be found worldwide. In 2008, Russia began a cyber attack on the Georgian government website, which was carried out along with Georgian military operations in South Ossetia. In 2008, Chinese 'nationalist hackers' attacked CNN as it reported on Chinese repression on Tibet.[37]

Jobs in cyberwarfare have become increasingly popular in the military. The United States Navy actively recruits for cyber warfare engineers.[38] The US Army has their Cyber Command where they actively recruit for cryptologic network warfare specialists.

6.2.2 Civil

Potential targets in internet sabotage include all aspects of the Internet from the backbones of the web, to the Internet Service Providers, to the varying types of data communication mediums and network equipment. This would include: web servers, enterprise information systems, client server systems, communication links, network equipment, and the desktops and laptops in businesses and homes. Electrical grids and telecommunication systems are also deemed vulnerable, especially due to current trends in automation.

6.2.3 Hacktivism

Politically motivated hacktivism, involves the subversive use of computers and computer networks to promote an agenda, and can potential extend to attacks, theft and virtual sabotage that could be seen as cyberwarfare - or mistaken for it.[39]

6.2.4 Private sector

Computer hacking represents a modern threat in ongoing industrial espionage and as such is presumed to widely occur. It is typical that this type of crime is underreported. According to McAfee's George Kurtz, corporations around the world face millions of cyberattacks a day. "Most of these attacks don't gain any media attention or lead to strong political statements by victims."[40] This type of crime is usually financially motivated.

6.2.5 Non-profit research

But not all examinations with the issue of cyberwarfare are achieving profit or personal gain. There are still institutes and companies like the University of Cincinnati or the Kaspersky Security Lab which are trying to increase the sensibility of this topic by researching and publishing of new security threats.

6.3 Cyberwarfare by country

The Internet security company McAfee stated in their 2007 annual report that approximately 120 countries have been developing ways to use the Internet as a weapon and target financial markets, government computer systems and utilities.[41]

6.3.1 Cyberwarfare in China

Main article: Cyberwarfare in the People's Republic of China
See also: Chinese intelligence activity abroad, Chinese intelligence operations in the United States and Chinese Information Operations and Information Warfare

Diplomatic cables highlight US concerns that China is using access to Microsoft source code and 'harvesting the talents of its private sector' to boost its offensive and defensive capabilities.[42]

A 2008 article in the *Culture Mandala: The Bulletin of the Centre for East-West Cultural and Economic Studies* by Jason Fritz alleges that the Chinese government from 1995 to 2008 was involved in a number of high-profile cases of espionage, primarily through the use of a "decentralized net-

work of students, business people, scientists, diplomats, and engineers from within the Chinese Diaspora".[43] A defector in Belgium, purportedly an agent, claimed that there were hundreds of spies in industries throughout Europe, and on his defection to Australia Chinese diplomat Chen Yonglin said there were over 1,000 such in that country. In 2007, a Russian executive was sentenced to 11 years for passing information about the rocket and space technology organization to China. Targets in the United States have included 'aerospace engineering programs, space shuttle design, C4ISR data, high-performance computers, Nuclear weapon design, cruise missile data, semiconductors, integrated circuit design, and details of US arms sales to Taiwan'.[43]

While China continues to be held responsible for a string of cyber-attacks on a number of public and private institutions in the United States, India, Russia, Canada, and France, the Chinese government denies any involvement in cyber-spying campaigns. The administration maintains the position that China is not the threat but rather the victim of an increasing number of cyber-attacks. Most reports about China's cyber warfare capabilities have yet to be confirmed by the Chinese government.[44]

According to Fritz, China has expanded its cyber capabilities and military technology by acquiring foreign military technology.[45] Fritz states that the Chinese government uses "new space-based surveillance and intelligence gathering systems, Anti-satellite weapon, anti-radar, infrared decoys, and false target generators" to assist in this quest, and that they support their "informationization" of the their military through "increased education of soldiers in cyber warfare; improving the information network for military training, and has built more virtual laboratories, digital libraries and digital campuses.'[45] Through this informationization, they hope to prepare their forces to engage in a different kind of warfare, against technically capable adversaries.[46] Many recent news reports link China's technological capabilities to the beginning of a new 'cyber cold war.'[47]

In response to reports of cyberattacks by China against the United States, Amitai Etzioni of the Institute for Communitarian Policy Studies has suggested that China and the United States agree to a policy of mutually assured restraint with respect to cyberspace. This would involve allowing both states to take the measures they deem necessary for their self-defense while simultaneously agreeing to refrain from taking offensive steps; it would also entail vetting these commitments.[48]

6.3.2 Cyberwarfare in Germany

In 2013, Germany revealed the existence of their 60-person Computer Network Operation unit.[49] The German intelligence agency, BND, announced it was seeking to hire 130 "hackers" for a new "cyber defence station" unit. In March 2013, BND president Gerhard Schindler announced that his agency had observed up to five attacks a day on government authorities, thought mainly to originate in China. He confirmed the attackers had so far only accessed data and expressed concern that the stolen information could be used as the basis of future sabotage attacks against arms manufacturers, telecommunications companies and government and military agencies.[50] Shortly after Edward Snowden leaked details of the U.S. National Security Agency's cyber surveillance system, German Interior Minister Hans-Peter Friedrich announced that the BND would be given an additional budget of 100 million Euros to increase their cyber surveillance capability from 5% of total internet traffic in Germany to 20% of total traffic, the maximum amount allowed by German law.[51]

6.3.3 Cyberwarfare in India

See also: National Cyber Security Policy 2013

The Department of Information Technology created the Indian Computer Emergency Response Team (CERT-In) in 2004 to thwart cyber attacks in India.[52] That year, there were 23 reported cyber security breaches. In 2011, there were 13,301. That year, the government created a new subdivision, the National Critical Information Infrastructure Protection Centre (NCIIPC) to thwart attacks against energy, transport, banking, telecom, defence, space and other sensitive areas.

The Executive Director of the Nuclear Power Corporation of India (NPCIL) stated in February 2013 that his company alone was forced to block up to ten targeted attacks a day. CERT-In was left to protect less critical sectors.

A high-profile cyber attack on 12 July 2012 breached the email accounts of about 12,000 people, including those of officials from the Ministry of External Affairs, Ministry of Home Affairs, Defence Research and Development Organisation (DRDO), and the Indo-Tibetan Border Police (ITBP).[52] A government-private sector plan being overseen by National Security Advisor (NSA) Shivshankar Menon began in October 2012, and intends to beef up India's cyber security capabilities in the light of a group of experts findings that India faces a 470,000 shortfall of such experts despite the country's reputation of being an IT and software powerhouse.[53]

In February 2013, Information Technology Secretary J. Satyanarayana stated that the NCIIPC was finalizing policies related to national cyber security that would focus on domestic security solutions, reducing exposure through foreign technology.[52] Other steps include the isolation of various security agencies to ensure that a synchronised attack could not succeed on all fronts and the planned appointment of a National Cyber Security Coordinator. As of that month, there had been no significant economic or physical damage to India related to cyber attacks.

6.3.4 Cyberwarfare in Iran

Main article: Cyberwarfare in Iran
See also: Iranian Cyber Army
Further information: Operation Olympic Games, Operation Ababil, Operation Cleaver and Operation Newscaster

Iran has been both victim and predator of several cyberwarfare operations. Iran is considered an emerging military power in the field.[54]

6.3.5 Cyberwarfare in South Korea

Main article: 2013 South Korea cyberattack

With ongoing tensions on the Korean Peninsula, South Korea's defense ministry stated that South Korea was going to improve cyber-defense strategies in hopes of preparing itself from possible cyber attacks. In March 2013, South Korea's major banks – Shinhan Bank, Woori Bank and NongHyup Bank – as well as many broadcasting stations – KBS, YTN and MBC – were hacked and more than 30,000 computers were affected; it is one of the biggest attacks South Korea has faced in years.[55] Although it remains uncertain as to who was involved in this incident, there has been immediate assertions that North Korea is connected, as it threatened to attack South Korea's government institutions, major national banks and traditional newspapers numerous times – in reaction to the sanctions it received from nuclear testing and to the continuation of Foal Eagle, South Korea's annual joint military exercise with the United States. North Korea's cyber warfare capabilities raise the alarm for South Korea, as North Korea is increasing its manpower through military academies specializing in hacking. Current figures state that South Korea only has 400 units of specialized personnel, while North Korea has more than 3,000 highly trained hackers; this portrays a huge gap in cyber warfare capabilities and sends a message to South Korea that it has to step up and strengthen its Cyber Warfare Command forces. Therefore, in order to be prepared from future attacks, South Korea and the United States will discuss further about deterrence plans at the Security Consultative Meeting (SCM). At SCM, they plan on developing strategies that focuses on accelerating the deployment of ballistic missiles as well as fostering its defense shield program, known as the Korean Air and Missile Defense.[56]

6.3.6 Cyberwarfare in the Netherlands

In the Netherlands Cyber Defense is nationally coordinated by the National Cyber Security Center (NCSC).[57] The Dutch Ministry of Defense laid out a cyber strategy in 2011.[58] The first focus is to improve the cyber defense handled by the Joint IT branch (JIVC). To improve intel operations the intel community in the Netherlands (including the military intel organization MIVD) has set up the Joint Sigint Cyber Unit (JSCU). The ministry of Defense is furthermore setting up an offensive cyber force, called Defensie Cyber Command (DCC),[59] which will be operational in the end of 2014.

6.3.7 Cyberwarfare in Russia

Main article: Cyberwarfare in Russia

6.3.8 Cyberwarfare in the UK

MI6 reportedly infiltrated an Al Qaeda website and replaced the recipe for a pipe bomb with the recipe for making cupcakes.[60]

On 12 November 2013, financial organisations in London conducted cyber war games dubbed 'Waking Shark 2'[61] to simulate massive internet-based attacks against bank and other financial organisations. The Waking Shark 2 cyber war games followed a similar exercise in Wall Street.[62]

6.3.9 Cyberwarfare in the United States

Main article: Cyberwarfare in the United States

Cyberwarfare in the United States is a part of the American military strategy of proactive cyber defence and the use of cyberwarfare as a platform for attack.[63] The new United States military strategy makes explicit that a cyberattack is *casus belli* just as a traditional act of war.[64]

In 2013 Cyberwarfare was, for the first time, considered a larger threat than Al Qaeda or terrorism, by many U.S. intelligence officials.[65] Representative Mike Rogers, chairman of the U.S. House Permanent Select Committee on Intelligence, for instance, said in late July 2013, that "most Americans" do not realize that the United States is currently in the middle of a "cyber war."[66]

U.S. government security expert Richard A. Clarke, in his book *Cyber War* (May 2010), defines "cyberwarfare" as "actions by a nation-state to penetrate another nation's computers or networks for the purposes of causing damage or disruption."[1]:6 *The Economist* describes cyberspace as "the fifth domain of warfare,"[67] and William J. Lynn, U.S. Deputy Secretary of Defense, states that "as a doctrinal matter, the Pentagon has formally recognized cyberspace as a new domain in warfare . . . [which] has become just as critical to military operations as land, sea, air, and space."[7]

In 2009, President Barack Obama declared America's digital infrastructure to be a "strategic national asset," and in May 2010 the Pentagon set up its new U.S. Cyber Command (USCYBERCOM), headed by General Keith B. Alexander, director of the National Security Agency (NSA), to defend American military networks and attack other countries' systems. The EU has set up ENISA (European Union Agency for Network and Information Security) which is headed by Prof. Udo Helmbrecht and there are now further plans to significantly expand ENISA's capabilities. The United Kingdom has also set up a cyber-security and "operations centre" based in Government Communications Headquarters (GCHQ), the British equivalent of the NSA. In the U.S. however, Cyber Command is only set up to protect the military, whereas the government and corporate infrastructures are primarily the responsibility respectively of the Department of Homeland Security and private companies.[67]

In February 2010, top American lawmakers warned that the "threat of a crippling attack on telecommunications and computer networks was sharply on the rise."[68] According to The Lipman Report, numerous key sectors of the U.S. economy along with that of other nations, are currently at risk, including cyber threats to public and private facilities, banking and finance, transportation, manufacturing, medical, education and government, all of which are now dependent on computers for daily operations.[68] In 2009, President Obama stated that "cyber intruders have probed our electrical grids."[69]

The Economist writes that China has plans of "winning informationised wars by the mid-21st century". They note that other countries are likewise organizing for cyberwar, among them Russia, Israel and North Korea. Iran boasts of having the world's second-largest cyber-army.[67] James Gosler, a government cybersecurity specialist, worries that the U.S. has a severe shortage of computer security specialists, estimating that there are only about 1,000 qualified people in the country today, but needs a force of 20,000 to 30,000 skilled experts.[70] At the July 2010 Black Hat computer security conference, Michael Hayden, former deputy director of national intelligence, challenged thousands of attendees to help devise ways to "reshape the Internet's security architecture", explaining, "You guys made the cyberworld look like the north German plain."[71]

In January 2012, Mike McConnell, the former director of national intelligence at the National Security Agency under President George W. Bush told the Reuters news agency that the U.S. has already launched attacks on computer networks in other countries.[72] McConnell did not name the country that the U.S. attacked but according to other sources it may have been Iran.[72] In June 2012 *the New York Times* reported that President Obama had ordered the cyber attack on Iranian nuclear enrichment facilities.[73]

In August 2010, the U.S. for the first time warned publicly about the Chinese military's use of civilian computer experts in clandestine cyber attacks aimed at American companies and government agencies. The Pentagon also pointed to an alleged China-based computer spying network dubbed GhostNet that was revealed in a research report last year.[74] The Pentagon stated:

> "The People's Liberation Army is using "information warfare units" to develop viruses to attack enemy computer systems and networks, and those units include civilian computer professionals. Commander Bob Mehal, will monitor the PLA's buildup of its cyberwarfare capabilities and will continue to develop capabilities to counter any potential threat."[75]

The United States Department of Defense sees the use of computers and the Internet to conduct warfare in cyberspace as a threat to national security. The United States Joint Forces Command describes some of its attributes:

> Cyberspace technology is emerging as an "instrument of power" in societies, and is becoming more available to a country's opponents, who may use it to attack, degrade, and disrupt communications and the flow of information. With low barriers to entry, coupled with the anonymous nature of activities in cyberspace, the list of potential adversaries is broad. Furthermore, the globe-spanning range of cyberspace and its disregard for national borders will challenge legal systems and complicate a nation's ability to deter threats and respond to contingencies.[76]

In February 2010, the United States Joint Forces Command released a study which included a summary of the threats posed by the internet:[76]

> With very little investment, and cloaked in a veil of anonymity, our adversaries will inevitably attempt to harm our national interests. Cyberspace will become a main front in both irregular and traditional conflicts. Enemies in cyberspace will include both states and nonstates and will range from the unsophisticated amateur to highly trained professional hackers. Through cyberspace, enemies will target industry, academia, government, as well as the military in the air, land, maritime, and space domains. In much the same way that airpower transformed the battlefield of World War II, cyberspace has fractured the physical barriers that shield a nation from attacks on its commerce and communication. Indeed, adversaries have already taken advantage of computer networks and the power of information technology not only to plan and execute savage acts of terrorism, but also to influence directly the perceptions and will of the U.S. Government and the American population.

On 24 November 2014. The Sony hack was a release of confidential data belonging to Sony Pictures Entertainment (SPE)

American "*Kill switch bill*"

On 19 June 2010, United States Senator Joe Lieberman (I-CT) introduced a bill called "Protecting Cyberspace as a National Asset Act of 2010",[77] which he co-wrote with Senator Susan Collins (R-ME) and Senator Thomas Carper (D-DE). If signed into law, this controversial bill, which the American media dubbed the "*Kill switch bill*", would grant the President emergency powers over parts of the Internet. However, all three co-authors of the bill issued a statement that instead, the bill "[narrowed] existing broad Presidential authority to take over telecommunications networks".[78]

The United States has used cyberattacks for tactical advantage in Afghanistan.[79]

6.4 Cyber counterintelligence

Cyber counter-intelligence are measures to identify, penetrate, or neutralize foreign operations that use cyber means as the primary tradecraft methodology, as well as foreign intelligence service collection efforts that use traditional methods to gauge cyber capabilities and intentions.[80]

- On 7 April 2009, The Pentagon announced they spent more than $100 million in the last six months responding to and repairing damage from cyber attacks and other computer network problems.[81]

- On 1 April 2009, U.S. lawmakers pushed for the appointment of a White House cyber security "czar" to dramatically escalate U.S. defenses against cyber attacks, crafting proposals that would empower the government to set and enforce security standards for private industry for the first time.[82]

- On 9 February 2009, the White House announced that it will conduct a review of the nation's cyber security to ensure that the Federal government of the United States cyber security initiatives are appropriately integrated, resourced and coordinated with the United States Congress and the private sector.[83]

- In the wake of the 2007 cyberwar waged against Estonia, NATO established the Cooperative Cyber Defence Centre of Excellence (CCD CoE) in Tallinn, Estonia, in order to enhance the organization's cyber defence capability. The center was formally established on 14 May 2008, and it received full accreditation by NATO and attained the status of International Military Organization on 28 October 2008.[84] Since Estonia has led international efforts to fight cybercrime, the United States Federal Bureau of Investigation says it will permanently base a computer crime expert in Estonia in 2009 to help fight international threats against computer systems.[85]

One of the hardest issues in cyber counterintelligence is the problem of "Attribution". Unlike conventional warfare, figuring out who is behind an attack can be very difficult.[86] However Defense Secretary Leon Panetta has claimed that the United States has the capability to trace attacks back to their sources and hold the attackers "accountable".[87]

In 2015, the Department of Defense released an updated cyber strategy memorandum detailing the present and future tactics deployed in the service of defense against cyberwarfare. In this memorandum, three cybermissions are laid out. The first cybermission seeks to arm and maintain existing capabilities in the area of cyberspace, the second cybermission focuses on prevention of cyberwarfare, and the third cybermission includes strategies for retaliation and preemption (as distinguished from prevention).[9]

6.5   Controversy over terms

There is debate on whether the term "cyberwarfare" is accurate.

Eugene Kaspersky, founder of Kaspersky Lab, concludes that "cyberterrorism" is a more accurate term than "cyberwar." He states that "with today's attacks, you are clueless about who did it or when they will strike again. It's not

cyber-war, but cyberterrorism."[88] He also equates large-scale cyber weapons, such as Flame and NetTraveler which his company discovered, to biological weapons, claiming that in an interconnected world, they have the potential to be equally destructive.[88][89]

In October 2011 the *Journal of Strategic Studies*, a leading journal in that field, published an article by Thomas Rid, "Cyber War Will Not Take Place" which argued that all politically motivated cyber attacks are merely sophisticated versions of sabotage, espionage, or subversion[90] - and that it is unlikely that cyber war will occur in the future.

Howard Schmidt, an American cybersecurity expert, argued in March 2010 that "there is no cyberwar... I think that is a terrible metaphor and I think that is a terrible concept. There are no winners in that environment."[30]

Other experts, however, believe that this type of activity already constitutes a war. The warfare analogy is often seen intended to motivate a militaristic response when that is not necessarily appropriate. Ron Deibert, of Canada's Citizen Lab, has warned of a "militarization of cyberspace."[91]

The European cybersecurity expert Sandro Gaycken argued for a middle position. He considers cyberwar from a legal perspective an unlikely scenario, due to the reasons lined out by Rid (and, before him, Sommer),[92] but the situation looks different from a strategic point of view. States have to consider military-led cyber operations an attractive activity, within and without war, as they offer a large variety of cheap and risk-free options to weaken other countries and strengthen their own positions. Considered from a long-term, geostrategic perspective, cyber offensive operations can cripple whole economies, change political views, agitate conflicts within or among states, reduce their military efficiency and equalize the capacities of high-tech nations to that of low-tech nations, and use access to their critical infrastructures to blackmail them.[93]

6.6   Incidents

- On 21 November 2011, it was widely reported in the U.S. media that a hacker had destroyed a water pump at the Curran-Gardner Township Public Water District in Illinois.[94] However, it later turned out that this information was not only false, but had been inappropriately leaked from the Illinois Statewide Terrorism and Intelligence Center.[95]

- On 6 October 2011, it was announced that Creech AFB's drone and Predator fleet's command and control data stream had been keylogged, resisting all attempts to reverse the exploit, for the past two weeks.[96] The Air Force issued a statement that the virus had "posed no threat to our operational mission".[97]

- In July 2011, the South Korean company SK Communications was hacked, resulting in the theft of the personal details (including names, phone numbers, home and email addresses and resident registration numbers) of up to 35 million people. A trojaned software update was used to gain access to the SK Communications network. Links exist between this hack and other malicious activity and it is believed to be part of a broader, concerted hacking effort.[98]

- Operation Shady RAT is an ongoing series of cyber attacks starting mid-2006, reported by Internet security company McAfee in August 2011. The attacks have hit at least 72 organizations including governments and defense contractors.[99]

- On 4 December 2010, a group calling itself the Pakistan Cyber Army hacked the website of India's top investigating agency, the Central Bureau of Investigation (CBI). The National Informatics Center (NIC) has begun an inquiry.[100]

- On 26 November 2010, a group calling itself the Indian Cyber Army hacked the websites belonging to the Pakistan Army and the others belong to different ministries, including the Ministry of Foreign Affairs, Ministry of Education, Ministry of Finance, Pakistan Computer Bureau, Council of Islamic Ideology, etc. The attack was done as a revenge for the Mumbai terrorist attacks.[101]

- In October 2010, Iain Lobban, the director of the Government Communications Headquarters (GCHQ), said Britain faces a "real and credible" threat from cyber attacks by hostile states and criminals and government systems are targeted 1,000 times each month, such attacks threatened Britain's economic future, and some countries were already using cyber assaults to put pressure on other nations.[102]

- In September 2010, Iran was attacked by the Stuxnet worm, thought to specifically target its Natanz nuclear enrichment facility. The worm is said to be the most advanced piece of malware ever discovered and significantly increases the profile of cyberwarfare.[103][104]

- In July 2009, there were a series of coordinated denial of service attacks against major government, news media, and financial websites in South Korea and the United States.[105] While many thought the attack was directed by North Korea, one researcher traced the attacks to the United Kingdom.[106]

- Russian, South Ossetian, Georgian and Azerbaijani sites were attacked by hackers during the 2008 South Ossetia War.[107]

- In 2007 the website of the Kyrgyz Central Election Commission was defaced during its election. The message left on the website read "This site has been hacked by Dream of Estonian organization". During the election campaigns and riots preceding the election, there were cases of Denial-of-service attacks against the Kyrgyz ISPs.[108]

- In September 2007, Israel carried out an airstrike on Syria dubbed Operation Orchard. U.S. industry and military sources speculated that the Israelis may have used cyberwarfare to allow their planes to pass undetected by radar into Syria.[109][110]

- In April 2007, Estonia came under cyber attack in the wake of relocation of the Bronze Soldier of Tallinn.[111] The largest part of the attacks were coming from Russia and from official servers of the authorities of Russia.[112] In the attack, ministries, banks, and media were targeted.[113][114] This attack on Estonia, a seemingly small Baltic nation, was so effective because of how most of the nation is run online. Estonia has implemented an e-government, where bank services, political elections and taxes are all online.This attack really hurt Estonia's economy and the people of Estonia. At least 150 people were injured on the first day due to riots in the streets.[115]

- In the 2006 war against Hezbollah, Israel alleges that cyber-warfare was part of the conflict, where the Israel Defense Forces (IDF) intelligence estimates several countries in the Middle East used Russian hackers and scientists to operate on their behalf. As a result, Israel attached growing importance to cyber-tactics, and became, along with the U.S., France and a couple of other nations, involved in cyber-war planning. Many international high-tech companies are now locating research and development operations in Israel, where local hires are often veterans of the IDF's elite computer units.[116] Richard A. Clarke adds that "our Israeli friends have learned a thing or two from the programs we have been working on for more than two decades."[1]:8

It should also be worthy to note that a Spy Drone was shot down by a team Egyptian White/Grey Hat Hackers near the Libyan borders,which was later delivered to the Egyptian government.

6.7 Legality, rules

Various parties have attempted to come up with international legal frameworks to clarify what is and is not acceptable, but none have yet to be widely accepted.

The Tallinn Manual, published in 2013, is an academic, non-binding study on how international law, in particular the jus ad bellum and international humanitarian law, apply to cyber conflicts and cyber warfare. It was written at the invitation of the Tallinn-based NATO Cooperative Cyber Defence Centre of Excellence by an international group of approximately twenty experts between 2009 and 2012.

The Shanghai Cooperation Organisation (members of which include China and Russia) defines cyberwar to include dissemination of information "harmful to the spiritual, moral and cultural spheres of other states". In September 2011, these countries proposed to the UN Secretary General a document called "International code of conduct for information security".[117]

In contrast, the United States' approach focuses on physical and economic damage and injury, putting political concerns under freedom of speech. This difference of opinion has led to reluctance in the West to pursue global cyber arms control agreements.[118] However, American General Keith B. Alexander did endorse talks with Russia over a proposal to limit military attacks in cyberspace.[119] In June 2013, Barack Obama and Vladimir Putin agreed to install a secure *Cyberwar-Hotline* providing "a direct secure voice communications line between the US cybersecurity coordinator and the Russian deputy secretary of the security council, should there be a need to directly manage a crisis situation arising from an ICT security incident." (White House quote)[120]

A Ukrainian professor of International Law, Alexander Merezhko, has developed a project called the International Convention on Prohibition of Cyberwar in Internet. According to this project, cyberwar is defined as the use of Internet and related technological means by one state against political, economic, technological and information sovereignty and independence of any other state. Professor Merezhko's project suggests that the Internet ought to remain free from warfare tactics and be treated as an international landmark. He states that the Internet (cyberspace) is a "common heritage of mankind."[121]

6.8   See also

- Air Force Cyber Command (Provisional)
- Automated teller machine#Device operation integrity
- Cyber-arms industry
- Cyber-collection
- Cyber spying
- IT risk

- iWar
- List of cyber-attacks
- List of cyber attack threat trends
- Penetration test
- Signals intelligence
- Duqu
- United States Cyber Command
  - Air Force Cyber Command
  - United States Army Cyber Command
  - Fleet Cyber Command
  - Marine Corps Cyberspace Command
- Fifth Dimension Operations

6.9   Further reading

- Andress, Jason. Winterfeld, Steve. (2011). *Cyber Warfare: Techniques, Tactics and Tools for Security Practitioners*. Syngress. ISBN 1-59749-637-5

- Brenner, S. (2009). *Cyber Threats: The Emerging Fault Lines of the Nation State*. Oxford University Press. ISBN 0-19-538501-2

- Carr, Jeffrey. (2010). *Inside Cyber Warfare: Mapping the Cyber Underworld*. O'Reilly. ISBN 978-0-596-80215-8

- Cordesman, Anthony H., Cordesman, Justin G. *Cyber-threats, Information Warfare, and Critical Infrastructure Protection*, Greenwood Publ. (2002)

- Costigan, Sean S.; Perry, Jake (2012). *Cyberspaces and global affairs*. Farnham, Surrey: Ashgate. ISBN 9781409427544.

- Gaycken, Sandro. (2012). *Cyberwar – Das Wettrüsten hat längst begonnen*. Goldmann/Randomhouse. ISBN 978-3442157105

- Geers, Kenneth. (2011). *Strategic Cyber Security*. NATO Cyber Centre. *Strategic Cyber Security*, ISBN 978-9949-9040-7-5, 169 pages

- Shane Harris (2014). *@War: The Rise of the Military-Internet Complex*. Eamon Dolan/Houghton Mifflin Harcourt. ISBN 978-0544251793.

- Hunt, Edward (2012). "US Government Computer Penetration Programs and the Implications for Cyberwar". *IEEE Annals of the History of Computing* **34** (3): 4–21. doi:10.1109/mahc.2011.82.

- Janczewski, Lech; Colarik, Andrew M. Cyber Warfare and Cyber Terrorism IGI Global (2008)

- Rid, Thomas (2011) "Cyber War Will Not Take Place," *Journal of Strategic Studies*, doi:10.1080/01402390.2011.608939

- Ventre, D. (2007). *La guerre de l'information.* Hermes-Lavoisier. 300 pages

- Ventre, D. (2009). *Information Warfare.* Wiley – ISTE. ISBN 978-1-84821-094-3

- Ventre, D. (Edit.) (2010). *Cyberguerre et guerre de l'information. Stratégies, règles, enjeux.* Hermes-Lavoisier. ISBN 978-2-7462-3004-0

- Ventre, D. (2011). *Cyberespace et acteurs du cyberconflit.* Hermes-Lavoisier. 288 pages

- Ventre, D. (Edit.) (2011). *Cyberwar and Information Warfare.* Wiley. 460 pages

- Ventre, D. (2011). *Cyberattaque et Cyberdéfense.* Hermes-Lavoisier. 336 pages

- Ventre, D. (Edit.) (2012). *Cyber Conflict. Competing National Perspectives.* Wiley-ISTE. 330 pages

- Woltag, Johann-Christoph: 'Cyber Warfare' in *Rüdiger Wolfrum (Ed.) Max Planck Encyclopedia of Public International Law (Oxford University Press 2012).*

6.10   References

[1] Clarke, Richard A. *Cyber War*, HarperCollins (2010) ISBN 9780061962233

[2] Blitz, James (1 November 2011). "Security: A huge challenge from China, Russia and organised crime". Financial Times. Retrieved 6 June 2015.

[3] Arquilla, John (1999). "Can information warfare ever be just?". *Ethics and Information Technology* **1** (3): 203–212. doi:10.1023/A:1010066528521.

[4] Collins, Sean (April 2012). "Stuxnet: the emergence of a new cyber weapon and its implications". *Journal of Policing, Intelligence and Counter Terrorism* **7** (1). Retrieved 6 June 2015.

[5] "Critical infrastructure vulnerable to attack, warns cyber security expert". *gsnmagazine.com*. Government Security News. 2014. Retrieved 6 June 2015.

[6] Maniscalchi, Jago (4 September 2011). "What is Cyberwar?". Retrieved 6 June 2015.

[7] Lynn, William J. III. "Defending a New Domain: The Pentagon's Cyberstrategy", *Foreign Affairs*, Sept/Oct. 2010, pp. 97–108

[8] Clapper, James R. "Worldwide Threat Assessment of the US Intelligence Community ", Senate Armed Services Committee, Feb. 26, 2015 p. 1

[9] Lisa Lucile Owens, Justice and Warfare in Cyberspace, The Boston Review (2015), available at

[10] Poole-Robb, Stuart. "Turkish blackout sparks fears of cyber attack on the West", ITProPortal.com, May 19, 2015

[11] "Cyberattacks, Terrorism Top U.S. Security Threat Report". *NPR.org.* 12 March 2013.

[12] "A Note on the Laws of War in Cyberspace", James A. Lewis, April 2010

[13] Rayman, Noah (December 18, 2013). "Merkel Compared NSA To Stasi in Complaint To Obama". *Time.* Retrieved February 1, 2014.

[14] Devereaux, Ryan; Greenwald, Glenn; Poitras, Laura (May 19, 2014). "Data Pirates of the Caribbean: The NSA Is Recording Every Cell Phone Call in the Bahamas". *The Intercept.* First Look Media. Retrieved May 21, 2014.

[15] Schonfeld, Zach (May 23, 2014). "The Intercept Wouldn't Reveal a Country the U.S. Is Spying On, So WikiLeaks Did Instead". *Newsweek.* Retrieved May 26, 2014.

[16] Bodmer, Kilger, Carpenter, & Jones (2012). Reverse Deception: Organized Cyber Threat Counter-Exploitation. New York: McGraw-Hill Osborne Media. ISBN 0071772499, ISBN 978-0071772495

[17] Sanders, Sam (4 June 2015). "Massive Data Breach Puts 4 Million Federal Employees' Records At Risk". *NPR.* Retrieved 5 June 2015.

[18] Liptak, Kevin (4 June 2015). "U.S. government hacked; feds think China is the culprit". *CNN.* Retrieved 5 June 2015.

[19] "Clarke: More defense needed in cyberspace" HometownAnnapolis.com, 24 September 2010

[20] "Malware Hits Computerized Industrial Equipment". *The New York Times*, 24 September 2010

[21] Shiels, Maggie. (9 April 2009) BBC: Spies 'infiltrate US power grid'. BBC News. Retrieved 8 November 2011.

[22] Meserve, Jeanne (8 April 2009). "Hackers reportedly have embedded code in power grid". CNN. Retrieved 8 November 2011.

[23] "US concerned power grid vulnerable to cyber-attack". In.reuters.com (9 April 2009). Retrieved 8 November 2011.

[24] Gorman, Siobhan. (8 April 2009) Electricity Grid in U.S. Penetrated By Spies. *The Wall Street Journal.* Retrieved 8 November 2011.

[25] NERC Public Notice. (PDF). Retrieved 8 November 2011.

[26] Xinhua: China denies intruding into the U.S. electrical grid. 9 April 2009

[27] 'China threat' theory rejected. *China Daily* (9 April 2009). Retrieved 8 November 2011.

[28] ABC News: Video. ABC News. (20 April 2009). Retrieved 8 November 2011.

[29] Disconnect electrical grid from Internet, former terror czar Clarke warns. The Raw Story (8 April 2009). Retrieved 8 November 2011.

[30] "White House Cyber Czar: 'There Is No Cyberwar'". *Wired,* 4 March 2010

[31] "Cyber-War Nominee Sees Gaps in Law", *The New York Times,* 14 April 2010

[32] Cyber ShockWave Shows U.S. Unprepared For Cyber Threats. Bipartisanpolicy.org. Retrieved 8 November 2011.

[33] Drogin, Bob (17 February 2010). "In a doomsday cyber attack scenario, answers are unsettling". *Los Angeles Times.*

[34] Ali, Sarmad (16 February 2010). "Washington Group Tests Security in 'Cyber ShockWave'". *The Wall Street Journal.*

[35] Cyber ShockWave CNN/BPC wargame: was it a failure?. *Computerworld* (17 February 2010). Retrieved 8 November 2011.

[36] Steve Ragan Report: The Cyber ShockWave event and its aftermath. *The Tech Herald.* 16 February 2010

[37] Lee, Andy (1 May 2012). "International Cyber Warfare: Limitations and Possibilities". Jeju Peace Institute.

[38] U.S. Navy Recruiting - Cyber Warfare Engineer.

[39] Denning, D. E. (2008). The ethics of cyber conflict. The Handbook of Information and Computer Ethics. 407–429.

[40] "Google Attack Is Tip Of Iceberg", McAfee Security Insights, 13 January 2010

[41] Government-sponsored cyberattacks on the rise, McAfee says. *Network World* (29 November 2007). Retrieved 8 November 2011.

[42] "US embassy cables: China uses access to Microsoft source code to help plot cyber warfare, US fears". *The Guardian* (London). 4 December 2010. Retrieved 31 December 2010.

[43] "How China will use cyber warfare to leapfrog in military competitiveness". *Culture Mandala: The Bulletin of the Centre for East-West Cultural and Economic Studies* **8** (1 [October 2008]). p. 37. Retrieved January 2013.

[44] "China to make mastering cyber warfare A priority (2011)". Washington, D.C.: NPR. Retrieved January 2013.

[45] "How China will use cyber warfare to leapfrog in military competitiveness". *Culture Mandala: The Bulletin of the Centre for East-West Cultural and Economic Studies* **8** (1 [October 2008]). p. 42. Retrieved January 2013.

[46] "How China will use cyber warfare to leapfrog in military competitiveness". *Culture Mandala: The Bulletin of the Centre for East-West Cultural and Economic Studies* **8** (1 [October 2008]). p. 43. Retrieved January 2013.

[47] "Washington, Beijing In Cyber-War Standoff". Yahoo! News. 12 February 2013. Retrieved January 2013.

[48] Etzioni, Amitai (20 September 2013). "MAR: A Model for US-China Relations", *The Diplomat.*

[49] "Germany's 60-person Computer Network Operation (CNO) unit has been practicing for cyber war for years."

[50] "Hackers wanted to man front line in cyber war", *The Local,* 24 March 2013

[51] "Germany to invest 100 million euros on internet surveillance: report", Kazinform, 18 June 2013

[52] "Beware of the bugs: Can cyber attacks on India's critical infrastructure be thwarted?". *BusinessToday.* Retrieved January 2013.

[53] "5 lakh cyber warriors to bolster India's e-defence". *The Times of India* (India). 16 October 2012. Retrieved 18 October 2012.

[54] "Iran's military is preparing for cyber warfare". Flash//CRITIC Cyber Threat News. Retrieved 18 March 2015.

[55] Lee, Se Young. "South Korea raises alert after hackers attack broadcasters, banks". *Global Post.* Retrieved 6 April 2013.

[56] Kim, Eun-jung. "S. Korean military to prepare with U.S. for cyber warfare scenarios". Yonhap News Agency. Retrieved 6 April 2013.

[57] "Nationaal Cyber Security Centrum – NCSC".

[58] "Defensie Cyber Strategie".

[59] "Cyber commando".

[60] "Al Qaeda rocked by apparent cyberattack. But who did it?". *The Christian Science Monitor.*

[61] "Attack the City: why the banks are 'war gaming'".

[62] "Wall Street banks learn how to survive in staged cyber attack". Reuters. 21 October 2013.

[63] American Forces Press Service: Lynn Explains U.S. Cybersecurity Strategy. Defense.gov. Retrieved 8 November 2011.

[64] "Pentagon to Consider Cyberattacks Acts of War". *The New York Times*. 31 May 2006

[65] Dilanian, Ken. "Cyber-attacks a bigger threat than Al Qaeda, officials say", *Los Angeles Times*, 12 March 2013

[66] "Intelligence Chairman: U.S. Fighting Cyber War 'Every Day'", *PJ Media*, 29 July 2013

[67] "Cyberwar: War in the Fifth Domain" *Economist*, 1 July 2010

[68] The Lipman Report, 15 October 2010

[69] Clarke, Richard. "China's Cyberassault on America", *The Wall Street Journal*, 15 June 2011

[70] "Cyberwarrior Shortage Threatens U.S. Security". NPR, 19 July 2010

[71] "U.S. military cyberwar: What's off-limits?" CNET, 29 July 2010

[72] "US Launched Cyber Attacks on Other Nations". RT, 26 January 2012.

[73] Sanger, David E. "Obama Order Sped Up Wave of Cyberattacks Against Iran." *The New York Times*, 1 June 2012.

[74] ANNUAL REPORT TO CONGRESS Military and Security Developments Involving the People's Republic of China 2010. US Defense Department (PDF). Retrieved 8 November 2011.

[75] AP: Pentagon takes aim at China cyber threat Archived 23 August 2010 at the Wayback Machine

[76] "The Joint Operating Environment", Joint Forces Command, 18 February 2010, pp. 34–36

[77] A Bill. To amend the Homeland Security Act of 2002 and other laws to enhance the security and resiliency of the cyber and communications infrastructure of the United States.. Senate.gov. 111th Congress 2D Session

[78] Senators Say Cybersecurity Bill Has No 'Kill Switch', *Information Week*, 24 June 2010. Retrieved 25 June 2010.

[79] Satter, Raphael. "US general: We hacked the enemy in Afghanistan.". Associated Press, 24 August 2012.

[80] DOD – Cyber Counterintelligence. Dtic.mil. Retrieved 8 November 2011.

[81] Pentagon Bill To Fix Cyber Attacks: ,0M. CBS News. Retrieved 8 November 2011.

[82] "Senate Legislation Would Federalize Cybersecurity". *The Washington Post*. Retrieved 8 November 2011.

[83] "White House Eyes Cyber Security Plan". CBS News (10 February 2009). Retrieved 8 November 2011.

[84] CCD COE – Cyber Defence. Ccdcoe.org. Retrieved 8 November 2011.

[85] Associated Press (11 May 2009) FBI to station cybercrime expert in Estonia. *Boston Herald*. Retrieved 8 November 2011.

[86] Reed, John. "Is the 'holy grail' of cyber security within reach?". *Foreign Policy Magazine*, 6 September 2012.

[87] Carroll, Chris. "US can trace cyberattacks, mount preemptive strikes, Panetta says". *Stars and Stripes*, 11 October 2012.

[88] "Latest viruses could mean 'end of world as we know it,' says man who discovered Flame", *The Times of Israel*, 6 June 2012

[89] "Cyber espionage bug attacking Middle East, but Israel untouched — so far", *The Times of Israel*, 4 June 2013

[90] Rid, Thomas (October 2011). "Cyber War Will Not Take Place". *Journal of Strategic Studies* **35**: 5–32. doi:10.1080/01402390.2011.608939. Retrieved 21 October 2011.

[91] Deibert, Ron (2011). "Tracking the emerging arms race in cyberspace". *Bulletin of the Atomic Scientists* **67** (1): 1–8. doi:10.1177/0096340210393703.

[92] Sommer, Peter (January 2011). "Reducing Systemic Cybersecurity Risk" (PDF). *OECD Multi-Displinary Issues*. Retrieved 21 May 2012.

[93] Gaycken, Sandro (2010). "Cyberwar – Das Internet als Kriegsschauplatz".

[94] Mathew J. Schwartz (21 November 2011). "Hacker Apparently Triggers Illinois Water Pump Burnout". *InformationWeek*.

[95] Kim Zetter (30 November 2011). "Exclusive: Comedy of Errors Led to False 'Water-Pump Hack' Report". *Wired*.

[96] U.S. drone and predator fleet is being keylogged. *Wired*, October 2011. Retrieved 6 October 2011

[97] Hennigan, W.J. "Air Force says drone computer virus poses 'no threat'". *Los Angeles Times*, 13 October 2011.

[98] "SK Hack by an Advanced Persistent Threat" (PDF). Command Five Pty Ltd. Retrieved 24 September 2011.

[99] Jim Finkle (3 August 2011). "State actor seen in "enormous" range of cyber attacks". Reuters. Retrieved 3 August 2011.

[100] "Hacked by 'Pakistan cyber army', CBI website still not restored". Ndtv.com (4 December 2010). Retrieved 8 November 2011.

[101] "36 government sites hacked by 'Indian Cyber Army'". *The Express Tribune*. Retrieved 8 November 2011.

[102] Britain faces serious cyber threat, spy agency head warns. *The Globe and Mail* (13 October 2010). Retrieved 8 November 2011.

[103] AFP (1 October 2010). Stuxnet worm brings cyber warfare out of virtual world. Google. Retrieved 8 November 2011.

[104] Ralph Langner: Cracking Stuxnet, a 21st-century cyber weapon | Video on. Ted.com. Retrieved 8 November 2011.

[105] Sudworth, John. (9 July 2009) "New cyberattacks hit South Korea". BBC News. Retrieved 8 November 2011.

[106] Williams, Martin. UK, Not North Korea, Source of DDOS Attacks, Researcher Says. *PC World.*

[107] Danchev, Dancho (11 August 2008). "Coordinated Russia vs Georgia cyberattack". ZDNet. Retrieved 25 November 2008.

[108] Website of Kyrgyz Central Election Commission hacked by Estonian hackers, Regnum, 14 December 2007

[109] Fulghum, David A. "Why Syria's Air Defenses Failed to Detect Israelis", *Aviation Week & Space Technology*, 3 October 2007. Retrieved 3 October 2007.

[110] Fulghum, David A. "Israel used electronic attack in air strike against Syrian mystery target", *Aviation Week & Space Technology*, 8 October 2007. Retrieved 8 October 2007.

[111] "War in the fifth domain. Are the mouse and keyboard the new weapons of conflict?". *The Economist.* 1 July 2010. Retrieved 2 July 2010. Important thinking about the tactical and legal concepts of cyber-warfare is taking place in a former Soviet barracks in Estonia, now home to NATO's "centre of excellence" for cyber-defence. It was established in response to what has become known as "Web War 1", a concerted denial-of-service attack on Estonian government, media and bank web servers that was precipitated by the decision to move a Soviet-era war memorial in central Tallinn in 2007.

[112] Estonia accuses Russia of 'cyber attack'. *The Christian Science Monitor.* (17 May 2007). Retrieved 8 November 2011.

[113] Ian Traynor, 'Russia accused of unleashing cyberwar to disable Estonia", *The Guardian*, 17 May 2007

[114] Boyd, Clark. (17 June 2010) "Cyber-war a growing threat warn experts". BBC News. Retrieved 8 November 2011.

[115] Scott J. Shackelford, From Nuclear War to Net War: Analogizing Cyber Attacks in International Law, 27 Berkeley J. Int'l Law. 192 (2009).

[116] "Israel Adds Cyber-Attack to IDF", Military.com, 10 February 2010

[117] Russian Embassy to the UK . Retrieved 25 May 2012.

[118] Tom Gjelten (23 September 2010). "Seeing The Internet As An 'Information Weapon'". NPR. Retrieved 23 September 2010.

[119] Gorman, Siobhan. (4 June 2010) WSJ: U.S. Backs Talks on Cyber Warfare. *The Wall Street Journal.* Retrieved 8 November 2011.

[120] Sean Gallagher, *US, Russia to install "cyber-hotline" to prevent accidental cyberwar*, Arstechnica, 18 June 2013

[121] Український центр політичного менеджменту – Зміст публікації – Конвенция о запрещении использования кибервойны. Politik.org.ua. Retrieved 8 November 2011.

6.11   External links

6.11.1   Books

- Bodmer, Kilger, Carpenter, & Jones (2012). Reverse Deception: Organized Cyber Threat Counter-Exploitation. New York: McGraw-Hill Osborne Media. ISBN 0071772499, ISBN 978-0071772495

6.11.2   Websites

- NATO Cooperative Cyber Defence Centre of Excellence (CCDCOE)
- Cyberwar Twitter feed from Richard Stiennon

6.11.3   Videos

- "Sabotaging the System" video, "60 Minutes", 8 November 2009, CBS News, 15 minutes

Articles

- ABC: Former White House security advisor warns of cyber war
- Wall Street Journal: Fighting Wars in Cyberspace
- Will There Be An Electronic Pearl Harbor, PC World by Ira Winkler, 1 December 2009
- Senate panel: 80 percent of cyberattacks preventable, Wired, 17 November 2009
- Consumer Reports Online Security Guide
- Cyberwarfare reference materials
- Duncan Gardham, 26 June 2009, Hackers recruited to fight 'new cold war', Telegraph UK
- Stefano Mele, Jun 2013, Cyber-Weapons: Legal and Strategic Aspects (version 2.0)
- Stefano Mele, 30 September 2010, Cyberwarfare and its damaging effects on citizens
- History of Cyber Warfare

- Cybersecurity: Authoritative Reports and Resources, US Congressional Research Service

- Why the USA is Losing The Cyberwar Against China, by Joseph Steinberg, VentureBeat, 9 November 2011

- Michael Riley and Ashlee Vance, 20 July 2011, Cyber Weapons: The New Arms Race

- The Digital Arms Race: NSA Preps America for Future Battle, Der Spiegel, January 2015

Chapter 7

Domain name scams

Domain name scams are types of Intellectual property scams or confidence scams in which unscrupulous domain name registrars attempt to generate revenue by tricking businesses into buying, selling, listing or converting a domain name. The Office of Fair Trading in the United Kingdom has outlined two types of domain name scams which are "Domain name registration scams" and "Domain name renewal scams".[1][2]

7.1 Domain slamming

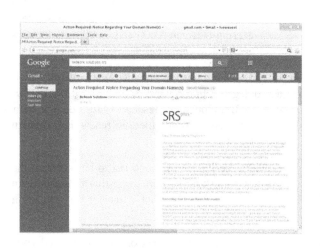

Domain slamming (also known as unauthorized transfers or domain name registration scams) is a scam in which the offending domain name registrar attempts to trick domain owners into switching from their existing registrar to theirs, under the pretense that the customer is simply renewing their subscription to their current register. The image on the right shows the initial domain slamming phishing email sent by Network Solutions to OpenSRS customers. The term derives from telephone slamming.

7.1.1 Prevention

In 2004, ICANN, the domain name governing body, made changes to its policy for transferring domains between registrars. They introduced a single protective measure that can help prevent unauthorized transfers: domain locking. Critics, although advising owners to apply the new feature, said that this was an "unnecessary and customer-unfriendly change".[3][4]

7.2 False offers to buy, or to find buyers

Scam methods may operate in reverse, with a stranger (not the registrar) communicating an offer to buy a domain name from an unwary owner. The offer is not genuine, but intended to lure the owner into a false sales process, with the owner eventually pressed to send money in advance to the scammer for appraisal fees or other purported services. By mimicking aspects of the legitimate sales process and agencies, the scheme appears genuine in the early stages. The prospect of an easy, lucrative sale disarms the owner's normal suspicion of an unsolicited offer from a stranger with no earnest value. Since an actual transfer through the registration system is never involved, legal safeguards built into the official transfer process provide no protection.

7.3 Fake trademark protection

Although less common than domain slamming, another domain name scam primarily coming from registrars based in China involves sending domain owners an e-mail claiming that another company has just attempted to register a number of domains with them which contain the targeted domain owner's trademark or has many keyword similarities to their existing domain name. Often, these domains will be the same as the one(s) owned by the targeted individual but with different TLDs (top-level domains). The scammer will claim to have halted the bulk registration in order to protect the targeted individual's intellectual property, and if the email recipient doesn't recognize the entity attempting to register these domain names, that they should respond immediately to protect their trademark. If the scam target does respond by email or by phone, the scammer will then try to get them to register these domain names for several years upfront with the registrar running this scam.[5]

Other variations of this type of scam include registrars that target their own existing customers with similar made-up threats of another entity trying to register the same domain as theirs under different TLDs. As well, some domainers are known to search for available TLDs for already registered domains, then emailing the owner of the registered domain and offering to sell the unregistered variations to him/her for a marked up amount. If the target agrees to the deal, the domainer will then purchase the domains on the spot for the regular $7~20 registration fee and immediately sell it back to the victim for a few hundred dollars.

7.4 Timeline

This section outlines reported domain scams as a timeline of events, showing how they have evolved, the companies involved and the outcome of complaints.

- In 2001, the federal Competition Bureau (of Canada) issued a warning about documents that appeared to be invoices sent out by a business called the *Internet Registry of Canada* (a Brandon Gray reseller[1]).[6]

  - "Complaints received by the Competition Bureau indicate that the mailings from the 'Internet Registry of Canada' give the impression that it is affiliated with the Government of Canada or that it is an officially sanctioned agency registering domain names in Canada. The 'Internet Registry of Canada' is not associated with any government agency," the Competition Bureau advisory stated.[7]

- VeriSign was sued in 2002 for their actions in sending ambiguous emails informing people, often incorrectly, that their domain was about to expire and inviting them to click on a link to renew it. Renewing the domain resulted in the registration company being transferred to VeriSign from the previous registrar.[8]

- In March 2002, the FTC shut down "TLD Network Ltd", "Quantum Management (GB) Ltd.", "TBS Industries Ltd." of London, England for selling bogus domain names ".USA", ".BRIT", which they deceptively marketed as usable suffixes.[9]

- In April 2002, the FTC charged *National Domain Name Registry*, *Electronic Domain Name Monitoring*, *Corporate Domain Name Monitoring*, and owner Darren J. Morgenstern, with making false and misleading statements to domain name holders whereby they duped consumers into needlessly registering variations of their existing domain names by deceptively contending that third parties were about to claim them.[10]

- On 2 July 2002, the "Domain Registry" served papers against Canada-based domain registrar Tucows Inc for alleged defamation and sought $21 m in damages.[11][12] Tucows later said: "The Company (Tucows) does not believe it will be liable for any damages and accordingly has not accrued any amounts at June 30, 2002."[13]

- In 2002, Register.com sued *Domain Registry of America* (a Brandon Gray reseller[1]), claiming the company illegally lured away thousands of customers by tricking them into transferring their domains.[14]

- In 2002, the UK Advertising Watchdog Authority (ASA) slammed *Domain Registry of Europe* (a Brandon Gray reseller[1]) over similar mail shots.[15][16]

  - In response to this, Alan Freeman, Relations Manager for *DRoE*, said that the company - which also trades as *Domain Registry of America* and *Domain Registry of Canada* - had registered 1.1 million domains for customers and was registering between 5,000 and 7,000 new domains a day.[11]

- In 2003, Dutch hosting provider Deinternetman pondered legal action against *Domain Registry of Europe* (a Brandon Gray reseller[1]) for sending their customers letters urging them to renew their domain contracts.[17]

- In 2003, VeriSign was found not to have broken the law but were barred from suggesting that a domain was about to expire or that a transfer was actually a renewal.[18]

- In 2003, the Federal Trade Commission reached a settlement with the *Domain Registry of America* (a Brandon Gray reseller[1]) for practices such as transferring domain registrations to their service under the guise of domain renewal, a practice known as *domain slamming*, and having hidden fees.[19][20][21][22]

- In July 2004, Daniel Klemann and *1480455 Ontario Incorporated*, operating as *Internet Registry of Canada* (a Brandon Gray reseller[1]), was sentenced to a $40,000 fine and a five-year prohibition order for deceptive Internet domain name renewal mailouts that targeted 73,000 businesses and non-profit organizations across Canada.[23]

- In April 2005, the Australian Competition & Consumer Commission warns of a domain name renewal scam where domain name holders have received a letter that looks like an invoice for the registration or renewal of a domain name, where the domain name in question is very similar to your actual domain name except has a different ending, for example it will end in ".net.au" instead of ".com" [24]

- In March 2006, Consumer Fraud Reporting reports about a company called "Domain Listing Service" sending out emails to domain name holders that look like a bill to register/renew their domain name listing a "final notice".[25]

- In 2006, reports appeared from New Zealand that Blair Rafferty had resurrected his bankrupt brother Chesley's domain name service, "domain slamming" New Zealand and Australian registrants.[26]

- In 2007, a company known as "Domain Renewal SA" operating from Brussels was sending out emails that told you that you need to renew your domain.[27]

- In August 2007, the Internet Centre reports of a wave of emails originating from China from "Asian Domain Registration Service", implying that a domain name will be lost, or all Asian TLDs of the domain name will be taken away shortly by a foreign company. The Internet Centre has found no indication that any of these are valid, and in fact they appear to be a scam.[28]

- In 2007, it was reported that a company under the name of *Liberty Names of America* (a Brandon Gray reseller[1]) had been sending out "Domain Name Expiration Notices", which one expert said is "not exactly *domain name slamming*. But it is sleazy marketing."[29]

- In March 2008, PC News Digest reports "Network Solutions Scam". When searching on the Network Solutions website to see if a name was available for registration, Network Solutions was actually registering the name and then attempting to sell that name at an inflated price.[30]

- In 2008, ICANN said: "we are aware of accredited registrars in North America with officers that have been convicted of mail fraud, that continue to be associated with the deceptive marketing practices employed by the *Domain Registry of America* (a Brandon Gray reseller[1]). We do not consider this an acceptable situation. Accreditation processes must be reviewed, and that review must be released for public scrutiny".[31]

- In 2009, ASA released an adjudication on *Domain Registry of America* t/a *Domain Renewal Group* (both Brandon Gray resellers[1]).[32]

- As of 2010, the company mailing as *DROA*, *French Internet Registry*, *Domain Renewal Group* or *Company Directory*, is doing so in order to achieve *domain slamming*.[33] McAfee Labs also reports that the *domain slamming* solicitations continue.[34]

- In September 2010, *Brandon Gray Internet Services Inc.* had its licence with the authority responsible for Canada's .ca domain names, Canadian Internet Registration Authority terminated as a result of *domain slamming* carried out under the name of *Domain Registry of Canada*.[35][36] The officer registered with the Ontario government for Brandon Gray Internet Services is Marilyn Benlolo.[37]

- In August 2010, the FTC charged *Internet Listing Service* with sending fake invoices to small business and others listing the existing domain name of the consumers Website or a slight variation on the domain name.[38]

- On March 31, 2011, the law office of Ostrolenk Faber LLP warned about Trademark and Domain Name Scams where its clients received fake warnings of usurpers of internet domain names. Clients were allegedly receiving phony "Trademark Office Notices" from the "United States Trademark Agency".[39]

- In Dec 2011, NameCheap accused GoDaddy of putting technical barriers to frustrate its customers from transferring their domains to Namecheap in breach of ICANN rules.[40]

- In July 2014, ICANN suspended *Brandon Gray Internet Services* (including its various resellers, like *Domain Registry of America* and *Namejuice.com*) for subjecting domain name holders to false advertising, deceptive practices, or deceptive notices.[41]

7.5 See also

- Copyfraud

- List of confidence tricks: Online scams

- Scams in intellectual property

- Telephone slamming

- Transfer secret

7.6 Notes

1.[a b c d e f g h i] Entities and resellers associated with Brandon Gray include Namejuice.com, Domain Registry of America, Domain Renewal Group, Domain Registry of Australia, Domain Registry of Canada, Domain Registry of Europe, Internet Registry of Canada, Liberty Names of America, Registration Services Inc, Yellow Business.ca and Internet Corporation Listing Service.[42]

7.7 References

[1] "Domain name scams". *Types of business scams*. Office of Fair Trading. Retrieved 27 July 2011.

[2] Richardson, Tim (12 July 2002). "Three domain name scams". *The Register*. Retrieved 27 July 2011.

[3] Rohde, Laura (November 12, 2004). "ICANN domain transfer policy takes effect". *InfoWorld*. Retrieved 22 July 2011.

[4] Lake, Matt (November 22, 2004). "Why it's easier than ever to lose your domain". *CNET*. Retrieved 22 July 2011.

[5] Lev, Amir (2009-12-09). "Beware Domain Registration Scams". PCWorld Communications, Inc. Retrieved 2012-05-04.

[6] MARRON, KEVIN (Nov 6, 2002). "'Domain slamming' surfaces on the Web". *The Globe and Mail*. Retrieved 12 July 2011.

[7] Charles, Bergeron. "Competition Bureau Issues Warning to Canadians about Misleading Mailings for Internet Domain Name Registrations". Competition Bureau.

[8] TheRegister.co.uk: VeriSign hit with slamming lawsuit

[9] Federal Trade Commission: Court Shuts Down Website Selling Bogus Domain Names ".USA," ".BRIT," Deceptively Marketed as Useable

[10] http://www.ftc.gov/opa/2002/04/morgenstern.shtm

[11] Richardson, Tim (17 July 2002). "Domain Registry of Europe defends tactics, sues Tucows". *The Register*. Retrieved 12 July 2011.

[12] Michener, Lang. "1446513 Ontario Limited v. Tucows Inc. et al.". TuCows. Retrieved 13 July 2011.

[13] COOPERMAN, MICHAEL. "Legal Proceedings". *QUARTERLY REPORT*. Tucows Inc. Retrieved 13 July 2011.

[14] Register.com says rival duped customers. By Lisa M. Bowman; Staff Writer, CNET News September 18, 2002 12:37 PM PDT

[15] Richardson, Tim (17 July 2002). "ASA slams 'intimidating' Domain Registry of Europe mailshots". *The Register*. Retrieved 12 July 2011.

[16] Richardson, Tim (16 August 2002). "Ad watchdog critical of Domain Registry of Europe". *The Register*. Retrieved 12 July 2011.

[17] Libbenga, Jan (6 August 2003). "Legal action threatened against domain slammer". *The Register*. Retrieved 12 July 2011.

[18] TheRegister.co.uk: VeriSign slammed for domain renewal scam

[19] Federal Trade Commission v. Domain Registry of America, Inc.

[20] Federal Trade Commission: Court Bars Canadian Company from Misleading Consumers in Marketing of Internet Domain Name Services

[21] The Register: Court bars Canadian domain slammer

[22] Stephen Lawson (31 December 2002). "Judge Halts Domain Deception". *PC World*. Retrieved 24 May 2008.

[23] King, Julie (July 2, 2004). "Toronto man sentenced in Bogus Invoice Scam". *CanadaOne*. Retrieved 14 July 2011.

[24] http://www.scamwatch.gov.au/content/index.phtml/tag/domainnamerenewalscams#h2_10

[25] http://www.consumerfraudreporting.org/domainnamescams.htm

[26] SAARINEN, JUHA (August 7, 2006). "Rafferty brother continues domain slamming scam". *Fairfax Media Business Group, Fairfax New Zealand Limited*. Retrieved 12 July 2011.

[27] Seltzer, Larry (2007-07-16). "Beware Fake Domain Renewal Notices". *eWeek*. Retrieved 21 July 2011.

[28] http://www.incentre.net/content/view/113/1

[29] Mitchell, Robert (November 7, 2007). "The not-quite-domain-name-slamming school of marketing". *Computerworld Inc*. Retrieved 13 July 2011.

[30] http://pcnewsdigest.com/network-solutions-scam/

[31] ICANN: ALAC Statement to the Board of ICANN on Amendments to the Registrar Accreditation Agreement Sun 14 Sep 2008

[32] "ASA Adjudication on Domain Registry of America". ASA. Retrieved 15 July 2011.

[33] Most of the renewal of a domain name Posted May 26, 2010 by Marina Legrand

[34] Schmugar, Craig (30 March 2010). "Persistent Domain-Renewal Scam Alive and Kicking". *McAfee Labs Blog*. Retrieved 6 May 2010. External link in |work= (help)

[35] Jackson, Brian (2010-09-22). "Alleged 'domain slammers'
     lose dot-ca licence, sue CIRA $10 million". *ITworldcanada*.
     Retrieved 12 July 2011.

[36] Shea, Dave. "Domain Registry Scam". *mezzoblue*. Dave
     Shea/mezzoblue. Retrieved 15 July 2011.

[37] Jackson, Brian (2010-09-22). "Alleged 'domain slammers'
     lose dot-ca licence, sue CIRA $10 million". *ITworldcanada*.
     Retrieved 7 August 2011.

[38] http://www.ftc.gov/opa/2010/08/ils.shtm

[39] http://www.ostrolenk.com/publications/trademark_
     articles.html?PID=75

[40] http://www.investopedia.com/ask/answers/052315/
     who-are-godaddys-gddy-main-competitors.asp?partner=
     YahooSA

[41] Neylon, Michele (19 July 2014). "Domain Registry Of
     America Suspended By ICANN". Domain Industry & In-
     ternet News. Retrieved 20 July 2014.

[42] Chirgwin, Richard (20 July 2014). "Brandon Gray aka
     Namejuice suspended by ICANN". The Register. Retrieved
     4 August 2014.

Chapter 8

Fakesysdef (malware)

Trojan:Win32/FakeSysdef, originally dispersed as an application called "HDD Defragmenter" hence the name "FakeSysdef" or "Fake System Defragmenter", is a Computer Trojan type of computer virus targeting the Microsoft Windows operating system that was first documented in late 2010.[1]

Win32/FakeSysdef manifests as one or more of an array of programs that purport to scan your computer for hardware failures related to system memory, hard drives and system functionality as a whole. They scan the computer, show false hardware issues, and present a remedy to defrag the hard drives and fine-tune the system performance. They then request, from the user, a payment in order to download the repair update and to activate the program in order to repair these contrived hardware issues.[2]

The fictitious scanning program detects one or more of the most widespread varieties of risks prevalent on the internet today. Everyday numerous fake antivirus and security applications are published and released to unsuspecting end-users via a large assortment of distribution channels. Many times such software turn out to be clones of each other – developed from the same code base but packaged with a unique title and design through the use of a "skin".[3]

The branding strategy may look legitimate to computer users as the names are usually a combination of technical words such as "HDD", "Disk", "Memory" and action words such as "Scanner", "Defragmenter", "Diagnostics", "Repair", and "Fix".[1]

8.1 Operation

Users may encounter this kind of threat when they visit websites that attempt to convince them to remove non-existent malware or security risks from their computers by installing the bogus software. The Trojan can also be installed by other malware, drive-by downloads, and when downloading and installing other software.

- Users may be directed to these sites by way of the following methods:
- Spam emails that contain links or attachments
- Blogs and forums that are spammed with links to adult videos
- User-generated content spam (e.g. fake videos)
- Malicious banner advertisements
- Pirated software ('warez') and pornography sites
- Search engine optimization (SEO) poisoning
- Fake torrent files or files on file sharing networks
- Web pages containing exploits

These programs intentionally misrepresent the security status of a computer by continually presenting fake scan dialog boxes and alert messages that prompt the user to buy the product.

The programs often have an icon in the notification area of the operating system desktop and constantly display pop-up messages alerting the user about fake security issues such as virus infections. These pop-up windows only disappear once the user has purchased the product and the non-existent threats have supposedly been removed from the compromised computer.

If the user decides to purchase the product, they are presented with a form within the application or are redirected to a Web site that requests credit card information.[3]

8.1.1 Initial Infection

The Win32/FakeSysdef installer may arrive in the computer with various file names. When run, the installer drops and injects a DLL file (or sometimes and EXE file) into common processes, for example "EXPLORER.EXE", "WINLOGON.EXE", and "WININET.EXE".

In some instances, the main executable drops both DLL and EXE components. In this case, the EXE is set to run at every Windows restart and the DLL is injected into "EXPLORER.EXE" by the "EXE" component.

To ensure that it automatically runs every time Windows starts, it drops a copy of itself or its EXE component using a random file name into the *%APPDATA%* folder.[4]

Win32/FakeSysdef may make widespread changes to the system including: modifying several Internet Explorer settings, enabling submitting non-encrypted form data, changing the desktop wallpaper, displaying or hiding all shortcuts, hiding desktop and start menu links, disabling Windows Task Manager, disabling checking for signatures on downloaded programs, setting low risk file types

Additionally, some Win32/FakeSysdef variants that may terminate running processes during installation and may block launched application after the computer restarts. During the installation process, they may terminate all running processes and force the computer to restart. After the restart, FakeSysdef attempts to block every launched program, and may then display fake error messages offering to fix the problem.[5] It then repeatedly restarts the computer until the user agrees to buy the fake software.[1][6] It then overwrites data on the hard drive/hard drive disk/HDD.

8.2 Symptoms

Win32/FakeSysdef displays numerous false alerts indicating system errors while displaying the appearance of scanning the hard disk and defragmenting it, then prompts the user, with a "Fix Errors" button, to buy and activate it to fix discovered errors.

When the "Fix Errors" button is selected, FakeSysdef pretends to scan and defragment the hard disk. It then displays more fake error messages, and tells the user that he needs to purchase an "Advanced Module" for the fix. If the user chooses to do so, the browser opens. It will open a custom web browser where the user can input card information to buy the software.[1]

8.3 Removal and Detection

To detect and remove this threat and other malicious software that may be installed on your computer, run a full-system scan with an appropriate, up-to-date, security solution.

This virus may make lasting changes to a computer's configuration that are not restored by detecting and removing this threat. Full recovery includes: configuring Security Zone

settings for Internet Explorer and enabling Task Manager, and repairing infected system services.

8.4 Prevention

- Enable a firewall on your computer.

- Get the latest computer updates for all your installed software.

- Use up-to-date antivirus software.

- Use caution when opening attachments and accepting file transfers.

- Use caution when clicking on hyperlinks to web pages.

- Protect yourself against social engineering attacks.

- Avoid downloading pirated software.

8.5 References

[1] *Malware Encyclopedia: Trojan:Win32/FakeSysdef*, Microsoft, 2010-11-10, retrieved 2013-03-15

[2] *FakeSysdef*, Spyware Remove, 2010-11-30, retrieved 2013-03-15

[3] *Security Response: Trojan.FakeAV*, Symantec, 2013-03-13, retrieved 2013-03-19

[4] *MSRT August '11: FakeSysdef*, TechNet Blogs, 2011-08-10, retrieved 2013-03-15

[5] Vincentas (9 July 2013). "Fakesysdef in SpyWareLoop.com". Spyware Loop. Retrieved 28 July 2013.

[6] *Evaluation and extraction of the potent and tricky Fakesysdef Aka Alureon Rootkit*, Rapid Whiz, 2012-03-19, retrieved 2013-03-15

Chapter 9

Gh0st RAT

Gh0st RAT is a Trojan horse for the Windows platform that the operators of GhostNet used to hack into some of the most sensitive computer networks on Earth.[2] It is a cyber spying computer program. The "Rat" part of the name refers to the software's ability to operate as a "Remote Administration Tool".

The GhostNet system disseminates malware to selected recipients via computer code attached to stolen emails and addresses, thereby expanding the network by allowing more computers to be infected.[3] According to the Infowar Monitor (IWM), "GhostNet" infection causes computers to download a Trojan known as "Gh0st RAT" that allows attackers to gain complete, real-time control.[4] Such a computer can be controlled or inspected by its hackers, and the software even has the ability to turn on the camera and audio-recording functions of an infected computer that has such capabilities, enabling monitors to see and hear what goes on in a room.

9.1 See also

- Computer surveillance

- Computer insecurity

- Cyber-security regulation

- Cyber-warfare

- Proactive Cyber Defence

- GhostNet

- Surveillance

- Espionage

- Phishing

9.2 References

[1] 该软件没有作者,没有版权 (This software has no authors and no copyright). Gh0st RAT Beta 2.5 红狼-网络神偷

[2] "Cyberspies' code a click away - Simple Google search quickly finds link to software for Ghost Rat program used to target governments". *Toronto Star (Canada)* (Toronto, Ontario, Canada). March 31, 2009. Retrieved 2009-04-04.

[3] Markoff, John (March 28, 2009). "Vast Spy System Loots Computers in 103 Countries". New York Times. Retrieved March 29, 2009.

[4] Harvey, Mike (March 29, 2009). "Chinese hackers 'using ghost network to control embassy computers'". London: The Times. Retrieved March 29, 2009.

- Walton, Gregory (April 2008). "Year of the Gh0st RAT". World Association of Newspapers. Retrieved 2009-04-01.

9.3 External links

- Information Warfare Monitor - Tracking Cyberpower (University of Toronto, Canada/Munk Centre)

Chapter 10

In-session phishing

In-session phishing is a form of phishing attack which relies on one web browsing session being able to detect the presence of another session (such as a visit to an online banking website) on the same web browser, and to then launch a pop-up window that pretends to have been opened from the targeted session. This pop-up window, which the user now believes to be part of the targeted session, is then used to steal user data in the same way as with other phishing attacks.

The advantage of in-session phishing to the attacker is that it does not need the targeted website to be compromised in any way, relying instead on a combination of data leakage within the web browser, the capacity of web browsers to run active content, the ability of modern web browsers to support more than one session at a time, and social engineering of the user.

The technique was originally documented by Amit Klein, CTO of security vendor Trusteer, Ltd.[1]

10.1 Process

Initial process of how phishers prepare the ground for their attacks. Phishing attacks can be subdivided into three phases:[2]

- Creation of a bogus web site that mimics the website of the bank that is the target of the attack.

- Uploading of the web page onto one's own site or else the compromising of an existing site.

- Mass emailing to lure the unwary to the bogus site.

Using the combination of all three techniques allows the attacker to carry out his plan. The attack's success, however, depends on factors such as; credibility of the site, contents of the email message, and the user's critical analysis capacity and IT proficiency.

10.2 References

[1] http://www.trusteer.com/files/
In-session-phishing-advisory-2.pdf

[2] http://www.sciencedirect.com/science/article/pii/
S1353485809700558

10.3 External links

- New Phishing Attack Targets Online Banking Sessions With Phony Popups

- New in-session phishing attack could fool experienced users

Chapter 11

List of rogue security software

The following is a partial list of rogue security software, most of which can be grouped into *families*. These are functionally identical versions of the same program repackaged as successive new products by the same vendor.[1][2]

11.1 References

[1] Stewart, Joe (2008-10-22), *Rogue Antivirus Dissected - Part 2*, SecureWorks

[2] Howes, Eric L (2008-11-21), *Spyware Warrior - Family Resemblances*, retrieved 2009-05-02

[3] Precise Security - Advanced Cleaner

[4] Kaspersky - AKM Antivirus 2010 Pro

[5] Spyware Warrior - AlfaCleaner

[6] Alpha AntiVirus - Spyware-Review

[7] BleepingComputer.com - ANG Antivirus

[8] Remove Antimalware Doctor - Spyware-Review

[9] 2 viruses - Remove Antimalware Pro

[10] Virus Removal Guru - AntiMalware GO

[11] Spyware-Fix - AntiMalware Go

[12] BleepingComputer - AntiSpyCheck 2.1

[13] BleepingComputer - AntispyStorm

[14] BleepingComputer - AntiSpyware 2008

[15] BleepingComputer - AntiSpyware Shield

[16] Virus Removal Guru - AntiSpyware Soft

[17] Precise Security - AntiSpywareSuite

[18] BleepingComputer - AntiVermins

[19] Virus Removal Guru - Antivir Solution Pro

[20] Spyware-Fix - Antivira AV

[21] BleepingComputer - Antivirii 2011

[22] Virus Removal Guru - Antivirus Action

[23] Virus Removal Guru - Antivirus Monitor

[24] BleepingComputer - Antivirus 7

[25] Remove Antivirus 8 - Spyware-Review

[26] Spyware-Fix - Antivirus 8

[27] BleepingComputer - Antivirus360

[28] BleepingComputer - Antivirus 2008

[29] Article noting that Antivirus 2010 and Anti-virus-1 are the same

[30] BleepingComputer - Antivirus 2010

[31] Symantec - AntiVirus Gold

[32] PCinDanger - Antivirus Live

[33] BleepingComputer - Antivirus Live

[34] BleepingComputer - Antivirus Master

[35] Spyware-Fix - Antivirus .NET

[36] BleepingComputer - AntivirusPro2009

[37] SpywareFixPro - Antivirus Pro 2010

[38] SpywareFixPro - Antivirus Pro 2010

[39] Remove-malware.net

[40] BleepingComputer - Antivirus Smart Protection

[41] BleepingComputer - Antivirus Soft

[42] Bleeping Computer - Antivirus Studio 2010

[43] BleepingComputer - Antivirus Suite

[44] remove-pcvirus.com - Antivirus Security Pro

[45] Faster, PC! Clean! Clean! - Antivirus System PRO

[46] Symantec - Antivirus XP

[47] MyAntispyware "How to remove Antivirus XP 2010"

[48] Spyware Fix - AV Antivirus Suite

[49] Spyware-Fix - AVG Antivirus 2011

[50] BleepingComputer - AV Security Essentials

[51] Virus Removal Guru - AV Security Suite

[52] SpywareRemove - Awola

[53] SpywareRemove - BestsellerAntivirus

[54] MyAntispyware "How to remove ByteDefender"

[55] Spyware-Fix - CleanThis

[56] BleepingComputer.com - Cloud Protection

[57] McAfee - ContraVirus

[58] Destroy Malware - Control Center

[59] SpywareFixPro - Cyber Security

[60] BleepingComputer - Data Protection

[61] Spyware-Fix - Defense Center

[62] Defru virus

[63] Sophos-Desktop Security 2010

[64] antivirus.about.com - "What is Disc Antivirsus Profes-
      sional?"

[65] Spyware-Fix - Disk Doctor

[66] Spyware Fix Dr. Guard

[67] Symantec Symantec - DriveCleaner

[68] MalwareBytes - EasySpywareCleaner

[69] BleepingComputer - eco Antivirus

[70] Symantec - Errorsafe

[71] Destroy Malware - Essential Cleaner

[72] Markoff, John (May 30, 1989). "Virus Outbreaks Thwart
      Computer Experts". *The New York Times*. Retrieved April
      3, 2010.

[73] Kabay, M. E. (August 17–23, 2005), "Some Notes on Mal-
      ware", *Ubiquity* (New York: ACM) **6** (30), ISSN 1530-
      2180, OCLC 43723524, retrieved April 3, 2010

[74] Faster, PC! Clean! Clean! - GreenAV2009

[75] Spyware Fix - Hard Drive Diagnostic

[76] Spyware-Fix - HDD Fix

[77] Spyware-Fix - HDD Plus

[78] Virus Removal Guru - HDD Rescue

[79] Spyware Fix - HDD Rescue

[80] BleepingComputer - Home Security Solutions

[81] MalwareBytes - IEDefender

[82] SpywareRemove - InfeStop

[83] Symantec - Internet Antivirus

[84] Spyware Fix - Internet Antivirus 2011

[85] Spyware-Fix - Internet Defender 2011

[86] Precisesecurity.com

[87] PCindanger.com

[88] BleepingComputer - Internet Security 2011

[89] BleepingComputer - Internet Security 2012

[90] Virus Removal Guru - Internet Security Essentials

[91] BleepingComputer - Internet Security Guard

[92] BleepingComputer - Live PC Care

[93] MyAntispyware "How to remove Live Security Platinum"

[94] MyAntispyware "How to remove Live Security Suite"

[95] Bleeping Computer - Mac Defender

[96] Bleeping Computer - Mac Protector

[97] Symantec - MacSweeper

[98] MalwareBytes - Malware Alarm

[99] MalwareBytes - MalwareCore

[100] MalwareBytes - MalwareCrush

[101] BleepingComputer - Malware Defense

[102] Kaspersky - Malware Protection Center

[103] Spyware-Fix - Memory Fixer

[104] BleepingComputer MS Antispyware 2009

[105] BleepingComputer - MS Antivirus

[106] Spyware-Fix - MS Removal Tool

[107] Microsoft Windows Blog - Fake Microsoft Security Essen-
       tials

[108] Spyware Fix - My Security Engine

[109] Spyware Fix - My Security Shield

[110] BleepingComputer - My Security Wall

[111] Dunkelstern Software - Review

[112] Sunbelt Security - Netcom3 Cleaner

[113] BleepingComputer - Paladin Antivirus

[114] SpywareWarrior - PAL Spyware Remover

[115] BleepingComputer - PC Antispy

[116] MalwareBytes - PC Clean Pro

[117] SpywareRemove - PC Privacy Cleaner

[118] ComputerAssociates - PCPrivacy Tools

[119] Faster, PC! Clean! Clean! - PCSecureSystem

[120] MalwareBytes - PerfectCleaner

[121] BleepingComputer - Perfect Defender 2009

[122] BleepingComputer - PersonalAntiSpy Free

[123] BleepingComputer - Personal Antivirus

[124] Spyware-Fix - Personal Internet Security 2011

[125] Spyware Fix - Personal Security

[126] Malwarebytes - Personal Shield Pro

[127] SpywareRemove - PC Antispyware

[128] Spyware Fix - PC Defender Antivirus

[129] http://www.safebro.com/pckeeper-virus-remove

[130] BleepingComputer - Privacy Center

[131] BleepingComputer - Protection Center

[132] SpywareRemove - PSGuard

[133] Spyware-Fix - Quick Defragmenter

[134] BleepingComputer - Rapid AntiVirus

[135] BleepingComputer - Real Antivirus

[136] Precise Security - Registry Great

[137] Bleeping Computer - Safety Alerter 2006

[138] bleepingcomputer - remove-security-center

[139] SpywareFixPro - SafetyKeeper

[140] Emsi Soft - SaliarAR

[141] BleepingComputer - Secure Fighter

[142] SpywareRemove - SecurePCCleaner

[143] Bleeping Computer - SecureVeteran

[144] Spyware-Fix - Security Master AV

[145] BleepingComputer - Security Monitor 2012

[146] BleepingComputer - Security Protection

[147] Spywarevoid.com

[148] BleepingComputer - Security Scanner

[149] BleepingComputer - Security Shield

[150] BleepingComputer - Security Solution 2011

[151] Virus Removal Guru - Security Suite

[152] Spyware-Review Security Tool

[153] Spyware-Fix - Security Tool

[154] Precise Security - Security Toolbar 7.1

[155] PcinDanger - Security Essentials 2010

[156] http://botcrawl.com/slimcleaner-virus-removal/

[157] Remove the Smart Anti-Malware Protection Virus (Removal Guide) Bleeping Computer

[158] Virus Removal Guru - Smart Engine

[159] Virus Removal Guru - Smart HDD

[160] BleepingComputer - Smart Protection 2012

[161] http://malwaretips.com - ITExpert

[162] SpywareFixPro - Soft Soldier

[163] - Speedypc Pro

[164] Spyware Warrior - Spy Away

[165] Symantec

[166] BleepingComputer - SpyCrush

[167] Symantec - SpyDawn

[168] Youtube.com

[169] Precise Security - SpyGuarder

[170] BleepingComputer - SpyHeal

[171] Symantec - Spylocked

[172] Faster, PC! Clean! Clean! - SpyMarshal

[173] Symantec - SpyRid

[174] Symantec - SpySheriff

[175] Symantec - SpySpotter

[176] Should I Remove It - SpywareBot

[177] Spyware Warrior - Spyware Cleaner

[178] BleepingComputer - SpywareGuard 2008

[179] Javacool Blog - Fake "SpywareGuard2008? rogue – beware

[180] Faster, PC! Clean! Clean! - Spyware Protect 2009

[181] Symantec - Spyware Quake

[182] Spyware Warrior - Spyware Sheriff

[183] Sunbelt Security - Spyware Stormer

[184] Spyware Warrior - SpywareStrike

[185] MalwareBytes - Spyware Striker Pro

[186] McAfee - SpyWiper

[187] BleepingComputer - Super AV

[188] SysGuard

[189] Spyware Fix - Sysinternals Antivirus

[190] Faster, PC! Clean! Clean! - System Antivirus 2008

[191] MyAntispyware "How to remove SystemArmor"

[192] Remove System Check (Uninstall Guide)

[193] System Defender

[194] BleepingComputer - System Defragmenter

[195] Symantec - SystemDoctor

[196] BleepingComputer - System Live Protect

[197] - System Security

[198] System Tool Removal Guide

[199] Spyware-Fix - System Tool 2011

[200]

[201] Symantec - TheSpyBot

[202] Virus Removal Guru - ThinkPoint

[203] (aka total security) BleepingComputer - Total Secure 2009

[204] BleepingComputer - Total Win 7 Security

[205] BleepingComputer - Total Win Vista Security

[206] BleepingComputer - Total Win XP Security

[207] BleepingComputer - UltimateCleaner

[208] Spyware-Fix - Ultra Defragger

[209] Symantec - VirusHeat

[210] Symantec - VirusIsolator

[211] BleepingComputer - VirusLocker

[212] Symantec - VirusMelt

[213] Symantec - VirusProtectPro

[214] Sunbelt Security - Virus Ranger

[215] Symantec - VirusRemover2008

[216] ComputerAssociates - VirusRemover2009

[217] Virus Removal Guru - Virus Response Lab 2009

[218] BleepingComputer - VirusTrigger

[219] Spyware-Fix - Vista Antimalware 2011

[220] BleepingComputer Antivirus Vista 2010

[221] Virus Removal Guru - Vista Antispyware 2011

[222] Bleeping Computer Vista Antispyware 2012

[223] Precise Security - Vista Antivirus 2008

[224] Virus Removal Guru - Vista Home Security 2011

[225] BleepingComputer - Vista Internet Security 2012

[226] BleepingComputer - Vista Security 2011

[227] Destroy Malware - Vista Security 2012

[228] BleepingComputer - Vista Smart Security 2010

[229] BleepingComputer - Volcano Security Suite

[230] virus/remove-win7-antispyware-2011.html Spyware-Fix - Win7 Antispyware 2011

[231] MyAntispyware "How to remove Win Antispyware Center"

[232] Virus Removal Guru - Win 7 Home Security 2011

[233] Faster, PC! Clean! Clean! - WinAntiVirus Pro 2006

[234] Spyware-Fix - Win Defrag

[235] Virus Removal Guru - Windows 7 Recovery

[236] Precise Security - Windows Anticrashes Utility

[237] Bleeping Computer - Windows Antidanger Center

[238]

[239] Precise Security - Windows Attention Utility

[240] Precise Security - Windows Cleaning Tool

[241] Spyware-Fix - Windows Efficiency Magnifier

[242] Spyware-Fix - Windows Emergency System

[243] Windows Expert Console

[244] Spyware-Fix - Windows Passport Utility

[245] SpywareFixPro - Windows Police Pro

[246] Spyware-Fix - Windows Power Expansion

[247] Spyware-Fix - Windows Privacy Agent

[248] BleepingComputer - Windows Pro Rescuer

[249] Spyware-Fix - Windows Processes Organizer

[250] BleepingComputer - Windows Protection Suite

[251] BleepingComputer - Windows Protection Master

[252] Virus Removal Guru - Windows Recovery

[253] Spyware-Fix - Windows Remedy

[254] Spyware-Fix - Windows Repair

[255] Precise Security - Windows Restore

[256] BleepingComputer - Win 7 Security 2012

[257] Spyware-Fix - Windows Scan

[258] Kaspersky - Windows Shield Center

[259] Spyware-Fix - Windows Stability Center

[260] Bleeping Computer - Windows Steady Work

[261] Spyware-Fix - Windows Support System

[262] Bleeping Computer - Windows Tasks Optimizer

[263] Spyware-Fix - Windows Threats Removing

[264] Spyware-Fix - Windows Tool

[265] Bleeping Computer - Windows Tweaking Utility

[266] Spyware-Fix - Windows Utility Tool

[267] Virus Removal Guru - Windows Vista Recovery

[268] remove-pcvirus.com

[269] Bleepingcomputer.com

[270] Virus Removal Guru - Windows XP Recovery

[271] Symantec - WinFixer

[272] Spyware-Fix - Win HDD

[273] Symantec - WinHound

[274] Winpc Antivirus

[275] Winpc Defender

[276] Symantec - WinSpywareProtect

[277] BleepingComputer - WinWeb Security 2008

[278] Spyware Fix - Wireshark Antivirus

[279] Symantec - WorldAntiSpy

[280] Precise Security - XP Antimalware

[281] SpywareRemove - XP AntiSpyware 2009

[282] MyAntispyware - "How to remove XP AntiSpyware 2010"

[283] Bleeping Computer - XP Antispyware 2012

[284] BleepingComputer - XP Antivirus

[285] Destroy Malware - XP Antivirus 2012

[286] MyAntispyware "How to remove XP Antivirus Pro 2010"

[287] Bleeping Computer - XP Defender Pro

[288] Virus Removal Guru - XP Home Security 2011

[289] BleepingComputer - XP Internet Security 2010

[290] Destroy Malware - XP Security 2012

[291] MyAntspyware "How to remove XP Security Tool"

[292] Pandasecurity.com

[293] MyAntispyware "How to remove XJR Antivirus"

[294] BleepingComputer - Your Protection

[295] BleepingComputer - Your PC Protector

[296] Precise Security - Zinaps AntiSpyware 2008

[297] Security Shield Removal

Chapter 12

Lottery scam

A **lottery scam** is a type of advance-fee fraud which begins with an unexpected email notification, phone call, or mailing (sometimes including a large check) explaining that "You have won!" a large sum of money in a lottery. The recipient of the message—the target of the scam—is usually told to keep the notice secret, "due to a mix-up in some of the names and numbers," and to contact a "claims agent." After contacting the agent, the target of the scam will be asked to pay "processing fees" or "transfer charges" so that the winnings can be distributed, but will never receive any lottery payment.[1] Many email lottery scams use the *names* of legitimate lottery organizations or other legitimate corporations/companies, but this does not mean the legitimate organizations are in any way involved with the scams.

12.1 Identification

There are several ways of identifying a fake lottery email:[2]

- Unless someone has bought a ticket, one cannot have won a prize. There are no such things as "email" draws or any other lottery where "no tickets were sold". This is simply another invention by the scammer to make the victims believe that they have won.

- The scammer will ask the victims to pay a fee in advance to receive their prize. All genuine lotteries simply subtract any fees and tax from the prize. Regardless of what the scammer claims this fee is for (such as courier charges, bank charges, or various imaginary certificates), these are all fabricated by the scammer to obtain money from victims.

- Scam lottery emails will nearly always come from free email accounts such as Outlook, Yahoo!, Hotmail, Live, MSN, Gmail etc.

Most email lottery scams are a type of advance fee fraud.[2] A typical scam email will read like this:

12.2 Mis-selling by lottery "win"

Another type of lottery scam is a scam email or web page where the recipient had won a sum of money in the lottery. The recipient is instructed to contact an agent very quickly but the scammers are just using a third party company, person, email or names to hide their true identity, in some cases offering extra prizes (such as a *7 Day/6 Night Bahamas Cruise Vacation,* if the user rings within 4 minutes). After contacting the "agent", the recipient will be asked to come to an office, where during one hour or more, the conditions of receiving the offer are revealed. For example, the prize recipient is encouraged to spend as much as 30 times the prize money in order to receive the prize itself. In other words, although the offer is in fact genuine, it is really only a discount of a few percent on an extremely expensive purchase. This type of scam is legal in many jurisdictions.

Sometimes lottery scam messages are sent by ordinary postal mail;[3] their content and style is similar to the e-mail versions. For example some scams by letter misuse the names of the legal Spanish lotteries, such as El Gordo de la Primitiva.[4]

In the UK, lottery scams have become such a major problem that many legitimate lottery sites now have dedicated pages on the subject.[5]

12.3 Blackmail variation

This variation relies on the target agreeing to accept a sum of money that they know that they are not entitled to and then, when they refuse to pay the advance fee, the scammers then threaten to report them unless blackmail is paid.

A typical scenario is when the emails are sent to staff of a multinational corporation with offices/branches throughout the world using their work email address. The fraudsters will represent themselves as the agents of a scheme that the multinational has won. An example being the "winners" of a prize as a result of placing an advertisement with the supposed promoter of the scheme in an obscure (and sometimes fictional) trade magazine published in an equally obscure country. The scammers will allege that they have written to the corporation's headquarters and made every attempt to pass on the "prize" but without success. As they (the scammers) don't want to lose face with the promoters they are anxious to discharge their responsibilities to pass on the prize money. So they ask for the target's personal banking details to allow the "prize" to be sent and (of course) they will trust the target will pass it on to their employers. This immediately makes the target vulnerable to a phishing attack but, more significantly, to blackmail attempts. When they refuse to pay any advance fee the fraudsters threaten to report the matter to their employers and/or the police.

12.4 References

[1] "How to identify and avoid hoax or fraudulent e-mail scams," *Microsoft* Archived January 18, 2008 at the Wayback Machine

[2] "FBI Common Fraud Schemes". US Federal Bureau of Investigation. Retrieved 2 August 2013.

[3] "Lottery scams by email or sms- Know their truth". InfoChacha. 2013-09-04. Retrieved 2013-12-07.

[4] "Top 10 List of Current Scams - 2008". Consumer Fraud Reporting. Retrieved 2 August 2013.

[5] "Lottery Scams". Lottery.co.uk. Retrieved 2013-12-07.

12.5 External links

- World Lottery Association warns of foreign lottery fraud risks, the World Lottery Association

- The Rundown on Lottery Scams

- Lottery Scams (information by the Bureau of Consular Affairs of the U.S. Department of State)

- Site fighting Online Lottery scams

Chapter 13

Man-in-the-browser

Man-in-the-Browser (**MITB**, **MitB**, **MIB**, **MiB**), a form of Internet threat related to man-in-the-middle (MITM), is a proxy Trojan horse[1] that infects a web browser by taking advantage of vulnerabilities in browser security to modify web pages, modify transaction content or insert additional transactions, all in a completely covert fashion invisible to both the user and host web application. A MitB attack will be successful irrespective of whether security mechanisms such as SSL/PKI and/or two or three-factor Authentication solutions are in place. A MitB attack may be countered by utilising out-of-band transaction verification, although SMS verification can be defeated by **man-in-the-mobile** (**MitMo**) malware infection on the mobile phone. Trojans may be detected and removed by antivirus software[2] with a 23% success rate against Zeus in 2009,[3] and still low rates in 2011.[4] The 2011 report concluded that additional measures on top of antivirus were needed.[4] A related, more simple attack is the **boy-in-the-browser** (**BitB**, **BITB**). The majority of financial service professionals in a survey considered MitB to be the greatest threat to online banking.

13.1 Description

The MitB threat was demonstrated by Augusto Paes de Barros in his 2005 presentation about backdoor trends "The future of backdoors - worst of all worlds".[5] The name "Man-in-the-Browser" was coined by Philipp Gühring on 27 January 2007.[6]

A MitB Trojan works by utilising common facilities provided to enhance browser capabilities such as Browser Helper Objects (a feature limited to Internet Explorer), browser extensions and user scripts (for example in JavaScript) etc.[6] Antivirus software can detect some of these methods.[2]

In a nutshell example exchange between user and host, such as an Internet banking funds transfer, the customer will always be shown, via confirmation screens, the exact payment information as keyed into the browser. The bank, however,

will receive a transaction with materially altered instructions, i.e. a different destination account number and possibly amount. The use of strong authentication tools simply creates an increased level of misplaced confidence on the part of both customer and bank that the transaction is secure. Authentication, by definition, is concerned with the validation of identity credentials. This should not be confused with transaction verification.

13.2 Examples

Examples of MitB threats on different operating systems and web browsers:

13.3 Protection

13.3.1 Antivirus

Known Trojans may be detected, blocked and removed by antivirus software.[2] In a 2009 study, the effectiveness of antivirus against Zeus was 23%,[3] and again low success rates were reported in a separate test in 2011.[4] The 2011 report concluded that additional measures on top of antivirus were needed.[4]

13.3.2 Hardened software

- Browser security software: MitB attacks may be blocked by in-browser security software such as Trusteer Rapport for Microsoft Windows and Mac OS X which blocks the APIs from browser extensions and controls communication.[12][11][15]

- Alternative software: Reducing or eliminating the risk of malware infection by using portable applications or using alternatives to Microsoft Windows like Mac OS X, Linux, or mobile OSes Android, iOS, Chrome OS, Windows Mobile, Symbian etc., and/or browsers Chrome, Opera.[25] Further protection can be achieved by running this alternative OS, like Linux, from a non-installed live CD, or Live USB.[26]

- Secure Web Browser: Several vendors can now provide a two-factor security solution where a Secure Web Browser is part of the solution. In this case MitB attacks are avoided as the user executes a hardened browser from their two-factor security device rather than executing the "infected" browser from their own machine.

13.3.3 Out-of-band transaction verification

A theoretically effective method of combating any MitB attack is through an out-of-band (OOB) transaction verification process. This overcomes the MitB trojan by verifying the transaction details, as received by the host (bank), to the user (customer) over a channel other than the browser; for example an automated telephone call, SMS, or a dedicated mobile app with graphical cryptogram.[27] OOB transaction verification is ideal for mass market use since it leverages devices already in the public domain (e.g. landline, mobile phone, etc.) and requires no additional hardware devices yet enables three-factor authentication (utilising voice biometrics), transaction signing (to non-repudiation level) and transaction verification. The downside is that the OOB transaction verification adds to the level of the end-user's frustration with more and slower steps.

Man-in-the-Mobile

Mobile phone mobile Trojan spyware **man-in-the-mobile** (**MitMo**)[28] can defeat OOB SMS transaction verification.[29]

- ZitMo (Zeus-In-The-Mobile) is not a MitB Trojan itself (although it performs a similar proxy function on the incoming SMSes), but is mobile malware suggested for installation on a mobile phone by a Zeus infected computer. By intercepting all incoming SMSes, it defeats SMS-based banking OOB two-factor authentication on Windows Mobile, Android, Symbian, BlackBerry.[29] ZitMo may be detected by Antivirus running on the mobile device.

- SpitMo (SpyEye-In-The-Mobile, SPITMO), is similar to ZitMo.[30]

13.3.4 Web fraud detection

Web Fraud Detection can be implemented at the bank to automatically check for anomalous behaviour patterns in transactions.[31]

13.4 Related attacks

13.4.1 Proxy trojans

Keyloggers are the most primitive form of **proxy trojans**, followed by browser-session recorders which capture more data, and lastly MitBs are the most sophisticated type.[1]

13.4.2 Man-in-the-middle

Main article: Man-in-the-middle

SSL/PKI etc. may offer protection in a man-in-the-middle attack, but offers no protection in a man-in-the-browser attack.

13.4.3 Boy-in-the-Browser

A related attack that is simpler and quicker for malware authors to set up is termed **boy-in-the-Browser** (**BitB** or **BITB**). Malware is used to change the client's computer network routing to perform a classic man-in-the-middle attack. Once the routing has been changed, the malware may completely remove itself, making detection more difficult.[32]

13.4.4 Clickjacking

Main article: Clickjacking

Clickjacking tricks a web browser user into clicking on something different from what the user perceives, by means of malicious code in the webpage.

13.5 See also

- Browser security

- Form grabbing

- IT risk

- Threat (computer)

- Timeline of computer viruses and worms

- Online banking

- Security token

- Transaction authentication number

- DNS hijacking

13.6 References

[1] Bar-Yosef, Noa (2010-12-30). "The Evolution of Proxy Trojans". Retrieved 2012-02-03.

[2] F-Secure (2007-02-11). "Threat Description: Trojan-Spy: W32/Nuklus.A". Retrieved 2012-02-03.

[3] Trusteer (2009-09-14). "Measuring the in-the-wild effectiveness of Antivirus against Zeus" (PDF). Archived from the original (PDF) on November 6, 2011. Retrieved 2012-02-05.

[4] Quarri Technologies, Inc (2011). "Web Browsers: Your Weak Link in Achieving PCI Compliance" (PDF). Retrieved 2012-02-05.

[5] Paes de Barros, Augusto (15 September 2005). "O futuro dos backdoors - o pior dos mundos" (PDF) (in Portuguese). Sao Paulo, Brazil: Congresso Nacional de Auditoria de Sistemas, Segurança da Informação e Governança - CNASI. Archived from the original (PDF) on July 6, 2011. Retrieved 2009-06-12.

[6] Gühring, Philipp (27 January 2007). "Concepts against Man-in-the-Browser Attacks" (PDF). Retrieved 2008-07-30.

[7] Dunn, John E (2010-07-03). "Trojan Writers Target UK Banks With Botnets". Retrieved 2012-02-08.

[8] Dunn, John E (2010-10-12). "Zeus not the only bank Trojan threat, users warned". Retrieved 2012-02-03.

[9] Curtis, Sophie (2012-01-18). "Facebook users targeted in Carberp man-in-the-browser attack". Retrieved 2012-02-03.

[10] Marusceac Claudiu Florin (2008-11-28). "Trojan.PWS.ChromeInject.B Removal Tool". Retrieved 2012-02-05.

[11] Nattakant Utakrit, School of Computer and Security Science, Edith Cowan University (2011-02-25). "Review of Browser Extensions, a Man-in-theBrowser Phishing Techniques Targeting Bank Customers". Retrieved 2012-02-03.

[12] Symantec Marc Fossi (2010-12-08). "ZeuS-style banking Trojans seen as greatest threat to online banking: Survey". Retrieved 2012-02-03.

[13] Ted Samson (2011-02-22). "Crafty OddJob malware leaves online bank accounts open to plunder". Retrieved 2012-02-06.

[14] Symantec Marc Fossi (2008-01-23). "Banking with Confidence". Retrieved 2008-07-30.

[15] Trusteer. "Trusteer Rapport". Retrieved 2012-02-03.

[16] CEO of Trusteer Mickey Boodaei (2011-03-31). "Man-in-the-Browser attacks target the enterprise". Retrieved 2012-02-03.

[17] www.net-security.org (2011-05-11). "Explosive financial malware targets Windows". Retrieved 2012-02-06.

[18] Jozsef Gegeny, Jose Miguel Esparza (2011-02-25). "Tatanga: a new banking trojan with MitB functions". Retrieved 2012-02-03.

[19] Borean, Wayne (2011-05-24). "The Mac OS X Virus That Wasn't". Retrieved 2012-02-08.

[20] Fisher, Dennis (2011-05-02). "Crimeware Kit Emerges for Mac OS X". Archived from the original on September 5, 2011. Retrieved 2012-02-03.

[21] F-secure. "Threat DescriptionTrojan-Spy:W32/Zbot". Retrieved 2012-02-05.

[22] Hyun Choi, Sean Kiernan (2008-07-24). "Trojan.Wsnpoem Technical Details". Symantec. Retrieved 2012-02-05.

[23] Microsoft (2010-04-30). "Encyclopedia entry: Win32/Zbot - Learn more about malware - Microsoft Malware Protection Center". Symantec. Retrieved 2012-02-05.

[24] Richard S. Westmoreland (2010-10-20). "Antisource - ZeuS". Retrieved 2012-02-05.

[25] Horowitz, Michael (2012-02-06). "Online banking: what the BBC missed and a safety suggestion". Retrieved 2012-02-08.

[26] Purdy, Kevin (2009-10-14). "Use a Linux Live CD/USB for Online Banking". Retrieved 2012-02-04.

[27] Finextra Research (2008-11-13). "Commerzbank to deploy Cronto mobile phone-based authentication technology". Retrieved 2012-02-08.

[28] Chickowski, Ericka (2010-10-05). "'Man In The Mobile' Attacks Highlight Weaknesses In Out-Of-Band Authentication". Retrieved 2012-02-09.

[29] Schwartz, Mathew J. (2011-07-13). "Zeus Banking Trojan Hits Android Phones". Retrieved 2012-02-04.

[30] Balan, Mahesh (2009-10-14). "Internet Banking & Mobile Banking users beware – ZITMO & SPITMO is here !!". Retrieved 2012-02-05.

[31] Sartain, Julie (2012-02-07). "How to protect online transactions with multi-factor authentication". Retrieved 2012-02-08.

[32] Imperva (2010-02-14). "Threat Advisory Boy in the Browser". Retrieved 2015-03-12.

13.7 External links

- Virus attack on HSBC Transactions with OTP Device

- Virus attack on ICICI Bank Transactions

- Virus attack on Citibank Transactions

- Hackers outwit online banking identity security systems BBC Click

- Antisource - ZeuS A summary of ZeuS as a Trojan and Botnet, plus vector of attacks

- Man-In-The-Browser Video on YouTube Entrust President and CEO Bill Conner

- Zeus: King of crimeware toolkits Video on YouTube The Zeus toolkit, Symantec Security Response

- How safe is online banking? Audio BBC Click

- Boy-in-the-Browser Cyber Attack Video on YouTube Imperva

Chapter 14

New Utopia

The **Principality of New Utopia**[1] is a micronation project established by the late Lazarus Long (a.k.a. Howard Turney).[2]

14.1 History

The project was publicised by various media outlets in Europe and the United States. In an article about fake nations, Quatloos.com called "New Utopia" a "fake nation scam".[1] The micronation was also briefly mentioned as a scam in a *Business Week e.biz* online article[3] and in a *Wired News* piece;[4] the latter noted, however, that "Turney... firmly maintains his intention to build the archipelago paradise once he raises enough cash".

Long operated a Web site to promote the so-called micronation tax haven, which he claimed was to be constructed on concrete platforms at the Misteriosa Bank 115 miles west of the Cayman Islands.[5][6][7] He offered US$350 million in unregistered bonds[8] and also promoted a currency purchase program by promising returns of up to 200 percent.[5]

The U.S. Securities and Exchange Commission (US SEC) termed New Utopia a "fraudulent nationwide Internet scheme",[1] and complained that Long had made "material misrepresentations and omissions concerning, among other things, the status of construction of the project, the companies associated with the project, the safety of the investment, and the status of the Commission's investigation into his activities."[2] The SEC's case against Long (SEC v. Lazarus Long) ruled against Long in 2000, ordering him to pay a disgorgement of US$24,000, the amount he had collected thus far.[2] The latter condition was subsequently waived due to Long's inability to pay.[8] Long continues to maintain that the project is real and offers 'charter citizenship' to individuals who "contribute" at least US$10,000 (recently increased from US$1,500).[9]

New Utopia's "UK Pro Consul" was interviewed by Danny Wallace for his 2005 BBC2 series about micronations, *How to Start Your Own Country* in which he claimed the country's sovereignty had been recognised by the 'Principality of Thaumaturgy'. Wallace questioned the existence of Thaumaturgy[10] New Utopia is also now recognised by The Principality of Vanuatu.

14.2 Structure

The social model and trade system would have been hyper-capitalistic, modelled after the writings of Ayn Rand, Napoleon Hill, Robert Heinlein, Dale Carnegie and Adam Smith.[11] Long also promised that the tiny nation would have a clinic better than the Mayo Clinic, a casino modelled after the Monte Carlo Casino, and "the ultimate luxury spa".[11] Residents would live in one of the 642 apartments and condos that would be built.[12] It would have been a tax haven, with all services paid by a 20% tax on imported consumable goods.[12]

14.3 Founder

Before creating New Utopia, Howard Turney had been introduced to the Human Growth Hormone (HGH) by an anti-aging doctor. He was so impressed with the results that he became an advocate of the hormone and he created in February 1993 a longevity spa called El Dorado Clinic in Playa del Carmen, Mexico. In 1995 he changed his name after Lazarus Long, a recurrent character in Heinlein's novels who goes through several rejuvenation treatments in order to live hundreds of years and eventually become immortal. Also around 1995 he stopped injecting HGH in the El Dorado clinic because of the corruption of local officers, and he moved to the US. A few years later he had to stop injecting HGH also in the US when doctors stopped prescribing due to illegal doping in sport. Then he tried to fund New Utopia, a place where the government couldn't tell him what he could do and what he couldn't. But in 1999 the SEC closed his bond offering because the bonds were unregistered with them.[13] He dedicated the rest of his life to the creation of New Utopia.

Lazarus Long died on 26 April 2012.

14.4 See also

- List of micronations

- Dominion of Melchizedek

- Republic of Minerva

14.5 References

[1] "EXHIBIT: Fake Nations", Quatloos.com. Retrieved 30 May 2007.

[2] US SEC ruling, Litigation Release No. 16425 / February 4, 2000. Securities and Exchange Commission v. Lazarus R. Long (a/k/a Howard Turney individually and doing business as New utopia,) USDC/NDOK/TULSA CA No. 99CV 0257BU(M)

[3] McNamee, Mike, "Invest in Freedonia!", *Business Week e.biz*, 11 December 2000. Retrieved 8 May 2007.

[4] Blumberg, Alex, "It's Good to Be King", *Wired* 8.03, March 2000. Retrieved 8 May 2007

[5] McMillan, Alex Frew (2000-04-25). "Beware of Net stock scams". CNN Money. Retrieved 2007-05-09.

[6] Perlman, Jay (2000-02-23). "Securities Fraud: Bogus Offerings". The Motley Fool. Retrieved 2007-05-09.

[7] Peter Lilley (2003), *Hacked, Attacked & Abused: Digital Crime Exposed*, Kogan Page Publishers, p. 90, ISBN 9780749438746

[8] Reagan, Brad (2002-01-14). "Strange -- but Not True". The Wall Street Journal. Retrieved 2007-05-09.

[9] "Citizenship & Nationality". *Principality of New Utopia*. United Earth Group of Companies. Retrieved 2007-05-09.

[10] http://www.youtube.com/watch?v=z-dv7V3esWo. Missing or empty |title= (help)

[11] Wheeler W. Dixon (2006), *Visions of Paradise: Images of Eden in the Cinema* (illustrated ed.), Rutgers University Press, pp. 40–41, ISBN 9780813537986

[12] John R. Wennersten (2008), *Leaving America: The New Expatriate Generation*, Greenwood Publishing Group, pp. 47–48, ISBN 9780313345067

[13] Arlene Weintraub (2011), *Selling the Fountain of Youth: How the Anti-Aging Industry Made a Disease Out of Getting Old-And Made Billions*, ReadHowYouWant.com, pp. 10–11, 13–14, 21–23, 28, ISBN 9781458732309

14.6 External links

- Official website

Chapter 15

Advance-fee scam

An **advance-fee scam** is a type of fraud and one of the most common types of confidence trick. The scam typically involves promising the victim a significant share of a large sum of money, which the fraudster requires a small up-front payment to obtain. If a victim makes the payment, the fraudster either invents a series of further fees for the victim, or simply disappears.

There are many variations on this type of scam, including 419 scam, Fifo's fraud, Spanish Prisoner scam, the black money scam and the Detroit-Buffalo scam.[1] The scam has been used with fax and traditional mail, and is now prevalent in online communications like emails.

Online versions of the scam originate primarily in the United States, the United Kingdom and Nigeria, with Ivory Coast, Togo, South Africa, the Netherlands, and Spain also having high incidences of such fraud. The scam messages often claim to originate in Nigeria, but usually this is not true. The number "419" refers to the section of the Nigerian Criminal Code dealing with fraud, the charges and penalties for offenders.[2]

15.1 History

The modern scam is similar to the Spanish Prisoner scam dating back to the late 18th century.[3][4] In that con, businessmen were contacted by an individual allegedly trying to smuggle someone connected to a wealthy family out of a prison in Spain. In exchange for assistance, the scammer promised to share money with the victim in exchange for a small amount of money to bribe prison guards.[5] One variant of the scam may date back to the 18th or 19th centuries, as a very similar letter, entitled "The Letter from Jerusalem", is seen in the memoirs of Eugène François Vidocq, a former French criminal and private investigator.[6] Another variant of the scam, dating back to circa 1830, appears very similar to what is passed via email today: "Sir, you will doubtlessly be astonished to be receiving a letter from a person unknown to you, who is about to ask a favour from you...", and goes on to talk of a casket con-

taining 16,000 francs in gold and the diamonds of a late marchioness.[7]

The modern scam became popular during the 1980s. There are many variants of the letters sent. One of these, sent via postal mail, was addressed to a woman's husband, and inquired about his health. It then asked what to do with profits from a $24.6 million investment, and ended with a telephone number.[8] Other official-looking letters were sent from a writer who said he was a director of the state-owned Nigerian National Petroleum Corporation. He said he wanted to transfer $20 million to the recipient's bank account – money that was budgeted but never spent. In exchange for transferring the funds out of Nigeria, the recipient would keep 30% of the total. To get the process started, the scammer asked for a few sheets of the company's letterhead, bank account numbers, and other personal information.[9][10] Yet other variants have involved mention of a Nigerian prince or other member of a royal family seeking to transfer large sums of money out of the country.[11]

The spread of e-mail and email harvesting software significantly lowered the cost of sending scam letters by using the Internet.[12][13] While Nigeria is most often the nation referred to in these scams, they may originate in other nations as well. For example, in 2006, 61% of Internet criminals were traced to locations in the United States, while 16% were traced to the United Kingdom and 6% to locations in Nigeria.[14] Other nations known to have a high incidence of advance-fee fraud include Ivory Coast,[15] Togo,[16] South Africa,[17] the Netherlands,[18] and Spain.[19]

One reason Nigeria may have been singled out is the apparently comical, almost ludicrous nature of the promise of West African riches from a Nigerian prince. According to Cormac Herley, a researcher for Microsoft, "By sending an email that repels all but the most gullible, the scammer gets the most promising marks to self-select."[20] Nevertheless, Nigeria has earned a reputation as being at the center of email scammers,[21] and the number 419 refers to the article of the Nigerian Criminal Code (part of Chapter 38: "Obtaining property by false pretenses; Cheating") dealing with fraud.[22] In Nigeria, scammers use computers in Internet cafés to send mass emails promising potential victims riches or romance, and to trawl for replies. They refer to their targets as *Magas*, slang developed from a Yoruba word meaning "fool". Some scammers have accomplices in the United States and abroad that move in to finish the deal once the initial contact has been made.[23]

In recent years, efforts have been made, by both governments and individuals, to combat scammers involved in advance-fee fraud and 419 scams. In 2004, the Nigerian government formed the Economic and Financial Crimes Commission (EFCC) to combat economic and financial crimes, such as advanced fee fraud.[24] In 2009, Nigeria's EFCC announced that they have adopted smart technology developed by Microsoft to track down fraudulent emails. They hoped to have the service, dubbed "Eagle Claw", running at full capacity to warn a quarter of a million potential victims.[21] Some individuals may also participate in a practice known as scam baiting, in which they pose as potential targets and engage the scammers in lengthy dialogue so as to waste their time and decrease the time they have available for real victims.[25] Details on the practice of scam baiting, and ideas, are chronicled on a website, 419eater.com, launched in 2003 by Michael Berry. One particularly notable case of scam baiting involved an American who identified himself to a Nigerian scammer as James T. Kirk. When the scammer — who apparently had never heard of the television series *Star Trek* — asked for his passport details, "Kirk" sent a copy of a fake passport with a photo of *Star Trek*'s Captain Kirk, hoping the scammer would attempt to use it and get arrested.[26]

Scam letter posted within South Africa

15.2 Implementation

This scam usually begins with a letter or email[5] purportedly sent to a selected recipient but actually sent to many, making an offer that would allegedly result in a large payoff for the victim. More recently, scammers have also used fake but plausible-seeming accounts on social networks to make contact with potential victims.

The email's subject line often says something like "From the desk of barrister [Name]", "Your assistance is needed", and so on. The details vary, but the usual story is that a person, often a government or bank employee, knows of a large amount of unclaimed money or gold which he cannot access directly, usually because he has no right to it. Such people, who may be real but impersonated people or fictitious characters played by the con artist, could include, for example, the wife or son of a deposed African leader who has amassed a stolen fortune, a bank employee who knows of a terminally ill wealthy person with no relatives, or a wealthy foreigner who deposited money in the bank just before dying in a plane crash (leaving no will or known next of kin),[27] a US soldier who has stumbled upon a hidden cache of gold in Iraq, a business being audited by the government, a disgruntled worker or corrupt government official who has embezzled funds, a refugee,[28] and similar characters. The money could be in the form of gold bullion, gold dust, money in a bank account, blood diamonds, a series of checks or bank drafts, and so forth. The sums involved are usually in the millions of dollars, and the investor is promised a large share, typically ten to forty percent, in return for assisting the fraudster to retrieve or expatriate the money. Although the vast majority of recipients do not respond to these emails, a very small percentage do, enough to make the fraud worthwhile, as many millions of messages can be sent daily.

To help persuade the victim to agree to the deal, the scammer often sends one or more false documents bearing official government stamps, and seals.[29] 419 scammers often mention false addresses and use photographs taken from the Internet or from magazines to falsely represent themselves. Often a photograph used by a scammer is not a picture of any person involved in the scheme. Multiple "people" involved in schemes are fictitious, and in many cases, one person controls many fictitious personas used in scams.[15]

Once the victim's confidence has been earned, the scammer then introduces a delay or monetary hurdle that prevents the deal from occurring as planned, such as "To transmit the money, we need to bribe a bank official. Could you help us with a loan?" or "For you to be a party to the transaction, you must have holdings at a Nigerian bank of $100,000 or more" or similar. This is the money being stolen from the victim; the victim willingly transfers the money, usually through some irreversible channel such as a wire transfer, and the scammer receives and pockets it. More delays and additional costs are added, always keeping the promise of an imminent large transfer alive, convincing the victim that the money the victim is currently paying is covered several times over by the payoff. The implication that these payments will be used for "white-collar" crime such as bribery, and even that the money they are being promised is being stolen from a government or royal/wealthy family, often prevents the victim from telling others about the "transaction", as it would involve admitting that they intended to be complicit in an international crime. Sometimes psychological pressure is added by claiming that the Nigerian side, to pay certain fees, had to sell belongings and borrow money on a house, or by comparing the salary scale and living conditions in Africa to those in the West. Much of the time, however, the needed psychological pressure is self-applied; once the victims have provided money toward the payoff, they feel they have a vested interest in seeing the "deal" through. Some victims even believe they can cheat the other party, and walk away with all the money instead of just the percentage they were promised.[15]

The essential fact in all advance-fee fraud operations is the promised money transfer to the victim never happens, because the money does not exist. The perpetrators rely on the fact that, by the time the victim realizes this (often only after being confronted by a third party who has noticed the transactions or conversation and recognized the scam), the victim may have sent thousands of dollars of their own money, and sometimes thousands more that has been borrowed or stolen, to the scammer via an untraceable and/or irreversible means such as wire transfer.[15] The scammer disappears, and the victim is left on the hook for the money sent to the scammer.

During the course of many schemes, scammers ask victims to supply bank account information. Usually this is a "test" devised by the scammer to gauge the victim's gullibility;[18] the bank account information isn't used directly by the scammer, because a fraudulent withdrawal from the account is more easily detected, reversed, and traced. Scammers instead usually request that payments be made using a wire transfer service like Western Union and MoneyGram.[30] The reason given by the scammer usually relates to the speed at which the payment can be received and processed, allowing quick release of the supposed pay-

off. The real reason is that wire transfers and similar methods of payment are irreversible, untraceable and, because identification beyond knowledge of the details of the transaction is often not required, completely anonymous.[15] However, bank account information obtained by scammers is sometimes sold in bulk to other fraudsters, who wait a few months for the victim to repair the damage caused by the initial scam, before raiding any accounts which the victim didn't close.

Telephone numbers used by scammers tend to come from burner phones. In Ivory Coast a scammer may purchase an inexpensive mobile phone and a pre-paid SIM card without submitting any identifying information. If the scammers believe they are being traced, they discard their mobile phones and purchase new ones.[15]

The spam emails used in these scams are often sent from Internet cafés equipped with satellite internet connection. Recipient addresses and email content are copied and pasted into a webmail interface using a stand-alone storage medium, such as a memory card. Certain areas of Lagos, such as Festac, contain many cyber cafés that serve scammers; cyber cafés often seal their doors outside hours, such as from 10:30pm to 7:00am, so that scammers inside may work without fear of discovery.[31]

Nigeria also contains many businesses that provide false documents used in scams; after a scam involving a forged signature of Nigerian President Olusegun Obasanjo in summer 2005, Nigerian authorities raided a market in the Oluwole section of Lagos. The police seized thousands of Nigerian and non-Nigerian passports, 10,000 blank British Airways boarding passes, 10,000 United States Postal money orders, customs documents, false university certificates, 500 printing plates, and 500 computers.[31]

The "success rate" of the scammers is also hard to gauge, since they are operating illegally and do not keep track of specific numbers. One individual estimated he sent 500 emails per day and received about seven replies, citing that when he received a reply, he was 70 percent certain he would get the money.[23] If tens of thousands of emails are sent every day by thousands of individuals, it doesn't take a very high success rate to be worthwhile.[32]

15.3 Common elements

15.3.1 Fake cheques

Fraudulent cheques and money orders are key elements in many advance-fee scams, such as auction/classified listing overpayment, lottery scams, inheritance scams, etc., and can be used in almost any scam when a "payment" to the victim is required to gain, regain or further solidify the victim's trust and confidence in the validity of the scheme.[33]

The use of cheques in a scam hinges on a US law (and common practice in other countries) concerning cheques: when an account holder presents a cheque for deposit or to cash, the bank must (or in other countries, usually) make the funds available to the account holder within 1–5 business days, regardless of how long it actually takes for the cheque to clear and funds to be transferred from the issuing bank.[34] The cheques clearing process normally takes 7–10 days, and can take up to a month when dealing with foreign banks. The time between the funds appearing as available to the account holder and the cheque clearing is known as the "float", during which time the bank could technically be said to have floated a loan to the account holder to be covered with the funds from the bank clearing the cheque.

The cheque given to the victim is typically counterfeit but drawn on a real account with real funds in it. With a piece of software like QuickBooks or pre-printed blank cheque stock, using the correct banking information, the scammer can easily print a cheque that is absolutely genuine-looking, passes all counterfeit tests, and may even clear the paying account if the account information is accurate and the funds are available. However, whether it clears or not, it eventually becomes apparent either to the bank or the account holder that the cheque is a forgery. This can be as little as three days after the funds are available if the bank supposedly covering the cheque discovers the cheque information is invalid, or it could take months for a business or individual to notice the fraudulent draft on their account. It has been suggested that in some cases the cheque is genuine — however the fraudster has a friend (or bribes an official) at the paying bank to claim it is a fake weeks or even months later when the physical cheque arrives back at the paying bank.

Regardless of the amount of time involved, once the cashing bank is alerted the cheque is fraudulent, the transaction is reversed and the money removed from the victim's account. In many cases, this puts victims in debt to their banks as the victim has usually sent a large portion of the cheque by some non-reversible 'wire transfer' means (typically Western Union) to the scammer and, since more uncollected funds have been sent than funds otherwise present in the victim's account, an overdraft results.

15.3.2   Western Union and MoneyGram wire transfers

A central element of advance-fee fraud is the transaction from the victim to the scammer must be untraceable and irreversible. Otherwise, the victim, once they become aware of the scam, can successfully retrieve their money and alert officials who can track the accounts used by the scammer.

Western Union, Avenue de Choisy, Paris 13ᵉ

Wire transfers via Western Union and MoneyGram are ideal for this purpose. International wire transfers cannot be cancelled or reversed, and the person receiving the money cannot be tracked. Other similar non-cancellable forms of payment include postal money orders and cashier's checks, but as wire transfer via Western Union or MoneyGram is the fastest method, it is the most common.

15.3.3   Anonymous communication

Since the scammer's operations must be untraceable to avoid identification, and because the scammer is often impersonating someone else, any communication between the scammer and his victim must be done through channels that hide the scammer's true identity. The following options in particular are widely used.

Web-based email

Because many free email services do not require valid identifying information, and also allow communication with many victims in a short span of time, they are the preferred method of communication for scammers. Some services go so far as to mask the sender's source IP address (Gmail being a common choice), making the scammer more difficult to trace to country of origin. While Gmail does indeed strip headers from emails, it is in fact possible to trace an IP address from such an email. Scammers can create as many accounts as they wish, and often have several at a time. In addition, if email providers are alerted to the scammer's activities and suspend the account, it is a trivial matter for the scammer to simply create a new account to resume scamming.

Email hijacking/friend scams

Suspected Web Forgery

This page has been reported as a web forgery designed to trick users into sharing personal or financial information. Entering any personal information on this page may result in identity theft or other fraud.

These types of web forgeries are used in scams known as phishing attacks, in which fraudulent web pages and emails are used to imitate sources you may trust. You can find out more about how Firefox protects you from phishing attacks.

Get me out of here! Ignore this warning

[This isn't a web forgery]

Screenshot of Firefox 2.0.0.1[35] phishing suspicious site warning

Some fraudsters hijack existing email accounts and use them for advance-fee fraud purposes. The fraudsters email associates, friends, or family members of the legitimate account owner in an attempt to defraud them.[36] Variety of techniques such as phishing, keyloggers, computer viruses are used to gain login information for the email address.

Fax transmissions

Facsimile machines are commonly used tools of business, whenever a client requires a hard copy of a document. They can also be simulated using web services, and made untraceable by the use of prepaid phones connected to mobile fax machines or by use of a public fax machine such as one owned by a document processing business like FedEx Office/Kinko's. Thus, scammers posing as business entities often use fax transmissions as an anonymous form of communication. This is more expensive, as the prepaid phone and fax equipment cost more than email, but to a skeptical victim it can be more believable.

SMS messages

Abusing SMS bulk senders such as WASPs, scammers subscribe to these services using fraudulent registration details and paying either via cash or stolen credit card details. They then send out masses of unsolicited SMSes to victims stating they have won a competition, lottery, reward, or like event, and they have to contact somebody to claim their prize. Typically the details of the party to be contacted will be an equally untraceable email address or a virtual telephone number. These messages may be sent over a weekend when abuse staff at the service providers are not working, enabling the scammer to be able to abuse the services for a whole weekend. Even when traceable, they give out long and winding procedures for procuring the reward (real or unreal) and that too with the impending huge cost of transportation and tax or duty charges. The origin of such SMS messages are often from fake websites/addresses.

A recent (mid-2011) innovation is the use of a Premium Rate 'call back' number (instead of a web site or email) in the SMS. On calling the number, the victim is first reassured that 'they are a winner' and then subjected to a long series of instructions on how to collect their 'winnings'. During the message, there will be frequent instructions to 'ring back in the event of problems'. The call is always 'cut off' just before the victim has the chance to note all the details. Some victims call back multiple times in an effort to collect all the details. The scammer thus makes their money out of the fees charged for the calls.

Telecommunications relay services

Many scams use telephone calls to convince the victim that the person on the other end of the deal is a real, truthful person. The scammer, possibly impersonating a US citizen or other person of a nationality, or gender, other than their own, would arouse suspicion by telephoning the victim. In these cases, scammers use TRS, a US federally funded relay service where an operator or a text/speech translation program acts as an intermediary between someone using an ordinary telephone and a deaf caller using TDD or other teleprinter device. The scammer may claim they are deaf, and that they must use a relay service. The victim, possibly drawn in by sympathy for a disabled caller, might be more susceptible to the fraud.

FCC regulations and confidentiality laws require operators to relay calls verbatim, and adhere to a strict code of confidentiality and ethics. Thus, no relay operator may judge the legality and legitimacy of a relay call, and must relay it without interference. This means the relay operator may not warn victims, even when they suspect the call is a scam. MCI said about one percent of their IP Relay calls in 2004 were scams.[37]

Tracking phone-based relay services is relatively easy, so scammers tend to prefer Internet Protocol-based relay services such as IP Relay. In a common strategy, they bind their overseas IP address to a router or server located on US soil, allowing them to use US-based relay service providers without interference.

TRS is sometimes used to relay credit card information to make a fraudulent purchase with a stolen credit card. In many cases however, it is simply a means for the con artist to further lure the victim into the scam.

15.3.4 Invitation to visit the country

Sometimes, victims are invited to a country to meet government officials, an associate of the scammer, or the scammer themselves. Some victims who travel are instead held for ransom. Scammers may tell a victim he or she does not need to get a visa or that the scammers will provide the visa.[38] If the victim does this, the scammers have the power to extort money from the victim.[38] Sometimes victims are ransomed or, as in the case of the Greek George Makronalli, who was lured to South Africa, killed.[39][40] In 1999, Norwegian millionaire Kjetil Moe was also lured to South Africa by 419 scam-artists, and murdered.[41][42] According to a 1995 U.S. State Department report, over fifteen persons between 1992 and 1995, including one U.S. citizen, have been murdered in Nigeria after following-through on advance-fee frauds.[43]

15.4 Variants

See also: Internet fraud, List of email scams and phishing

There are many variations on the most common stories, and also many variations on the way the scam works. Some of the more commonly seen variants involve employment scams, lottery scams, online sales and rentals, and romance scams. Many scams involve online sales, such as those advertised on websites such as Craigslist and eBay, or even with rental properties. It is important to keep in mind that it is beyond the scope of this article to list every single type of known advanced fee fraud or 419 scheme. Rather, this only covers some of the major types. Additional examples may be available in the *external links* section at the end of this article.

15.4.1 Employment scams

Main article: Employment scams

This scam targets people who have posted their resumes on e.g. job sites. The scammer sends a letter with a falsified company logo. The job offer usually indicates exceptional salary and benefits, and requests that the victim

needs a "work permit" for working in the country, and includes the address of a (fake) "government official" to contact. The "government official" then proceeds to fleece the victim by extracting fees from the unsuspecting user for the work permit and other fees. A variant of the job scam recruits freelancers seeking legitimate gigs (such as in editing or translation), then offers "pre-payment" for their work.

Many legitimate (or at least fully registered) companies work on a similar basis, using this method as their primary source of earnings. Some modelling and escort agencies will tell applicants that they have a number of clients lined up, but that they require a "registration fee" of sorts to account for processing and marketing expenses, or so it is claimed, which is paid in a number of untraceable methods, most often by cash; once the fee is paid, the applicant is informed the client has cancelled, and thereafter they never contact the applicant again.

The scammer contacts the victim to interest them in a "work-at-home" opportunity, or asks them to cash a check or money order that for some reason cannot be redeemed locally. In one cover story, the perpetrator of the scam wishes the victim to work as a "mystery shopper", evaluating the service provided by MoneyGram or Western Union locations within major retailers such as Wal-Mart.[44] The scammer sends the victim a forged check or money order, the victim cashes it, sends the cash to the scammer via wire transfer, and the scammer disappears. Later the forgery is discovered and the bank transaction is reversed, leaving the victim liable for the balance. Schemes based solely on check cashing usually offer only a small part of the check's total amount, with the assurance that many more checks will follow; if the victim buys into the scam and cashes all the checks, the scammer can win big in a very short period of time.

15.4.2 Lottery scam

Main article: Lottery scam

The lottery scam involves fake notices of lottery wins. The winner is usually asked to send sensitive information such as name, residential address, occupation/position, lottery number etc. to a free email account which is at times untraceable or without any link. The scammer then notifies the victim that releasing the funds requires some small fee (insurance, registration, or shipping). Once the victim sends the fee, the scammer invents another fee.

Much like the various forms of overpayment fraud detailed above, a new variant of the lottery scam involves fake or stolen checks being sent to the 'winner' of the lottery (these checks representing a part payment of the winnings). The winner is more likely to assume the win is legitimate, and thus more likely to send the fee (which he does not realize is an advance fee). The check and associated funds are flagged by the bank when the fraud is discovered, and debited from the victim's account.

In 2004 a variant of the lottery scam appeared in the United States. Fraud artists using the scheme call victims on telephones; a scammer tells a victim a government has given them a grant and they must pay an advance fee, usually around $250, to receive the grant.[45]

15.4.3 Online sales and rentals

Many scams involve the purchase of goods and services via classified advertisements, especially on sites like Craigslist, eBay, or Gumtree. These typically involve the scammer contacting the seller of a particular good or service via telephone or email expressing interest in the item. They will typically then send a fake check written for an amount greater than the asking price, asking the seller to send the difference to an alternate address, usually by money order or Western Union. A seller eager to sell a particular product may not wait for the check to clear, and when the bad check bounces, the funds wired have already been lost.[46]

Some scammers advertise phony academic conferences in exotic or international locations, complete with fake websites, scheduled agendas and advertising experts in a particular field that will be presenting there. They offer to pay the airfare of the participants, but not the hotel accommodations. They will extract money from the victims when they attempt to reserve their accommodations in a non-existent hotel.[47]

Sometimes, an inexpensive rental property is advertised by a fake landlord, who is typically out of state (or the country) and asking for the rent and/or deposit to be wired to them.[48] Or the con artist finds a property, pretends to be the owner, lists it online, and communicates with the would-be renter to make a cash deposit.[49] The scammer may also be the renter as well, in which case they pretend to be a foreign student and contact a landlord seeking accommodation. They usually state they are not yet in the country and wish to secure accommodations prior to arriving. Once the terms are negotiated, a forged check is forwarded for a greater amount than negotiated, and the fraudster asks the landlord to wire some of the money back.[50]

15.4.4 Pet scams

This is a variation of the online sales scam where high-value, scarce pets are advertised as bait on online advertising websites using little real seller verification like Craigslist, Gumtree, and JunkMail. The pet may either be advertised as being for-sale or up for adoption. Typically the pet is advertised on online advertising pages complete with photographs taken from various sources such as real advertisements, blogs or where ever an image can be stolen. Upon the potential victim contacting the scammer, the scammer responds by asking for details pertaining to the potential victim's circumstances and location under the pretense of ensuring that the pet would have a suitable home. By determining the location of the victim, the scammer ensures he is far enough from the victim so as to not allow the buyer to physically view the pet. Should the scammer be questioned, as the advertisement claimed a location initially, the scammer will claim work circumstances having forced him to relocate. This forces a situation whereby all communication is either via email, telephone (normally untraceable numbers) and SMS. Upon the victim deciding to adopt or purchase the pet, a courier has to be used which is in reality part of the scam. If this is for an adopted pet, typically the victim is expected to pay some fee such as insurance, food or shipping. Payment is via MoneyGram, Western Union or money mules' bank accounts where other victims have been duped into work from home scams.[51]

Numerous problems are encountered in the courier phase of the scam. The crate is too small and the victim has the option of either purchasing a crate with air conditioning or renting one while also paying a deposit, typically called a caution or cautionary fee. The victim may also have to pay for insurance if such fees have not been paid yet. If the victim pays these fees, the pet may become sick and a veterinarian's assistance is sought for which the victim has to repay the courier. Additionally, the victim may be asked to pay for a health certificate needed to transport the pet, and for kennel fees during the recuperation period. The further the scam progresses, the more similar are the fictitious fees to those of typical 419 scams. It is not uncommon to see customs or like fees being claimed if such charges fit into the scam plot.[52]

Numerous scam websites may be used for this scam. This scam has been linked to the classical 419 scams in that the fictitious couriers used, as are also used in other types of 419 scams such as lotto scams.

15.4.5 Romance scam

Main article: Romance scam

One of the variant is the *Romance Scam*, a money-for-romance angle.[53] The con artist approaches the victim on an online dating service, an instant messenger, or a social networking site. The scammer claims an interest in the victim, and posts pictures of an attractive person.[54] The scammer uses this communication to gain confidence, then asks for money.[53] The con artist may claim to be interested in meeting the victim, but needs cash to book a plane, buy a bus ticket, rent a hotel room, pay for personal-travel costs such as gasoline or a vehicle rental, or to cover other expenses. In other cases, they claim they're trapped in a foreign country and need assistance to return, to escape imprisonment by corrupt local officials, to pay for medical expenses due to an illness contracted abroad, and so on.[54] The scammer may also use the confidence gained by the romance angle to introduce some variant of the original Nigerian Letter scheme,[54] such as saying they need to get money or valuables out of the country and offer to share the wealth, making the request for help in leaving the country even more attractive to the victim.

In a newer version of the scam, the con artist claims to have information about the fidelity of a person's significant other, which they will share for a fee. This information is garnered through social networking sites by using search parameters such as 'In a relationship' or 'Married'. Anonymous emails are first sent to attempt to verify receipt, then a new web based email account is sent along with directions on how to retrieve the information.

A scam from Malaysia involves a "woman" alleging to be half American and half Asian with a father who is American but has died. After communication begins the target is immediately asked for money to pay for the woman's sick mother's hospital bills. Also, requests are made to help her get back to the United States. In every case the scammer does not use a webcam so the target can't verify the woman is truly in the picture they have sent. Offers to send a camera to the woman by postal mail (instead of money to buy it) are met with hostility.

Domestic scams often involve meeting someone on an online match making service.[53] The scammer initiates contact with their target who is out of the area and requests money for transportation fare.[54] One "woman" scamming had money sent to a generic name like Joseph Hancock alleging she could not collect the money due to losing her international passport. After sending the money the victim is given bad news the woman was robbed on the way to the bus stop and the victim feels compelled to send more money. The fraudster never visits the victim and is willing to chat with the victim through a chat client as long as the victim is still willing to send more money.

In another variation on the romance scam, the scammer contacts women, either in Nigeria or elsewhere, for example, Ghana, offering to "find a man" for them on Internet dating or social media sites. The scammer will charge the woman a fee for his services or may even offer to sell her a computer so she can have direct access to Internet and e-mail. The scammer then runs the traditional scam to lure a man into a relationship, again using false names, stories and photos.

15.4.6 Other scams

Other scams involve unclaimed property, also called "bona vacantia" in the United Kingdom. In England and Wales (other than the Duchy of Lancaster and the Duchy of Cornwall), this property is administered by the Bona Vacantia Division of the Treasury Solicitor's Department. Fraudulent emails and letters claiming to be from this department have been reported, informing the recipient they are the beneficiary of a legacy but requiring the payment of a fee before sending more information or releasing the money.[55] In the United States, messages may appear to come from the National Association of Unclaimed Property Administrators (NAUPA). Interestingly, this is a real organization of unclaimed property chiefs from around the nation, but it does not have control over any actual money – much less the authority to dole it out to people.[56]

In one variant of 419 fraud, an alleged hitman writes to someone explaining he has been targeted to kill them. He tells them he knows the allegations against them are false, and asks for money so the target can receive evidence of the person who ordered the hit.[57]

Another variant of advanced fee fraud is known as a pigeon drop. This is a confidence trick in which the mark, or "pigeon", is persuaded to give up a sum of money in order to secure the rights to a larger sum of money, or more valuable object. In reality, the scammers make off with the money and the mark is left with nothing. In the process, the stranger (actually a confidence trickster) puts his money with the mark's money (in an envelope, briefcase, or sack) which the mark is then entrusted with. The money is actually not put into the sack or envelope, but is switched for a bag full of newspaper or other worthless material. Through various theatrics, the mark is given the opportunity to leave with the money without the stranger realising. In actuality, the mark would be fleeing from his own money, which the con man still has (or has handed off to an accomplice).[58]

Some scammers will go after the victims of previous scams; known as a reloading scam. For example, they may contact a victim saying they can track and apprehend the scammer and recover the money lost by the victim, for a price. Or they may say a fund has been set up by the Nigerian government to compensate victims of 419 fraud, and all that is required is proof of the loss, personal information, and a processing and handling fee. The recovery scammers obtain lists of victims by buying them from the original scammers.[59]

15.5 Consequences

Estimates of the total losses due to the scam vary widely since many people may be too embarrassed to admit that they were gullible enough to be scammed to report the crime. A United States government report in 2006 indicated that Americans lost $198.4 million to Internet fraud in 2006, averaging a loss of $5,100 per incident.[14] That same year, a report in the United Kingdom claimed that these scams cost the United Kingdom economy £150 million per year, with the average victim losing £31,000.[60] In addition to the financial cost, many victims also suffer a severe emotional and psychological cost, such as losing their ability to trust people. One man from Cambridgeshire, UK, committed suicide by lighting himself on fire with petrol after realizing that the $1.2 million "internet lottery" that he won was actually a scam.[61] In 2007, a Chinese student at the University of Nottingham killed herself after she discovered that she had fallen for a similar lottery scam.[62]

Other victims lose wealth and friends, become estranged from family members, deceive partners, get divorced, or commit other criminal offenses in the process of either fulfilling their "obligations" to the scammers or obtaining more money.[63] In 2008, an Oregon woman lost $400,000 to a Nigerian advance-fee fraud scam, after an email told her she had inherited money from her long-lost grandfather. Her curiosity was piqued because she actually had a grandfather whom her family had lost touch with, and whose initials matched those given in the email. She sent hundreds of thousands of dollars over a period of more than two years, despite her family, bank staff and law enforcement officials all urging her to stop.[64] The elderly are also particularly susceptible to online scams such as this, as they typically come from a generation that was more trusting, and are often too proud to report the fraud. They also may be concerned that relatives might see it as a sign of declining mental capacity, and they are afraid to lose their independence.[65]

Even though the United States Federal Trade Commission and other government agencies are well aware of the Nigerian and advance-fee fraud, victims can still be tried and convicted of crimes themselves. They may end up borrowing or stealing money to pay the advance fees, believing an early payday is imminent. Some of the crimes committed by victims include Credit-card fraud, check kiting, and embezzlement.[66][67][68] One San Diego-based businessman, James Adler, lost over $5 million in a Nigeria-based advance-fee scam. While a court affirmed that various Nigerian government officials (including a governor of the Central Bank of Nigeria) were directly or indirectly involved and that Nigerian government officials could be sued in U.S. courts under the "commercial activity" exception to the Foreign Sovereign Immunities Act, he was unable to

get his money back due to the doctrine of unclean hands because he had knowingly entered into a contract that was illegal.[69]

Some 419 scams involve even more serious crimes, such as kidnapping or murder. One such case, in 2008, involves Osamai Hitomi, a Japanese businessman who was lured to Johannesburg, South Africa and kidnapped on September 26, 2008. The kidnappers took him to Alberton, south of Johannesburg, and demanded a $5 million ransom from his family. Seven people were ultimately arrested.[70] In July 2001, Joseph Raca, a former mayor of Northampton, UK, was kidnapped by scammers in Johannesburg, South Africa, who demanded a ransom of £20,000. The captors released Raca after they became nervous.[71] One 419 scam that ended in murder occurred in February 2003, when Jiří Pasovský, a 72-year-old scam victim from the Czech Republic, shot and killed 50-year-old Michael Lekara Wayid, an official at the Nigerian embassy in Prague, and injured another person, after the Nigerian Consul General explained he could not return the $600,000 that Pasovský had lost to a Nigerian scammer.[26][72][73][74]

The international nature of the crime, combined with the fact that many victims do not want to admit that they bought into an illegal activity, has made tracking down and apprehending these criminals difficult. Furthermore, the government of Nigeria has been slow to take action, leading some investigators to believe that some Nigerian government officials are involved in some of these scams.[75] The government's establishment of the Economic and Financial Crimes Commission (EFCC) in 2004 has helped with the issue to some degree, although there are still issues with corruption.[24][76] A notable case which the EFCC pursued was the case of Emmanuel Nwude, who was convicted for defrauding $242 million out of the director of a Brazilian bank, Banco Noroeste, which ultimately lead to the bank's collapse.

Despite this, there has been some recent success in apprehending and prosecuting these criminals. In 2004, fifty-two suspects were arrested in Amsterdam after an extensive raid, after which, almost no 419 emails were reported being sent by local internet service providers.[77] In November 2004, Australian authorities apprehended Nick Marinellis of Sydney, the self-proclaimed head of Australian 419ers who later boasted that he had "220 African brothers worldwide" and that he was "the Australian headquarters for those scams".[78] In 2008, US authorities in Olympia, Washington, sentenced Edna Fiedler to two years in prison with 5 years of supervised probation for her involvement in a $1 million Nigerian check scam. She had an accomplice in Lagos, Nigeria, who shipped her up to $1.1 million worth of counterfeit checks and money orders with instructions on where to ship them.[79]

15.6 In popular culture

Due to the increased use of the 419 scam on the Internet, it has been used as a plot device in many films, television shows and books. A song, "I Go Chop Your Dollar", performed by Nkem Owoh, also became internationally known as an anthem for 419 scammers.[80] Other appearances in popular media include:

- The novel *I Do Not Come To You By Chance* by Nigerian author Adaobi Tricia Nwaubani explores the phenomenon.

- The 2006 direct-to-DVD kid flick *EZ Money* features an instance of this scam as its central premise.[81]

- In the 2007 *Futurama* straight-to-DVD film *Bender's Big Score*, Professor Farnsworth falls for a lottery scam, giving away his personal details on the Internet after believing he has won the Spanish national lottery. Later, Nixon's Head falls for a "sweepstakes" letter by the same scammers, while Zoidberg is taken by an advance-fee fraud, thinking he is next of kin to a Nigerian Prince.

- In series 6, episode 3 of the BBC television series *The Real Hustle*, the hustlers demonstrated the 419 Scam to the hidden cameras in the "High Stakes" episodes of the show.[82]

- In the HBO comedy series *Flight of the Conchords* episode "The New Cup", the band's manager, Murray, uses the band's emergency funds for what appears to be a 419 scam—an investment offer made by a Mr. Nigel Soladu, who had e-mailed him from Nigeria. However, it turns out that Nigel Soladu is a real Nigerian businessman and the investment offer is legitimate, although Murray notes that, despite Mr. Soladu having e-mailed many people for an investment, only he had taken him up on it. The band receives a 1000% profit, which they use to get bailed out of jail.

- The Residents included a song called "My Nigerian Friend" in their 2008 multimedia production *The Bunny Boy*.

- A segment of the 2008 *This American Life* episode *Enforcers* discusses scammers from Nigeria and a group of activists that try to scam the scammers.[83]

- In the pilot episode, "The Nigerian Job", of *Leverage*, the group uses the reputation of the Nigerian Scam to con a deceitful businessman.

- In *The Office* episode "Michael's Birthday" it is revealed that Michael fell for a 419 scam because he thought he was helping the "son of the deposed king of Nigeria".

- The 2012 novel *419* by Will Ferguson is the story of a daughter looking for the persons she believes responsible for her father's death. A follow-up to earlier novels about con men and frauds (*Generica* and *Spanish Fly*), *419* won the 2012 Giller Prize, Canada's most distinguished literary award.[84][85]

- An episode of *30 Rock* shows Tracy Jordan reminding his entourage about an email they previously received from a group of Nigerians trying to get a large sum of money out of the country. Tracy explains that a check from them had just arrived, but that he would have been happy just helping the dethroned Nigerian Prince.

- In the video game Warframe, Nef Anyo ran an advance-fee fraud during Operation False Profit, where players attempted to reverse the scam and steal credits from him in order to bankrupt him and prevent his creation of a robotic army.

- In the song, Lame Claim To Fame by "Weird Al" Yankovic, The singer mentions getting an e-mail from the prince of Nigeria.

15.7 See also

- Canadian Anti-Fraud Centre Canadian law enforcement project combating advance-fee fraud

- Causes and correlates of crime

- Email spam

- Nigerian organized crime

- True-believer syndrome

15.8 References

[1] "FBI — Financial Fraud". *FBI*.

[2] "Nigerian scam". Encyclopedia Britannica. Retrieved 2012-07-14.

[3] "An old swindle revived; The "Spanish Prisoner" and Buried Treasure Bait Again Being Offered to Unwary Americans". *The New York Times*. 20 March 1898. p. 12. Retrieved 2010-07-01.

[4] Old Spanish Swindle Still Brings In New U.S. Dollars, Sarasota Herald-Tribune, October 2, 1960, pg 14

[5] Mikkelson, Barbara & David P. (February 1, 2010). "Nigerian Scam". *Snopes*. Retrieved June 22, 2012.

[6] Vidocq, Eugène François (1834). *Memoirs of Vidocq: Principal Agent of the French Police until 1827*. Baltimore, Maryland: E. L. Carey & A. Hart. p. 58.

[7] Harris, Misty (June 21, 2012). "Nigerian email scams royally obvious for good reason, study says". *The Province*. Retrieved June 23, 2012.

[8] Buse, Uwe (November 7, 2005). "Africa's City of Cyber Gangsters.". *Der Spiegel*. Retrieved June 22, 2012.

[9] Lohr, Steve (May 21, 1992). "'Nigerian Scam' Lures Companies.". *New York Times*. Retrieved June 22, 2012.

[10] "International Financial Scams". United States Department of State, Bureau of Consular Affairs. Retrieved 2015-01-12.

[11] "The Nigerian Prince: Old Scam, New Twist". Better Business Bureau. Retrieved February 26, 2015.

[12] Andrews, Robert (August 4, 2006). "Baiters Teach Scammers a Lesson.". *Wired*. Retrieved June 22, 2012.

[13] Stancliff, Dave (February 12, 2012). "As It Stands: Why Nigeria became the scam capital of the world". *Times-Standard*. Retrieved June 22, 2012.

[14] Rosenberg, Eric (March 31, 2007). "U.S. Internet fraud at all-time high". *San Francisco Chronicle*. Retrieved June 22, 2012.

[15] "West African Advance Fee Scams.". United States Department of State. Retrieved June 23, 2012.

[16] "Togo: Country Specific Information". United States Department of State. Retrieved June 23, 2012.

[17] "Advance Fee Fraud.". Hampshire Constabulary. Retrieved June 23, 2012.

[18] "Fraud Scheme Information.". United States Department of State. Retrieved June 23, 2012.

[19] "Advance Fee Fraud.". BBA. Retrieved June 23, 2012. External link in |publisher= (help)

[20] Herley, Cormac (2012). "Why do Nigerian Scammers Say They are from Nigeria?" (PDF). *Microsoft*. Retrieved June 23, 2012.

[21] Staff Writer (October 22, 2009). "Nigeria's anti graft police shuts 800 scam websites.". *Agence France-Presse*. Retrieved June 22, 2012.

[22] "Nigeria Laws: Part 6: Offences Relating to property and contracts.". Nigeria Law. Retrieved June 22, 2012. External link in |publisher= (help)

[23] Dixon, Robyn (October 20, 2005). "I Will Eat Your Dollars.". *Los Angeles Times*. Retrieved June 22, 2012.

[24] "Economic and Financial Crimes Commission (Establishment) Act of 2004" (PDF). Economic and Financial Crimes Commission (Nigeria). Retrieved June 22, 2012. External link in |publisher= (help)

[25] Cheng, Jacqui (May 11, 2009). "Baiting Nigerian scammers for fun (not so much for profit).". *Ars technica*. Retrieved June 22, 2012.

[26] Corbin, Jane (January 15, 2010). "A mysterious email and a split-second mistake: That's all it took for internet gangsters to hijack my life...". *Daily Mail*. Retrieved June 22, 2012.

[27] "Latest e-mail uses Alaska Airlines crash victims to scam | Consumer News - seattlepi.com". Blog.seattlepi.nwsource.com. 2007-11-09. Retrieved 2012-02-22.

[28] "Zimbabwe appeal". *Department of Commerce - WA ScamNet*. Retrieved 2015-11-09.

[29] Longmore-Etheridge, Ann (August 1996). "Nigerian scam goes on". *Security Management* **40** (8): 109. Retrieved 12 February 2013.

[30] "Advance Fee Loan Scams | DirectLendingSolutions.com®". *www.directlendingsolutions.com*. Retrieved 2015-09-24.

[31] "Internet Archive Wayback Machine". Web.archive.org. 2005-10-29. Retrieved 2012-02-22.

[32] Grinker, Roy R.; Lubkemann, Stephen C.; Steiner, Christopher B. (2010). *Perspectives on Africa: A Reader in Culture, History and Representation*. New York City: John Wiley & Sons. pp. 618–621. ISBN 978-1-4443-3522-4.

[33] Stevenson, Joseph A. (2010-08-11). "Bogus Cheques Writing Jobs". Careerfield. Archived from the original on 5 February 2014. Retrieved 2014-02-05.

[34] Mayer, Caroline E. (2006-06-01). "Banks Honor Bogus Cheques and Scam Victims Pay". Washington Post. p. A01. Retrieved 2006-07-09.

[35] "Firefox Release Notes". Mozilla. Retrieved 14 September 2010.

[36] Gallagher, David F. (2007-11-09). "E-Mail Scammers Ask Your Friends for Money". Bits.blogs.nytimes.com. Retrieved 2012-02-22.

[37] "Con artists target phone system for deaf". MSNBC. 2004-04-20. Retrieved 2012-02-22.

[38] http://www.state.gov/www/regions/africa/naffpub.pdf

[39] Philip de Braun (2004-12-31). "SA cops, Interpol probe murder". News24. Retrieved 2010-11-27.

[40] "Scam Bait - Don't let greed get you scammed". Freebies.about.com. 2010-06-17. Retrieved 2012-02-22.

[41] Kjetil Moe found dead.

[42] "The 419 Scam, or Why a Nigerian Prince Wants to Give You Two Million Dollars". *informit.com*.

[43] "U.S. State Department 1995 report on Advance-fee Fraud" (PDF). *state.gov*.

[44] "Denton Woman Says Mystery Shopper Job Was Scam". Nbc5i.com. November 6, 2007. Archived from the original on 2008-09-27. Retrieved 2009-06-10.

[45] "Government Grant Scam". snopes.com. Retrieved 2012-02-22.

[46] "Craigslist Scams.". fraudguides.com. Retrieved June 24, 2012.

[47] Grant, Bob (November 24, 2009). "Another fake conference?". *The Scientist*. Retrieved June 24, 2012.

[48] Sichelman, Lew (March 25, 2012). "Rental scams can target either landlords or tenants". *Los Angeles Times*. Retrieved June 23, 2012.

[49] Aho, Karen. "Renters: Beware of new twists on an old scam". *MSN*. Retrieved June 24, 2012.

[50] McKee, Chris (March 27, 2011). "Room rental internet scam takes Eugene college students for thousands". *KMTR*. Retrieved June 24, 2012.

[51] "AKC and Better Business Bureau Warn Consumers to Be Wary of Puppy Scams". Retrieved May 29, 2007.

[52] Weisbaum, Herb. "Hound hoax: Con artists target dog lovers". *MSNBC*. Retrieved June 18, 2007.

[53] "Online Romance Scams Continue To Grow - Project Economy News Story". Kmbc.com. 2006-05-19. Retrieved 2012-02-22.

[54] "Singles seduced into scams online". MSNBC. 2005-07-28. Retrieved 2012-02-22.

[55] "Scam Email Warnings.". Bona Vacantia. Retrieved June 24, 2012. External link in |publisher= (help)

[56] Leamy, Elisabeth (August 16, 2011). "Beware of Unclaimed Money Scams". *ABC News*. Retrieved June 23, 2012.

[57] Mikkelson, Barbara. "Hitman Scam.". Snopes. Retrieved June 23, 2012.

[58] Zak, Paul J. (November 13, 2008). "How to Run a Con". *Psychology Today*. Retrieved June 23, 2012.

[59] Mikkelson, Barbara & David P. "Scam Me Twice, Shame On Me, ...". Snopes. Retrieved June 24, 2012.

[60] "Nigeria scams 'cost UK billions'.". *BBC News*. November 20, 2006. Retrieved June 22, 2012.

[61] "Suicide of internet scam victim.". *BBC News*. January 30, 2004. Retrieved June 22, 2012.

[62] "Web scam drove student to suicide.". *BBC News*. May 2, 2008. Retrieved June 22, 2012.

[63] "Nigerian scam victims maintain the faith.". *Sydney Morning Herald*. May 14, 2007. Retrieved June 22, 2012.

[64] Song, Anna (November 11, 2008). "Woman out $400K to 'Nigerian scam' con artists". KATU. Retrieved June 22, 2012.

[65] Harzog, Beverly Blair (May 25, 2012). "Protect Elderly Relatives from Credit Card Fraud.". *ABC News*. Retrieved June 23, 2012.

[66] Hills, Rusty; Frendewey, Matt (June 12, 2007). "Former Alcona County Treasurer Sentenced to 9-14 Years in Nigerian Scam Case.". *State of Michigan*. Retrieved June 23, 2012.

[67] Krajicek, David. "A "Perfect" Life: Mary Winkler Story". *TruTV*. Retrieved June 23, 2012.

[68] Liewer, Steve (July 5, 2007). "Navy officer gets prison for stealing from ship safe". *San Diego Union Tribune*. Retrieved June 23, 2012.

[69] Soto, Onell R. (August 15, 2004). "Fight to get money back a loss". *San Diego Union Tribune*. Retrieved June 22, 2012.

[70] "Seven in court for 419 kidnap.". *News 24*. September 30, 2008. Retrieved June 22, 2012.

[71] "Kidnapped Briton tells of terror.". *BBC News*. July 14, 2001. Retrieved June 22, 2012.

[72] Misha Glenny. *McMafia*. Vintage Books. pp. 138–141. ISBN 978-0-09-948125-6.

[73] Sullivan, Bob (March 5, 2003). "Nigerian scam continues to thrive". MSNBC. Retrieved June 22, 2012.

[74] Delio, Michelle (February 21, 2003). "Nigerian Slain Over E-Mail Scam". *Wired*. Retrieved June 22, 2012.

[75] Sine, Richard (May 2–8, 1996). "Just Deposit $28 Million". *Metroactive*. Retrieved June 23, 2012.

[76] Oluwarotimi, Abiodun (May 26, 2012). "Nigeria: Police Force Is Corrupt, EFCC Not Sincere - U.S.". *AllAfrica.com*. Retrieved June 23, 2012.

[77] Libbenga, Jan (July 5, 2004). "Cableco 'inside job' aided Dutch 419ers.". *The Register*. Retrieved June 23, 2012.

[78] Haines, Lester (November 8, 2012). "Aussie 419 ringleader jailed for four years.". *The Register*. Retrieved June 23, 2012.

[79] "Woman gets prison for 'Nigerian' scam.". *United Press International*. June 26, 2008. Retrieved June 23, 2012.

[80] Libbenga, Jan (July 2, 2007). "'I Go Chop Your Dollar' star arrested". *The Register*. Retrieved June 23, 2012.

[81] Carter, R.J. (August 26, 2006). "'DVD Review: EZ Money'". Retrieved December 7, 2012.

[82] "Episode 3 of 10, Series 6: High Stakes.". BBC. Retrieved June 22, 2012.

[83] "Enforcers - This American Life".

[84] LaLonde, Michelle (May 17, 2012). "Will Ferguson's new novel, 419, centres on an email scam based in Nigeria.". *Montreal Gazette*. Retrieved June 22, 2012.

[85] "Will Ferguson takes Giller Prize for novel 419". *Toronto Star*, October 30, 2012.

15.9   Further reading

- Apter, Andrew (2005). "The Politics of Illusion". *The Pan-African Nation: Oil and the Spectacle of Culture in Nigeria*. Chicago: University of Chicago Press. ISBN 0-226-02355-9.

- Berry, Michael (2006). *Greetings in Jesus Name!: The Scambaiter Letters*. Harbour Books. ISBN 1-905128-08-8.

- Dillon, Eamon (2008). "Chapter 6: The 419ers". *The Fraudsters — How Con Artists Steal Your Money*. Merlin Publishing. ISBN 978-1-903582-82-4.

- Edelson, Eve (2006). *Scamorama: Turning the Tables on Email Scammers*. Disinformation Company. ISBN 1-932857-38-9.

- Tive, Charles (2006). *419 Scam: Exploits of the Nigerian Con Man*. iUniverse.com. ISBN 0-595-41386-2.

- Van Wijk, Anton (2009). *Mountains of Gold; An Exploratory Research on Nigerian 419-fraud: Backgrounds*. SWP Publishing. ISBN 978-90-8850-028-2.

15.10   External links

- Scamdex: The Email Scam Resource

- RentScams: Rental Property Scams

- Scammed.by: Directory containing over 45,000 examples of scam emails and email addresses

- Federal Bureau of Investigation, United States

- Economic and Financial Crimes Commission, Nigeria

Chapter 16

Operation Newscaster

Logo designed by iSIGHT Partners

"**Operation Newscaster**", as labelled by American firm *iSIGHT Partners* in 2014, is a cyber espionage covert operation directed at military and political figures using social networking, allegedly done by Iran. The operation has been described as "creative",[1] "long-term" and "unprecedented".[2] According to *iSIGHT Partners*, it is "the most elaborate cyber espionage campaign using social engineering that has been uncovered to date from any nation".[2]

16.1 ISight's perceptions

On 29 May 2014, Texas-based cyber espionage research firm *iSIGHT Partners* released a report, uncovering an operation it labels "Newscaster" since at-least 2011, has targeted at least 2,000 people in United States, Israel, Britain, Saudi Arabia, Syria, Iraq and Afghanistan.[2][3]

The victims who are not identified in the document due to security reasons, are senior U.S. military and diplomatic personnel, congresspeople, journalists, lobbyists, think tankers and defense contractors, including a four-star admiral.[2][3]

The firm couldn't determine what data the hackers may have stolen.[3]

According to the *iSIGHT Partners* report, hackers used 14 "elaborated fake" personas claiming to work in journalism, government, and defense contracting and were active in Facebook, Twitter, LinkedIn, Google+, YouTube and Blogger. To establish trust and credibility, the users fab-

A screenshot from NewsOnAir.org

ricated a fictitious journalism website, *NewsOnAir.org*, using content from the media like Associated Press, BBC, Reuters and populated their profiles with fictitious personal content. They then tried to befriend target victims and sent them "friendly messages"[1] with Spear-phishing to steal email passwords[4] and attacks and infecting them to a "not particularly sophisticated" malware for data exfiltration.[2][3]

The report says *NewsOnAir.org* was registered in Tehran and likely hosted by an Iranian provider. The Persian language word "Parastoo" (Persian: پرستو; meaning *swallow*) was used as a password for malware associated with the group, which appeared to work during business hours in Tehran[2] as they took Thursday and Friday off.[1] *iSIGHT Partners* could not confirm whether the hackers had ties to the Iranian government.[4]

16.2 Analysis

According to *Al Jazeera*, Chinese army's cyber unit carried out scores of similar phishing schemes.[4]

Morgan Marquis-Boire, a researcher at the University of Toronto stated that the campaign "appeared to be the work of the same actors performing malware attacks on Iranian dissidents and journalists for at least two years".[4]

Franz-Stefan Gady, a senior fellow at the EastWest Institute and a founding member of the Worldwide Cybersecurity Initiative, stated that "They're not doing this for a quick buck, to extrapolate data and extort an organization. They're in it for the long haul. Sophisticated human engineering has been the preferred method of state actors".[4]

16.3 Reactions

- Facebook spokesman said the company discovered the hacking group while investigating suspicious friend requests and removed all of the fake profiles.[2]

- LinkedIn spokesman said they are investigating the report, though none of the 14 fake profiles uncovered were currently active.[2]

- Twitter declined to comment.[2]

- Federal Bureau of Investigation told *Al Jazeera* "it was aware of the report but that it had no comment".[4]

16.4 References

[1] Nakashima, Ellen (May 29, 2014). "Iranian hackers are targeting U.S. officials through social networks, report says". *The Washington Post*. Retrieved March 30, 2015.

[2] Finkle, Jim (May 29, 2014). Tiffany Wu, ed. "Iranian hackers use fake Facebook accounts to spy on U.S., others". *Reuters*. Retrieved March 30, 2015.

[3] Chumley, Cheryl K. (May 29, 2014). "Iranian hackers sucker punch U.S. defense officials with creative social-media scam". *The Washington Times*. Retrieved March 30, 2015.

[4] Pizzi, Michael (May 29, 2014). "Iran hackers set up fake news site, personas to steal U.S. secrets". *Al Jazeera*. Retrieved March 30, 2015.

16.5 External links

- NEWSCASTER – An Iranian Threat Inside Social Media

Chapter 17

Patched (malware)

Win32/Patched is a Computer Trojan targeting the Microsoft Windows operating system that was first detected in October 2008.[1] Files detected as "Trojan.Win32.Patched" are usually Windows components that are patched by a malicious application. The purpose of patching varies. For example, certain malware patches system components in order to disable security, such as the Windows Safe File Check feature. Other malware can add parts of its code to a system component and then patch certain functions of the original file to point to an appended code.[2]

17.1 Operation

This Trojan operates through modification to legitimate systems files on an infected system.[3] Additionally, malware can add parts of its code to a system component and then patch certain functions of the original file to point to an appended code. The most frequently patched components are:

- winlogon.exe

- wininet.dll

- kernel32.dll

- iexplore.exe

- services.exe.[2][4]

17.1.1 Initial Infection

- Variant R replace the original legitimate system file "sfc.dll" with a patched version. The original "sfc.dll" may have been placed by malware into another location within the same computer. Trojan:Win32/Patched.R is capable of loading other files. It may be installed by other malware.[5]

- Variant I represent malicious, and packed, Win32 programs. Many malicious programs are packed with particular utilities in an attempt to avoid detection.[6]

- Variant C defines corrupted DLL files that are modified to load an additional DLL. This variant may also attack and corrupt the services.exe executable[1]

- Variant A can modify a legitimate DLL file on an infected system.[3]

17.2 Symptoms

There are no obvious symptoms that indicate the presence of this malware on an affected machine. Additionally, There are no common symptoms associated with this threat. Alert notifications from installed antivirus software may be the only symptom(s).[1]

17.3 Removal And Detection

It is not advised to delete, rename or quarantine patched Windows components because it may affect system stability. Even though Windows locks its main files while it is active, it might be still possible to affect them.

If your Anti-Virus software detected a certain file as Trojan.Win32.Patched you can attempt to have it create a copy of a patched file, try to restore its contents, and then it will add a renaming command into the Windows Registry in order to replace the patched file with a cleaned one during the next Windows startup.

A restoration to one of the recent System Restore points may be advisable. In many cases a patched system component will be replaced with a clean one. Before restoring a System Restore point it is advised to backup all personal data to avoid losing it when Windows rolls back to a previously saved state.

Windows Installation discs contain a repair option that can replace the patched file.

Another course of action includes attaching a hard drive with a patched file as slave to a similar Windows-based system, boot up and to replace a patched file with a file taken from a clean system.[2]

17.4 Prevention

- Enable a firewall on your computer.

- Get the latest computer updates for all your installed software.

- Use up-to-date antivirus software.

- Use caution when opening attachments and accepting file transfers.

- Use caution when clicking on links to web pages.

- Protect yourself against social engineering attacks.

17.5 References

[1] *Malware Encyclopedia: Virus:Win32/Patched.C*, Microsoft, 2008-10-22, retrieved 2012-07-06

[2] *Virus and threat descriptions: Trojan:W32/Patched*, F-Secure, retrieved 2012-07-06

[3] *Malware Encyclopedia: Virus:Win32/Patched.A*, Microsoft, 2009-09-30, retrieved 2012-07-06

[4] *In-The-Field Analysis of "TrojanHorse:win32/Patched.c. LYT" Virus*, RapidWhiz, retrieved 2012-07-06

[5] *Malware Encyclopedia: Virus:Win32/Patched.R*, Microsoft, 2010-01-16, retrieved 2012-07-06

[6] *Malware Encyclopedia: Virus:Win32/Patched.I*, Microsoft, 2010-01-16, retrieved 2012-07-06

Chapter 18

PayPaI

This article is about a phishing scam. For the legitimate payment system, see PayPal.

Paypai (capitalised as **PayPaI**) is a phishing scam, which targets account holders of the widely used internet payment service, PayPal, taking advantage of the fact that a capital "i" may be difficult to distinguish from a lower-case "L" in some computer fonts. This is a form of a homograph attack.

The scam involves sending PayPal account holders a notification email claiming that PayPal has "temporarily suspended" their account. Instead of linking to paypal.com, the site links to a convincing duplicate of the site at paypai.com, in the hope that the user will enter their PayPal login details, which the owner of paypai.com can then store and use.

18.1 History

Paypai was first active in mid-2000. It sent account holders of PayPal bogus payment receipt notifications, mimicking those sent by PayPal, indicating that the account holder had received a large payment and directed recipients to paypai.com through a link in the message.[1][2]

The site, paypai.com, was an exact replica of the HTML source code and images that PayPal uses on its home page. While devious, this was not difficult, since the HTML and images are downloaded for display whenever a user visits a website. The site was registered with Network Solutions to a "Birykov" in South Ural, Russia.[1][2]

At the time, MS Sans Serif, a font similar to Arial that rendered capital "i" and lowercase "L" almost identically, was the default font in the address bar on most Windows applications. When Windows XP was released in 2001, Tahoma became the default; Tahoma places serifs on the capital "i" to easily distinguish it from lowercase "L".

Paypai scams resurfaced in 2011 and 2012.[3][4]

18.2 See also

- IDN homograph attack

18.3 References

[1] Knowles, William (July 22, 2000). "Scam artist copies PayPal Web site". *Information Security News mailing list archives*. SecLists.Org. Retrieved February 18, 2012.

[2] Sullivan, Bob (July 24, 2000). "PayPal alert! Beware the 'Paypai' scam". *ZDNet UK*. Retrieved February 18, 2012.

[3] Mustaca, Sorin (February 12, 2011). "Old tricks, new language: "Paypai" in German". *TechBlog*. Avira GmbH. Retrieved February 17, 2012.

[4] MinnieApolis (January 27, 2012). "New Twist on PayPaL Phishing is from PayPaI (with an i)". *Newsvine*. Retrieved February 17, 2012.

Chapter 19

Phishing

Not to be confused with Fishing.
For more information about Wikipedia-related phishing attempts, see Wikipedia:Phishing emails

Phishing is the attempt to acquire sensitive informa-

Dear valued customer of TrustedBank,

We have recieved notice that you have recently attempted to withdraw the following amount from your checking account while in another country: $135.25.

If this information is not correct, someone unknown may have access to your account. As a safety measure, please visit our website via the link below to verify your personal information:

http://www.trustedbank.com/general/custverifyinfo.asp

Once you have done this, our fraud department will work to resolve this discrepency. We are happy you have chosen us to do business with.

Thank you,
TrustedBank

Member FDIC © 2005 TrustedBank, Inc

An example of a phishing email, disguised as an official email from a (fictional) bank. The sender is attempting to trick the recipient into revealing confidential information by "confirming" it at the phisher's website. Note the misspelling of the words received and discrepancy. Also note that although the URL of the bank's webpage appears to be legitimate, the hyperlink would actually be pointed at the phisher's webpage.

tion such as usernames, passwords, and credit card details (and sometimes, indirectly, money), often for malicious reasons, by masquerading as a trustworthy entity in an electronic communication.[1][2] The word is a neologism created as a homophone of *fishing* due to the similarity of using fake bait in an attempt to catch a victim. Communications purporting to be from popular social web sites, auction sites, banks, online payment processors or IT administrators are commonly used to lure unsuspecting victims. Phishing emails may contain links to websites that are infected with malware.[3] Phishing is typically carried out by email spoofing[4] or instant messaging,[5] and it often directs users to enter details at a fake website whose look and feel are almost identical to the legitimate one. Phishing

is an example of social engineering techniques used to deceive users, and exploits the poor usability of current web security technologies.[6] Attempts to deal with the growing number of reported phishing incidents include legislation, user training, public awareness, and technical security measures. Many websites have now created secondary tools for applications, like maps for games, but they should be clearly marked as to who wrote them, and users should not use the same passwords anywhere on the internet.

Phishing is a continual threat, and the risk is even larger in social media such as Facebook, Twitter, and Google+. Hackers could create a clone of a website and tell you to enter personal information, which is then emailed to them. Hackers commonly take advantage of these sites to attack people using them at their workplace, homes, or in public in order to take personal and security information that can affect the user or company (if in a workplace environment). Phishing takes advantage of the trust that the user may have since the user may not be able to tell that the site being visited, or program being used, is not real; therefore, when this occurs, the hacker has the chance to gain the personal information of the targeted user, such as passwords, usernames, security codes, and credit card numbers, among other things.

19.1 History

A phishing technique was described in detail in a paper and presentation delivered to the 1987 International HP Users Group, Interex.[7] The first recorded mention of the term "phishing" is found in the hacking tool AOHell (according to its creator), which included a function for attempting to steal the passwords or financial details of America Online users.[8][9] According to Ghosh, there were "445,004 attacks in 2012 as compared to 258,461 in 2011 and 187,203 in 2010", showing that phishing has been increasingly threatening individuals.

19.1.1 Early phishing on AOL

Phishing on AOL was closely associated with the warez community that exchanged pirated software and the hacking scene that perpetrated credit card fraud and other online crimes. AOHell, released in early 1995, was a program designed to hack AOL users by allowing the attacker to pose as an AOL company representative. After AOL brought in measures in late 1995 to prevent using fake, algorithmically generated credit card numbers to open accounts, AOL crackers resorted to phishing for legitimate accounts[11] and exploiting AOL.

A phisher might pose as an AOL staff member and send an instant message to a potential victim, asking him to reveal his password.[12] In order to lure the victim into giving up sensitive information, the message might include imperatives such as "verify your account" or "confirm billing information". Once the victim had revealed the password, the attacker could access and use the victim's account for fraudulent purposes. Both phishing and warezing on AOL generally required custom-written programs, such as AOHell. Phishing became so prevalent on AOL that they added a line on all instant messages stating: "no one working at AOL will ask for your password or billing information", though even this didn't prevent some people from giving away their passwords and personal information if they read and believed the IM first. A user using both an AIM account and an AOL account from an ISP simultaneously could phish AOL members with relative impunity as internet AIM accounts could be used by non-AOL internet members and could not be actioned (i.e., reported to AOL TOS department for disciplinary action).[13]

Eventually, AOL's policy enforcement with respect to phishing and warez became stricter and forced pirated software off AOL servers. AOL simultaneously developed a system to promptly deactivate accounts involved in phishing, often before the victims could respond. The shutting down of the warez scene on AOL caused most phishers to leave the service.[14]

The origination of the term 'phishing' is said to be coined by the well known spammer and hacker in the mid-90s, Khan C Smith[15] and its use quickly adapted by warez groups throughout aol. AOL enforcement would detect words used in AOL chat rooms to suspend the accounts individuals involved in pirating software and trading stolen accounts. The term was used because '<><' is the single most common tag of HTML that was found in all chat transcripts naturally, and as such could not be detected or filtered by AOL staff. The symbol <>< was replaced for any wording that referred to stolen credit cards, accounts, or illegal activity. Since the symbol looked like a fish, and due to the popularity of phreaking it was adapted as 'Phishing'.

19.1.2 Transition to wider-range operations

The capture of AOL account information may have led phishers to misuse credit card information, and to the realization that attacks against online payment systems were feasible. The first known direct attempt against a payment system affected E-gold in June 2001, which was followed up by a "post-9/11 id check" shortly after the September 11 attacks on the World Trade Center.[16] Both were viewed at the time as failures, but can now be seen as early experiments towards more fruitful attacks against mainstream banks. In September 2003, the first known phishing attack against a retail bank was reported by The Banker in an article written by Kris Sangani titled Battle Against Identity Theft.[17] By 2004, phishing was recognized as a fully industrialized part of the economy of crime: specializations emerged on a global scale that provided components for cash, which were assembled into finished attacks.[18][19]

In 2011, a Chinese phishing campaign targeted Gmail accounts of highly ranked officials of the United States and South Korean governments and militaries, as well as Chinese political activists.[20] The Chinese government denied accusations of taking part in cyber-attacks from within its borders, but there is evidence that the People's Liberation Army has assisted in the coding of cyber-attack software.[21]

19.2 Phishing techniques

19.2.1 Notable phishing attacks

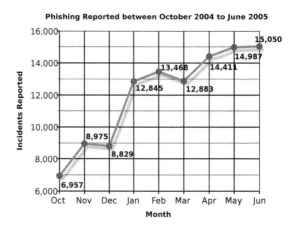

A chart showing the increase in phishing reports from October 2004 to June 2005

Phishers are targeting the customers of banks and online payment services. Emails, supposedly from the Internal Revenue Service, have been used to glean sensitive data from U.S. taxpayers.[29] While the first such examples were sent indiscriminately in the expectation that some would be received by customers of a given bank or service, recent research has shown that phishers may in principle be able to determine which banks potential victims use, and target bogus emails accordingly.[30] Social networking sites are now a prime target of phishing, since the personal details in such sites can be used in identity theft;[31] in late 2006 a computer worm took over pages on MySpace and altered links to direct surfers to websites designed to steal login details.[32] Experiments show a success rate of over 70% for phishing attacks on social networks.[33]

The RapidShare file sharing site has been targeted by phishing to obtain a premium account, which removes speed caps on downloads, auto-removal of uploads, waits on downloads, and cool down times between uploads.[34]

Attackers who broke into TD Ameritrade's database and took 6.3 million email addresses (though they were not able to obtain social security numbers, account numbers, names, addresses, dates of birth, phone numbers and trading activity) also wanted the account usernames and passwords, so they launched a follow-up spear phishing attack.[35]

Almost half of phishing thefts in 2006 were committed by groups operating through the *Russian Business Network* based in St. Petersburg.[36]

In the 3rd Quarter of 2009 the Anti-Phishing Working Group reported receiving 115,370 phishing email reports from consumers with US and China hosting more than 25% of the phishing pages each.[37]

There are anti-phishing websites which publish exact messages that have recently circulating the internet, such as FraudWatch International and Millersmiles. Such sites often provide specific details about the particular messages.[38][39] To avoid directly dealing with the source code of web pages, hackers are increasingly using a phishing tool called **Super Phisher** that makes the work easy when compared to manual methods of creating phishing websites.[40]

By December 2013, Cryptolocker ransomware infected 250,000 personal computers by first targeting businesses using a Zip archive attachment that claimed to be a customer complaint, and later targeting general public using a link in an email regarding a problem clearing a check. The ransomware scrambles and locks files on the computer and requests the owner make a payment in exchange for the key to unlock and decrypt the files. According to Dell SecureWorks, 0.4% or more of those infected likely agreed to the ransom demand.[41]

List of phishing types

Phishing An attempt to acquire information such as usernames, passwords, and credit card details by masquerading as a trustworthy entity in an electronic communication. In October 2013, emails purporting to be from American Express were sent to an unknown number of recipients. A simple DNS change could have been made to thwart this spoofed email, but American Express failed to make any changes.[42]

Spear phishing Phishing attempts directed at specific individuals or companies have been termed **spear phishing**.[43] Attackers may gather personal information about their target to increase their probability of success. This technique is, by far, the most successful on the internet today, accounting for 91% of attacks.[44]

Clone phishing A type of phishing attack whereby a legitimate, and previously delivered, email containing an attachment or link has had its content and recipient address(es) taken and used to create an almost identical or cloned email. The attachment or link within the email is replaced with a malicious version and then sent from an email address spoofed to appear to come from the original sender. It may claim to be a resend of the original or an updated version to the original. This technique could be used to pivot (indirectly) from a previously infected machine and gain a foothold on another machine, by exploiting the social trust associated with the inferred connection due to both parties receiving the original email.

Whaling Several recent phishing attacks have been directed specifically at senior executives and other high profile targets within businesses, and the term **whaling** has been coined for these kinds of attacks.[45] In the case of whaling, the masquerading web page/email will take a more serious executive-level form. The content will be crafted to target an upper manager and the person's role in the company. The content of a whaling attack email is often written as a legal subpoena, customer complaint, or executive issue. Whaling scam emails are designed to masquerade as a critical business email, sent from a legitimate business authority. The content is meant to be tailored for upper management, and usually involves some kind of falsified company-wide concern. Whaling phishermen have also forged official-looking FBI subpoena emails, and claimed that the manager needs to click a link and install special software to view the subpoena.[46]

19.2.2 Link manipulation

Most methods of phishing use some form of technical deception designed to make a link in an email (and the spoofed website it leads to) appear to belong to the spoofed organization. Misspelled URLs or the use of subdomains are the common tricks used by phishers. In the following example URL, http://www.yourbank.example.com/, it appears as though the URL will take you to the *example* section of the *yourbank* website; actually this URL points to the "*yourbank*" (i.e. phishing) section of the *example* website. Another common trick is to make the displayed text for a link (the text between the tags) suggest a reliable destination, when the link actually goes to the phishers' site. Many email clients or web browsers will show previews of where a link will take the user in the bottom left of the screen, while hovering the mouse cursor over a link.[47] This behaviour, however, may in some circumstances be overridden by the phisher.

A further problem with URLs has been found in the handling of internationalized domain names (IDN) in web browsers, that might allow visually identical web addresses to lead to different, possibly malicious, websites. Despite the publicity surrounding the flaw, known as IDN spoofing[48] or homograph attack,[49] phishers have taken advantage of a similar risk, using open URL redirectors on the websites of trusted organizations to disguise malicious URLs with a trusted domain.[50][51][52] Even digital certificates do not solve this problem because it is quite possible for a phisher to purchase a valid certificate and subsequently change content to spoof a genuine website, or, to host the phish site without SSL at all.[53]

19.2.3 Filter evasion

Phishers have even started using images instead of text to make it harder for anti-phishing filters to detect text commonly used in phishing emails.[54] However, this has led to the evolution of more sophisticated anti-phishing filters that are able to recover hidden text in images. These filters use OCR (optical character recognition) to optically scan the image and filter it.[55]

Some anti-phishing filters have even used IWR (intelligent word recognition), which is not meant to completely replace OCR, but these filters can even detect cursive, hand-written, rotated (including upside-down text), or distorted (such as made wavy, stretched vertically or laterally, or in different directions) text, as well as text on colored backgrounds.

19.2.4 Website forgery

Once a victim visits the phishing website, the deception is not over. Some phishing scams use JavaScript commands in order to alter the address bar.[56] This is done either by placing a picture of a legitimate URL over the address bar, or by closing the original bar and opening up a new one with the legitimate URL.[57]

An attacker can even use flaws in a trusted website's own scripts against the victim.[58] These types of attacks (known as cross-site scripting) are particularly problematic, because they direct the user to sign in at their bank or service's own web page, where everything from the web address to the security certificates appears correct. In reality, the link to the website is crafted to carry out the attack, making it very difficult to spot without specialist knowledge. Just such a flaw was used in 2006 against PayPal.[59]

A Universal Man-in-the-middle (MITM) Phishing Kit, discovered in 2007, provides a simple-to-use interface that allows a phisher to convincingly reproduce websites and capture log-in details entered at the fake site.[60]

To avoid anti-phishing techniques that scan websites for phishing-related text, phishers have begun to use Flash-based websites (a technique known as phlashing). These look much like the real website, but hide the text in a multimedia object.[61]

19.2.5 Covert Redirect

Covert Redirect is a subtle method to perform phishing attacks that makes links appear legitimate, but actually redirect a victim to an attacker's website. The flaw is usually masqueraded under a log-in popup based on an affected site's domain.[62] It can affect OAuth 2.0 and OpenID based on well-known exploit parameters as well. This often makes use of Open Redirect and XSS vulnerabilities in the third-party application websites.[63]

Normal phishing attempts can be easy to spot because the malicious page's URL will usually be different from the real site link. For Covert Redirect, an attacker could use a real website instead by corrupting the site with a malicious login popup dialogue box. This makes Covert Redirect different from others.[64][65]

For example, suppose a victim clicks a malicious phishing link beginning with Facebook. A popup window from Facebook will ask whether the victim would like to authorize the app. If the victim chooses to authorize the app, a "token" will be sent to the attacker and the victim's personal sensitive information could be exposed. These information may include the email address, birth date, contacts, and work history.[63] In case the "token" has greater privilege, the attacker could obtain more sensitive information including the mailbox, online presence, and friends list. Worse still, the attacker may possibly control and operate the user's account.[66] Even if the victim does not choose to authorize the app, he or she will still get redirected to a website controlled by the attacker. This could potentially further compromise the victim.[67] So Covert Redirect is a perfect phishing attack model.

This serious vulnerability is discovered by Wang Jing, a Mathematics Ph.D. student at School of Physical and Mathematical Sciences in Nanyang Technological University in Singapore.[68] Covert Redirect is a notable security flaw. It is a threat to the Internet that is worth attention.[69]

19.2.6 Phone phishing

Not all phishing attacks require a fake website. Messages that claimed to be from a bank told users to dial a phone number regarding problems with their bank accounts.[70] Once the phone number (owned by the phisher, and provided by a Voice over IP service) was dialled, prompts told users to enter their account numbers and PIN. Vishing (voice phishing) sometimes uses fake caller-ID data to give the appearance that calls come from a trusted organization.[71]

19.2.7 Other techniques

- Another attack used successfully is to forward the client to a bank's legitimate website, then to place a popup window requesting credentials on top of the page in a way that makes many users think the bank is requesting this sensitive information.[72]

- Tabnabbing takes advantage of tabbed browsing, with multiple open tabs. This method silently redirects the user to the affected site. This technique operates in reverse to most phishing techniques in that it doesn't directly take you to the fraudulent site, but instead loads their fake page in one of your open tabs.

- Evil twins is a phishing technique that is hard to detect. A phisher creates a fake wireless network that looks similar to a legitimate public network that may be found in public places such as airports, hotels or coffee shops. Whenever someone logs on to the bogus network, fraudsters try to capture their passwords and/or credit card information.

19.3 Damage caused by phishing

The damage caused by phishing ranges from denial of access to email to substantial financial loss. It is estimated that between May 2004 and May 2005, approximately 1.2 million computer users in the United States suffered losses caused by phishing, totaling approximately US$929 million. United States businesses lose an estimated US$2 billion per year as their clients become victims.[73] In 2007, phishing attacks escalated. 3.6 million adults lost US$3.2 billion in the 12 months ending in August 2007.[74] Microsoft claims these estimates are grossly exaggerated and puts the annual phishing loss in the US at US$60 million.[75] In the United Kingdom losses from web banking fraud—mostly from phishing—almost doubled to £23.2m in 2005, from £12.2m in 2004,[76] while 1 in 20 computer users claimed to have lost out to phishing in 2005.[77]

According to 3rd Microsoft Computing Safer Index Report released in February 2014, the annual worldwide impact of phishing could be as high as $5 billion.[78]

The stance adopted by the UK banking body APACS is that "customers must also take sensible precautions ... so that they are not vulnerable to the criminal."[79] Similarly, when the first spate of phishing attacks hit the Irish Republic's banking sector in September 2006, the Bank of Ireland initially refused to cover losses suffered by its customers,[80] although losses to the tune of €113,000 were made good.[81]

19.4 Anti-phishing

As recently as 2007, the adoption of anti-phishing strategies by businesses needing to protect personal and financial information was low.[82] Now there are several different techniques to combat phishing, including legislation and technology created specifically to protect against phishing.[83] These techniques include steps that can be taken by individuals, as well as by organizations. Phone, web site, and email phishing can now be reported to authorities, as described below.

19.4.1 Social responses

One strategy for combating phishing is to train people to recognize phishing attempts, and to deal with them. Education can be effective, especially where training provides direct feedback.[84] One newer phishing tactic, which uses phishing emails targeted at a specific company, known as *spear phishing*, has been harnessed to train individuals at various locations, including United States Military Academy at West Point, NY. In a June 2004 experiment with spear phishing, 80% of 500 West Point cadets who were sent a fake email from a non-existent Col. Robert Melville at West Point, were tricked into clicking on a link that would supposedly take them to a page where they would enter personal information. (The page informed them that they had been lured.)[85]

People can take steps to avoid phishing attempts by slightly modifying their browsing habits.[86] When contacted about an account needing to be "verified" (or any other topic used by phishers), it is a sensible precaution to contact the company from which the email apparently originates to check that the email is legitimate. Alternatively, the address that the individual knows is the company's genuine website can be typed into the address bar of the browser, rather than trusting any hyperlinks in the suspected phishing message.[87]

Nearly all legitimate e-mail messages from companies to their customers contain an item of information that is not readily available to phishers. Some companies, for example PayPal, always address their customers by their username in emails, so if an email addresses the recipient in a generic fashion ("*Dear PayPal customer*") it is likely to be an attempt at phishing.[88] Emails from banks and credit card companies often include partial account numbers. However, recent research[89] has shown that the public do not typically distinguish between the first few digits and the last few digits of an account number—a significant problem since the first few digits are often the same for all clients of a financial institution. People can be trained to have their suspicion aroused if the message does not contain any specific personal information. Phishing attempts in early 2006, however, used personalized information, which makes it unsafe to assume that the presence of personal information alone guarantees that a message is legitimate.[90] Furthermore, another recent study concluded in part that the presence of personal information does not significantly affect the success rate of phishing attacks,[91] which suggests that most people do not pay attention to such details.

The Anti-Phishing Working Group, an industry and law enforcement association, has suggested that conventional phishing techniques could become obsolete in the future as people are increasingly aware of the social engineering techniques used by phishers.[92] They predict that pharming and other uses of malware will become more common tools for stealing information.

Everyone can help educate the public by encouraging safe practices, and by avoiding dangerous ones. Unfortunately, even well-known players are known to incite users to hazardous behavior, e.g. by requesting their users to reveal their passwords for third party services, such as email.[93]

19.4.2 Technical responses

Anti-phishing measures have been implemented as features embedded in browsers, as extensions or toolbars for browsers, and as part of website login procedures.[3] Anti-phishing software is also available. The following are some of the main approaches to the problem.

Helping to identify legitimate websites

Most websites targeted for phishing are secure websites meaning that SSL with strong PKI cryptography is used for server authentication, where the website's URL is used as identifier. In theory it should be possible for the SSL authentication to be used to confirm the site to the user, and this was SSL v2's design requirement and the meta of secure browsing. But in practice, this is easy to trick.

The superficial flaw is that the browser's security user interface (UI) is insufficient to deal with today's strong threats. There are three parts to secure authentication using TLS and certificates: indicating that the connection is in authenticated mode, indicating which site the user is connected to, and indicating which authority says it is this site. All three are necessary for authentication, and need to be confirmed by/to the user.

Secure connection The standard display for secure browsing from the mid-1990s to mid-2000s was the padlock. In 2005, Mozilla fielded a yellow address bar as a better indication of the secure connection. This innovation was later reversed due to the EV certificates, which replaced certain certificates providing a high level of organization identity verification with a green display, and other certificates with an extended blue favicon box to the left of the URL bar (in addition to the switch from "http" to "https" in the url itself).

Which site The user is expected to confirm that the domain name in the browser's URL bar was in fact where they intended to go. URLs can be too complex to be easily parsed. Users often do not know or recognise the URL of the legitimate sites they intend to connect to, so that the authentication becomes meaningless.[6] A condition for meaningful server authentication is to have a server identifier that is meaningful to the user; many ecommerce sites will change the domain names within their overall set of websites, adding to the opportunity for confusion. Simply displaying the domain name for the visited website,[94] as some anti-phishing toolbars do, is not sufficient.

Some newer browsers, such as Internet Explorer 8, display the entire URL in grey, with just the domain name itself in black, as a means of assisting users in identifying fraudulent URLs.

An alternative approach is the petname extension for Firefox which lets users type in their own labels for websites, so they can later recognize when they have returned to the site. If the site is not recognised, then the software may either warn the user or block the site outright. This represents user-centric identity management of server identities.[95] Some suggest that a graphical image selected by the user is better than a petname.[96]

With the advent of EV certificates, browsers now typically display the organisation's name in green, which is much more visible and is hopefully more consistent with the user's expectations. Browser vendors have chosen to limit this prominent display only to EV certificates, leaving the user to fend for himself with all other certificates.

Who is the authority   The browser needs to state who the authority is that makes the claim of who the user is connected to. At the simplest level, no authority is stated, and therefore the browser is the authority, as far as the user is concerned. The browser vendors take on this responsibility by controlling a *root list* of acceptable CAs. This is the current standard practice.

The problem with this is that not all certification authorities (CAs) employ equally good nor applicable checking, regardless of attempts by browser vendors to control the quality. Nor do all CAs subscribe to the same model and concept that certificates are only about authenticating ecommerce organisations. *Certificate Manufacturing* is the name given to low-value certificates that are delivered on a credit card and an email confirmation; both of these are easily perverted by fraudsters. Hence, a high-value site may be easily spoofed by a valid certificate provided by another CA. This could be because the CA is in another part of the world, and is unfamiliar with high-value ecommerce sites, or it could be that no care is taken at all. As the CA is only charged with protecting its own customers, and not the customers of other CAs, this flaw is inherent in the model.

The solution to this is that the browser should show, and the user should be familiar with, the name of the authority. This presents the CA as a brand, and allows the user to learn the handful of CAs that she is likely to come into contact within her country and her sector. The use of brand is also critical to providing the CA with an incentive to improve their checking, as the user will learn the brand and demand good checking for high-value sites.

This solution was first put into practice in early IE7 versions, when displaying EV certificates.[97] In that display, the issuing CA is displayed. This was an isolated case, however. There is resistance to CAs being branded on the chrome, re-

sulting in a fallback to the simplest level above: the browser is the user's authority.

Fundamental flaws in the security model of secure browsing   Experiments to improve the security UI have resulted in benefits, but have also exposed fundamental flaws in the security model. The underlying causes for the failure of the SSL authentication to be employed properly in secure browsing are many and intertwined.

Users tend not to check security information, even when it is explicitly displayed to them. For example, the vast majority of warnings for sites are for misconfigurations, not a man-in-the-middle attack (MITM). Users have learned to bypass the warnings and treat all warnings with the same disdain, resulting in click-through syndrome. For example, Firefox 3 has a 4-click process for adding an exception, but it has been shown to be ignored by an experienced user in a real case of MITM.

Another underlying factor is the lack of support for virtual hosting. The specific causes are a lack of support for Server Name Indication in TLS web servers, and the expense and inconvenience of acquiring certificates. The result is that the use of authentication is too rare to be anything but a special case. This has caused a general lack of knowledge and resources in authentication within TLS, which in turn has meant that the attempts by browser vendors to upgrade their security UIs have been slow and lackluster.

The security model for secure browser includes many participants: user, browser vendor, developers, CA, auditor, web server vendor, ecommerce site, regulators (e.g., FDIC), and security standards committees. There is a lack of communication between different groups that are committed to the security model. E.g., although the understanding of authentication is strong at the protocol level of the IETF committees, this message does not reach the UI group. Web server vendors do not prioritize the Server Name Indication (TLS/SNI) fix, not seeing it as a security fix but instead a new feature. In practice, all participants look to the others as the source of the failures leading to phishing, hence the local fixes are not prioritized.

Matters improved slightly with the CAB Forum, as that group includes browser vendors, auditors and CAs. But the group did not start out in an open fashion, and the result suffered from commercial interests of the first players, as well as a lack of parity between the participants. Even today, CAB forum is not open, and does not include representation from small CAs, end-users, ecommerce owners, etc.

Vendors commit to standards, which results in an outsourcing effect when it comes to security. Although there have been many and good experiments in improving the security UI, these have not been adopted because they are not standard, or clash with the standards. Threat models can re-invent themselves in around a month; Security standards take around 10 years to adjust.

Control mechanisms employed by the browser vendors over the CAs have not been substantially updated; the threat model has. The control and quality process over CAs is insufficiently tuned to the protection of users and the addressing of actual and current threats. Audit processes are in great need of updating. The recent EV Guidelines documented the current model in greater detail, and established a good benchmark, but did not push for any substantial changes to be made.

There is no way to obscure or encrypt the IP address of an https request. This leaves the source and destination of all requests transparently visible on the network, providing detailed information about the online habits of users in a targeted organization.

Browsers alerting users to fraudulent websites

Another popular approach to fighting phishing is to maintain a list of known phishing sites and to check websites against the list. Microsoft's IE7 browser, Mozilla Firefox 2.0, Safari 3.2, and Opera all contain this type of anti-phishing measure.[3][98][99][100][101] Firefox 2 used Google anti-phishing software. Opera 9.1 uses live blacklists from Phishtank, cyscon and GeoTrust, as well as live whitelists from GeoTrust. Some implementations of this approach send the visited URLs to a central service to be checked, which has raised concerns about privacy.[102] According to a report by Mozilla in late 2006, Firefox 2 was found to be more effective than Internet Explorer 7 at detecting fraudulent sites in a study by an independent software testing company.[103]

An approach introduced in mid-2006 involves switching to a special DNS service that filters out known phishing domains: this will work with any browser,[104] and is similar in principle to using a hosts file to block web adverts.

To mitigate the problem of phishing sites impersonating a victim site by embedding its images (such as logos), several site owners have altered the images to send a message to the visitor that a site may be fraudulent. The image may be moved to a new filename and the original permanently replaced, or a server can detect that the image was not requested as part of normal browsing, and instead send a warning image.[105][106]

Augmenting password logins

The Bank of America's website[107][108] is one of several that ask users to select a personal image, and display this user-selected image with any forms that request a password. Users of the bank's online services are instructed to enter a password only when they see the image they selected. However, several studies suggest that few users refrain from entering their passwords when images are absent.[109][110] In addition, this feature (like other forms of two-factor authentication) is susceptible to other attacks, such as those suffered by Scandinavian bank Nordea in late 2005,[111] and Citibank in 2006.[112]

A similar system, in which an automatically generated "Identity Cue" consisting of a colored word within a colored box is displayed to each website user, is in use at other financial institutions.[113]

Security skins[114][115] are a related technique that involves overlaying a user-selected image onto the login form as a visual cue that the form is legitimate. Unlike the website-based image schemes, however, the image itself is shared only between the user and the browser, and not between the user and the website. The scheme also relies on a mutual authentication protocol, which makes it less vulnerable to attacks that affect user-only authentication schemes.

Still another technique relies on a dynamic grid of images that is different for each login attempt. The user must identify the pictures that fit their pre-chosen categories (such as dogs, cars and flowers). Only after they have correctly identified the pictures that fit their categories are they allowed to enter their alphanumeric password to complete the login. Unlike the static images used on the Bank of America website, a dynamic image-based authentication method creates a one-time passcode for the login, requires active participation from the user, and is very difficult for a phishing website to correctly replicate because it would need to display a different grid of randomly generated images that includes the user's secret categories.[116]

Eliminating phishing mail

Specialized spam filters can reduce the number of phishing emails that reach their addressees' inboxes, or provide post-delivery remediation, analyzing and removing spear phishing attacks upon delivery through email provider-level integration. These approaches rely on machine learning[117] and natural language processing approaches to classify phishing emails.[118][119] Email address authentication is another new approach.[4]

Monitoring and takedown

Several companies offer banks and other organizations likely to suffer from phishing scams round-the-clock services to monitor, analyze and assist in shutting down phishing websites.[120] Individuals can contribute by reporting phishing to both volunteer and industry groups,[121] such as cyscon or PhishTank.[122] Individuals can also contribute by reporting phone phishing attempts to Phone Phishing,Federal Trade Commission.[123] Phishing web pages and emails can be reported to Google.[124][125] The Internet Crime Complaint Center noticeboard carries phishing and ransomware alerts.

Transaction verification and signing

Solutions have also emerged using the mobile phone[126] (smartphone) as a second channel for verification and authorization of banking transactions.

Limitations of technical responses

An article in Forbes in August 2014 argues that the reason phishing problems persist even after a decade of anti-phishing technologies being sold is that phishing is "a technological medium to exploit human weaknesses" and that technology cannot fully compensate for human weaknesses.[127]

19.4.3   Legal responses

Video instruction on how to file a complaint with the Federal Trade Commission

On January 26, 2004, the U.S. Federal Trade Commission filed the first lawsuit against a suspected phisher. The defendant, a Californian teenager, allegedly created a webpage designed to look like the America Online website, and used it to steal credit card information.[128] Other countries have followed this lead by tracing and arresting phishers. A phishing kingpin, Valdir Paulo de Almeida, was arrested in Brazil for leading one of the largest phishing crime rings, which in two years stole between US$18 million and US$37 million.[129] UK authorities jailed two men in June 2005 for their role in a phishing scam,[130] in a case connected to the U.S. Secret Service Operation Firewall, which targeted notorious "carder" websites.[131] In 2006 eight people were ar-

rested by Japanese police on suspicion of phishing fraud by creating bogus Yahoo Japan Web sites, netting themselves ¥100 million (US$870,000).[132] The arrests continued in 2006 with the FBI Operation Cardkeeper detaining a gang of sixteen in the U.S. and Europe.[133]

In the United States, Senator Patrick Leahy introduced the *Anti-Phishing Act of 2005* in Congress on March 1, 2005. This bill, if it had been enacted into law, would have subjected criminals who created fake web sites and sent bogus emails in order to defraud consumers to fines of up to US$250,000 and prison terms of up to five years.[134] The UK strengthened its legal arsenal against phishing with the Fraud Act 2006,[135] which introduces a general offence of fraud that can carry up to a ten-year prison sentence, and prohibits the development or possession of phishing kits with intent to commit fraud.[136]

Companies have also joined the effort to crack down on phishing. On March 31, 2005, Microsoft filed 117 federal lawsuits in the U.S. District Court for the Western District of Washington. The lawsuits accuse "John Doe" defendants of obtaining passwords and confidential information. March 2005 also saw a partnership between Microsoft and the Australian government teaching law enforcement officials how to combat various cyber crimes, including phishing.[137] Microsoft announced a planned further 100 lawsuits outside the U.S. in March 2006,[138] followed by the commencement, as of November 2006, of 129 lawsuits mixing criminal and civil actions.[139] AOL reinforced its efforts against phishing[140] in early 2006 with three lawsuits[141] seeking a total of US$18 million under the 2005 amendments to the Virginia Computer Crimes Act,[142][143] and Earthlink has joined in by helping to identify six men subsequently charged with phishing fraud in Connecticut.[144]

In January 2007, Jeffrey Brett Goodin of California became the first defendant convicted by a jury under the provisions of the CAN-SPAM Act of 2003. He was found guilty of sending thousands of emails to America Online users, while posing as AOL's billing department, which prompted customers to submit personal and credit card information. Facing a possible 101 years in prison for the CAN-SPAM violation and ten other counts including wire fraud, the unauthorized use of credit cards, and the misuse of AOL's trademark, he was sentenced to serve 70 months. Goodin had been in custody since failing to appear for an earlier court hearing and began serving his prison term immediately.[145][146][147][148]

19.5   See also

• Advanced persistent threat

- Brandjacking
- Clickjacking
- Certificate authority
- Confidence trick
- Hacker (computer security)
- In-session phishing
- Internet fraud
- Penetration test
- SiteKey
- SMiShing
- Spy-phishing
- White-collar crime
- Typosquatting

19.6 Notes

[1] Ramzan, Zulfikar (2010). "Phishing attacks and countermeasures". In Stamp, Mark & Stavroulakis, Peter. *Handbook of Information and Communication Security.* Springer. ISBN 9783642041174.

[2] Van der Merwe, A J, Loock, M, Dabrowski, M. (2005), Characteristics and Responsibilities involved in a Phishing Attack, Winter International Symposium on Information and Communication Technologies, Cape Town, January 2005.

[3] "Safe Browsing (Google Online Security Blog)". Retrieved June 21, 2012.

[4] "Landing another blow against email phishing (Google Online Security Blog)". Retrieved June 21, 2012.

[5] Tan, Koontorm Center. "Phishing and Spamming via IM (SPIM)". Retrieved December 5, 2006.

[6] Jøsang, Audun; et al. "Security Usability Principles for Vulnerability Analysis and Risk Assessment." (PDF). *Proceedings of the Annual Computer Security Applications Conference 2007 (ACSAC'07).* Retrieved 2007.

[7] Felix, Jerry and Hauck, Chris (September 1987). "System Security: A Hacker's Perspective". *1987 Interex Proceedings* **8**: 6.

[8] Langberg, Mike (September 8, 1995). "AOL Acts to Thwart Hackers". *San Jose Mercury News.*

[9] Rekouche, Koceilah (2011). "Early Phishing". arXiv:1106.4692 [cs.CR].

[10] "APWG Phishing Attack Trends Reports". Retrieved April 21, 2015.

[11] "Phishing". *Word Spy.* Retrieved September 28, 2006.

[12] Stutz, Michael (January 29, 1998). "AOL: A Cracker's Momma!". Wired News.

[13] http://www.phishing.org/history-of-phishing/

[14] "History of AOL Warez". Archived from the original on January 31, 2011. Retrieved September 28, 2006.

[15] "EarthLink wins $25 million lawsuit against junk e-mailer".

[16] "GP4.3 – Growth and Fraud — Case #3 – Phishing". *Financial Cryptography.* December 30, 2005.

[17] Sangani, Kris (September 2003). "The Battle Against Identity Theft". *The Banker* **70** (9): 53–54.

[18] "In 2005, Organized Crime Will Back Phishers". *IT Management.* December 23, 2004. Archived from the original on January 31, 2011.

[19] Abad, Christopher (September 2005). "The economy of phishing: A survey of the operations of the phishing market". *First Monday.*

[20] Keizer, Greg. "Suspected Chinese spear-phishing attacks continue to hit Gmail users". *Computer World.* Retrieved December 4, 2011.

[21] Ewing, Philip. "Report: Chinese TV doc reveals cyber-mischief". *Dod Buzz.* Retrieved December 4, 2011.

[22] O'Connell, Liz. "Report: Email phishing scam led to Target breach". *BringMeTheNews.com.* Retrieved September 15, 2014.

[23] Ausick, Paul. "Target CEO Sack". Retrieved September 15, 2014.

[24] "Anatomy of an RSA attack". *RSA.com.* RSA FraudAction Research Labs. Retrieved September 15, 2014.

[25] Drew, Christopher; Markoff, John (May 27, 2011). "Data Breach at Security Firm Linked to Attack on Lockheed". The New York Times. Retrieved September 15, 2014.

[26] Krebs, Brian. "Data: Nearly All U.S. Home Depot Stores Hit". *Krebs on Security.* Retrieved September 15, 2014.

[27] Caruso, Joe. "Pishing data breach". Global Digital Forensics. Retrieved September 15, 2014.

[28] "ICANN Targeted in Spear Phishing Attack | Enhanced Security Measures Implemented". *icann.org.* Retrieved December 18, 2014.

[29] "Suspicious e-Mails and Identity Theft". *Internal Revenue Service.* Archived from the original on January 31, 2011. Retrieved July 5, 2006.

[30] "Phishing for Clues". Indiana University Bloomington. September 15, 2005.

[31] Kirk, Jeremy (June 2, 2006). "Phishing Scam Takes Aim at MySpace.com". IDG Network.

[32] "Malicious Website / Malicious Code: MySpace XSS QuickTime Worm". *Websense Security Labs*. Archived from the original on December 5, 2006. Retrieved December 5, 2006.

[33] Jagatic, Tom; Markus Jakobsson (October 2007). "Social Phishing". *Communications of the ACM* **50** (10): 94–100. doi:10.1145/1290958.1290968.

[34] "1-Click Hosting at RapidTec — Warning of Phishing!". Archived from the original on April 30, 2008. Retrieved December 21, 2008.

[35] "Torrent of spam likely to hit 6.3 million TD Ameritrade hack victims". Archived from the original on May 5, 2009.

[36] [http://www.washingtonpost.com/wp-dyn/content/story/2007/10/12/ST2007101202661.html?hpid=topnews Shadowy Russian Firm Seen as Conduit for Cybercrime, by Brian Krebs, Washington Post, October 13, 2007

[37] APWG. "Phishing Activity Trends Report" (PDF). Retrieved November 4, 2013.

[38] "Millersmiles Home Page". Oxford Information Services. Archived from the original on July 21, 2007. Retrieved January 3, 2010.

[39] "FraudWatch International Home Page". FraudWatch International. Retrieved January 3, 2010.

[40] "61 Super Phisher". Retrieved March 19, 2011.

[41] Kelion, Leo (December 24, 2013). "Cryptolocker ransomware has 'infected about 250,000 PCs'". *BBC*. Retrieved December 24, 2013.

[42] Paul, Andrew. "Phishing Emails: The Unacceptable Failures of American Express". Email Answers. Retrieved October 9, 2013.

[43] "What is spear phishing?". *Microsoft Security At Home*. Retrieved June 11, 2011.

[44] Stephenson, Debbie. "Spear Phishing: Who's Getting Caught?". Firmex. Retrieved July 27, 2014.

[45] "Fake subpoenas harpoon 2,100 corporate fat cats". The Register. Archived from the original on January 31, 2011. Retrieved April 17, 2008.

[46] "What Is 'Whaling'? Is Whaling Like 'Spear Phishing'?". About Tech. Archived from the original on March 28, 2015. Retrieved March 28, 2015.

[47] "HSBC Security and Fraud Center – Phishing Scams, Fraud Protection". Hsbcusa.com. Retrieved September 9, 2012.

[48] Johanson, Eric. "The State of Homograph Attacks Rev1.1". *The Shmoo Group*. Retrieved August 11, 2005.

[49] Evgeniy Gabrilovich and Alex Gontmakher (February 2002). "The Homograph Attack" (PDF). *Communications of the ACM* **45** (2): 128. doi:10.1145/503124.503156.

[50] Leyden, John (August 15, 2006). "Barclays scripting SNAFU exploited by phishers". The Register.

[51] Levine, Jason. "Goin' phishing with eBay". *Q Daily News*. Retrieved December 14, 2006.

[52] Leyden, John (December 12, 2007). "Cybercrooks lurk in shadows of big-name websites". The Register.

[53] "Black Hat DC 2009". May 15, 2011.

[54] Mutton, Paul. "Fraudsters seek to make phishing sites undetectable by content filters". *Netcraft*. Archived from the original on January 31, 2011.

[55] The use of Optical Character Recognition OCR software in spam filtering – PowerPoint PPT Presentation

[56] Mutton, Paul. "Phishing Web Site Methods". *FraudWatch International*. Archived from the original on January 31, 2011. Retrieved December 14, 2006.

[57] "Phishing con hijacks browser bar". BBC News. April 8, 2004.

[58] Krebs, Brian. "Flaws in Financial Sites Aid Scammers". *Security Fix*. Archived from the original on January 31, 2011. Retrieved June 28, 2006.

[59] Mutton, Paul. "PayPal Security Flaw allows Identity Theft". *Netcraft*. Archived from the original on January 31, 2011. Retrieved June 19, 2006.

[60] Hoffman, Patrick (January 10, 2007). "RSA Catches Financial Phishing Kit". eWeek.

[61] Miller, Rich. "Phishing Attacks Continue to Grow in Sophistication". *Netcraft*. Archived from the original on January 31, 2011. Retrieved December 19, 2007.

[62] "Serious security flaw in OAuth, OpenID discovered". CNET. May 2, 2014. Retrieved November 10, 2014.

[63] "Covert Redirect Vulnerability Related to OAuth 2.0 and OpenID". Tetraph. May 1, 2014. Retrieved November 10, 2014.

[64] "Facebook, Google Users Threatened by New Security Flaw". Tom's Guid. May 2, 2014. Retrieved November 11, 2014.

[65] "Facebook, Google users threatened by new security flaw". FOX NEWS. May 5, 2014. Retrieved November 10, 2014.

[66] "Nasty Covert Redirect Vulnerability found in OAuth and OpenID". The Hacker News. May 3, 2014. Retrieved November 10, 2014.

[67] "Facebook, Google Users Threatened by New Security Flaw". Yahoo. May 2, 2014. Retrieved November 10, 2014.

[68] "'Covert Redirect' vulnerability impacts OAuth 2.0, OpenID". SC Magazine. May 2, 2014. Retrieved November 10, 2014.

[69] "Covert Redirect Flaw in OAuth is Not the Next Heartbleed". Symantec. May 3, 2014. Retrieved November 10, 2014.

[70] Gonsalves, Antone (April 25, 2006). "Phishers Snare Victims With VoIP". Techweb.

[71] "Identity thieves take advantage of VoIP". Silicon.com. March 21, 2005. Archived from the original on March 24, 2005.

[72] "Internet Banking Targeted Phishing Attack". Metropolitan Police Service. June 3, 2005. Archived from the original (PDF) on February 18, 2010. Retrieved March 22, 2009.

[73] Kerstein, Paul (July 19, 2005). "How Can We Stop Phishing and Pharming Scams?". CSO. Archived from the original on March 24, 2008.

[74] McCall, Tom (December 17, 2007). "Gartner Survey Shows Phishing Attacks Escalated in 2007; More than $3 Billion Lost to These Attacks". Gartner.

[75] "A Profitless Endeavor: Phishing as Tragedy of the Commons" (PDF). *Microsoft*. Retrieved November 15, 2008.

[76] "UK phishing fraud losses double". Finextra. March 7, 2006.

[77] Richardson, Tim (May 3, 2005). "Brits fall prey to phishing". The Register.

[78] "20% Indians are victims of Online phishing attacks: Microsoft". *IANS*. news.biharprabha.com. Retrieved February 11, 2014.

[79] Miller, Rich. "Bank, Customers Spar Over Phishing Losses". *Netcraft*. Retrieved December 14, 2006.

[80] "Latest News". Archived from the original on October 7, 2008.

[81] "Bank of Ireland agrees to phishing refunds". vnunet.com. Archived from the original on October 28, 2008.

[82] Baker, Emiley; Wade Baker; John Tedesco (2007). "Organizations Respond to Phishing: Exploring the Public Relations Tackle Box". *Communication Research Reports* **24** (4): 327. doi:10.1080/08824090701624239.

[83] "Protect People against phishing". Retrieved February 3, 2015.

[84] Ponnurangam Kumaraguru, Yong Woo Rhee, Alessandro Acquisti, Lorrie Cranor, Jason Hong and Elizabeth Nunge (November 2006). "Protecting People from Phishing: The Design and Evaluation of an Embedded Training Email System" (PDF). *Technical Report CMU-CyLab-06-017, CyLab, Carnegie Mellon University*. Retrieved November 14, 2006.

[85] Bank, David (August 17, 2005). "Spear Phishing Tests Educate People About Online Scams". The Wall Street Journal.

[86] Hendric, William. "Steps to avoid phishing". Retrieved March 3, 2015.

[87] "Anti-Phishing Tips You Should Not Follow". *HexView*. Archived from the original on March 20, 2008. Retrieved June 19, 2006.

[88] "Protect Yourself from Fraudulent Emails". *PayPal*. Retrieved July 7, 2006.

[89] Markus Jakobsson, Alex Tsow, Ankur Shah, Eli Blevis, Youn-kyung Lim. 171850/http://www.informatics.indiana.edu/markus/papers/trust_USEC.pdf "What Instills Trust? A Qualitative Study of Phishing" Check |archiveurl= value (help) (PDF). *informatics.indiana.edu*. Archived from the original (PDF) on March 6, 2007.

[90] Zeltser, Lenny (March 17, 2006). "Phishing Messages May Include Highly-Personalized Information". The SANS Institute.

[91] Markus Jakobsson and Jacob Ratkiewicz. "Designing Ethical Phishing Experiments". *WWW '06*. Archived from the original on January 31, 2011.

[92] Kawamoto, Dawn (August 4, 2005). "Faced with a rise in so-called pharming and crimeware attacks, the Anti-Phishing Working Group will expand its charter to include these emerging threats.". ZDNet India.

[93] "Social networking site teaches insecure password practices". *Blog.anta.net*. November 9, 2008. ISSN 1797-1993. Retrieved November 9, 2008.

[94] Brandt, Andrew. "Privacy Watch: Protect Yourself With an Antiphishing Toolbar". *PC World – Privacy Watch*. Retrieved September 25, 2006.

[95] Jøsangm Audun and Pope, Simon. "User Centric Identity Management" (PDF). *Proceedings of AusCERT 2005*. Retrieved 2008.

[96] "Phishing – What it is and How it Will Eventually be Dealt With" by Ian Grigg 2005

[97] "Brand matters (IE7, Skype, Vonage, Mozilla)" Ian Grigg

[98] Franco, Rob. "Better Website Identification and Extended Validation Certificates in IE7 and Other Browsers". *IEBlog*. Archived from the original on January 16, 2010. Retrieved May 20, 2006.

[99] "Bon Echo Anti-Phishing". *Mozilla*. Archived from the original on August 23, 2011. Retrieved June 2, 2006.

[100] "Safari 3.2 finally gains phishing protection". *Ars Technica.* November 13, 2008. Archived from the original on August 23, 2011. Retrieved November 15, 2008.

[101] "Gone Phishing: Evaluating Anti-Phishing Tools for Windows". 3Sharp. September 27, 2006. Archived from the original on January 14, 2008. Retrieved October 20, 2006.

[102] "Two Things That Bother Me About Google's New Firefox Extension". *Nitesh Dhanjani on O'Reilly ONLamp.* Retrieved July 1, 2007.

[103] "Firefox 2 Phishing Protection Effectiveness Testing". Archived from the original on January 31, 2011. Retrieved January 23, 2007.

[104] Higgins, Kelly Jackson. "DNS Gets Anti-Phishing Hook". *Dark Reading.* Archived from the original on August 18, 2011. Retrieved October 8, 2006.

[105] Krebs, Brian (August 31, 2006). "Using Images to Fight Phishing". Security Fix.

[106] Seltzer, Larry (August 2, 2004). "Spotting Phish and Phighting Back". eWeek.

[107] Bank of America. "How Bank of America SiteKey Works For Online Banking Security". Archived from the original on August 23, 2011. Retrieved January 23, 2007.

[108] Brubaker, Bill (July 14, 2005). "Bank of America Personalizes Cyber-Security". Washington Post.

[109] Stone, Brad (February 5, 2007). "Study Finds Web Antifraud Measure Ineffective". New York Times. Retrieved February 5, 2007.

[110] Stuart Schechter, Rachna Dhamija, Andy Ozment, Ian Fischer (May 2007). "The Emperor's New Security Indicators: An evaluation of website authentication and the effect of role playing on usability studies" (PDF). *IEEE Symposium on Security and Privacy, May 2007.* Archived from the original (PDF) on April 6, 2008. Retrieved February 5, 2007.

[111] "Phishers target Nordea's one-time password system". Finextra. October 12, 2005.

[112] Krebs, Brian (July 10, 2006). "Citibank Phish Spoofs 2-Factor Authentication". Security Fix.

[113] Graham Titterington. "More doom on phishing". *Ovum Research, April 2006.*

[114] Schneier, Bruce. "Security Skins". *Schneier on Security.* Retrieved December 3, 2006.

[115] Rachna Dhamija, J.D. Tygar (July 2005). "The Battle Against Phishing: Dynamic Security Skins" (PDF). *Symposium On Usable Privacy and Security (SOUPS) 2005.* Archived from the original (PDF) on April 6, 2008. Retrieved February 5, 2007.

[116] "Dynamic, Mutual Authentication Technology for Anti-Phishing". Confidenttechnologies.com. Retrieved September 9, 2012.

[117] Cleber K., Olivo , Altair O., Santin , Luiz S., Oliveira (July 2011). "Obtaining the Threat Model for E-mail Phishing" (PDF). *Applied Soft Computing.* Archived from the original (PDF) on July 8, 2011.

[118] Madhusudhanan Chandrasekaran, Krishnan Narayanan, Shambhu Upadhyaya (March 2006). "Phishing E-mail Detection Based on Structural Properties" (PDF). *NYS Cyber Security Symposium.* Archived from the original (PDF) on February 16, 2008.

[119] Ian Fette, Norman Sadeh, Anthony Tomasic (June 2006). "Learning to Detect Phishing Emails" (PDF). *Carnegie Mellon University Technical Report CMU-ISRI-06-112.*

[120] "Anti-Phishing Working Group: Vendor Solutions". *Anti-Phishing Working Group.* Archived from the original on January 31, 2011. Retrieved July 6, 2006.

[121] McMillan, Robert (March 28, 2006). "New sites let users find and report phishing". LinuxWorld.

[122] Schneier, Bruce (October 5, 2006). "PhishTank". *Schneier on Security.* Archived from the original on January 31, 2011. Retrieved December 7, 2007.

[123] "Federal Trade Commission". *Federal Trade Commission.* Retrieved March 6, 2009.

[124] "Report phishing" page, Google

[125] How to report phishing scams to Google Consumer Scams.org

[126] Using the smartphone to verify and sign online banking transactions, SafeSigner.

[127] Joseph Steinberg. "Why You Are At Risk Of Phishing Attacks". *Forbes.* Retrieved November 14, 2014.

[128] Legon, Jeordan (January 26, 2004). "Phishing scams reel in your identity". CNN.

[129] Leyden, John (March 21, 2005). "Brazilian cops net 'phishing kingpin'". The Register.

[130] Roberts, Paul (June 27, 2005). "UK Phishers Caught, Packed Away". eWEEK.

[131] "Nineteen Individuals Indicted in Internet 'Carding' Conspiracy". justice.gov. Retrieved October 13, 2015.

[132] "8 held over suspected phishing fraud". The Daily Yomiuri. May 31, 2006.

[133] "Phishing gang arrested in USA and Eastern Europe after FBI investigation". Archived from the original on January 31, 2011. Retrieved December 14, 2006.

[134] "Phishers Would Face 5 Years Under New Bill". Information Week. March 2, 2005.

[135] "Fraud Act 2006". Archived from the original on August 23, 2011. Retrieved December 14, 2006.

[136] "Prison terms for phishing fraudsters". The Register. November 14, 2006.

[137] "Microsoft Partners with Australian Law Enforcement Agencies to Combat Cyber Crime". Archived from the original on November 3, 2005. Retrieved August 24, 2005.

[138] Espiner, Tom (March 20, 2006). "Microsoft launches legal assault on phishers". ZDNet.

[139] Leyden, John (November 23, 2006). "MS reels in a few stray phish". The Register.

[140] "A History of Leadership – 2006". Archived from the original on May 22, 2007.

[141] "AOL Takes Fight Against Identity Theft To Court, Files Lawsuits Against Three Major Phishing Gangs". Archived from the original on January 31, 2007. Retrieved March 8, 2006.

[142] "HB 2471 Computer Crimes Act; changes in provisions, penalty.". Retrieved March 8, 2006.

[143] Brulliard, Karin (April 10, 2005). "Va. Lawmakers Aim to Hook Cyberscammers". Washington Post.

[144] "Earthlink evidence helps slam the door on phisher site spam ring". Archived from the original on July 5, 2007. Retrieved December 14, 2006.

[145] Prince, Brian (January 18, 2007). "Man Found Guilty of Targeting AOL Customers in Phishing Scam". PC-Mag.com.

[146] Leyden, John (January 17, 2007). "AOL phishing fraudster found guilty". The Register.

[147] Leyden, John (June 13, 2007). "AOL phisher nets six years' imprisonment". The Register.

[148] Gaudin, Sharon (June 12, 2007). "California Man Gets 6-Year Sentence For Phishing". InformationWeek.

19.7 References

- Ghosh, Ayush (2013). "Seclayer: A plugin to prevent phishing attacks". *IUP Journal of Information Technology*, 9(4), 52–64.

19.8 External links

- Anti-Phishing Working Group

- Center for Identity Management and Information Protection—Utica College

- Plugging the "phishing" hole: legislation versus technology—*Duke Law & Technology Review*

- Know Your Enemy: Phishing—Honeynet project case study

- A Profitless Endeavor: Phishing as Tragedy of the Commons—Microsoft Corporation

- Reporting, Classification & Data Sharing of information on phishing sites reported by the public—PhishKiller

- Database for information on phishing sites reported by the public—PhishTank

- The Impact of Incentives on Notice and Take-down – Computer Laboratory, University of Cambridge (PDF, 344 kB)

- Information On and Archive of Phishing Emails—Scamdex.com

- Phishing Strategies—vpnanswers.com

- Phishing attack education game

Chapter 20

Pranknet

Pranknet, also known as **Prank University** ',[1] is a Canadian-based anonymous prank calling virtual community responsible for damage to hotels and fast food restaurants of more than $60,000 as well as multiple instances of telephone harassment. It was founded by a man who later referred to himself as "Dex" (alleged to be a Canadian man named Tariq Malik[2][3]).[4] The group has been linked to nearly 60 separate incidents.[5]

Posing as authority figures, such as fire alarm company representatives and hotel front-desk/corporate managers, Pranknet participants called unsuspecting employees and customers in the United States and tricked them into damaging property, setting off fire sprinklers, breaking out windows, and other humiliating acts such as disrobing and consumption of human urine. Pranknet members can listen in real-time and discuss the progress together in a private chat room.[6]

In 2009, a wave of the pranks across the United States prompted internal alerts by Choice Hotels, as well as advisories by the Orange County, Florida Sheriff's office, and others.[7] At that time, law enforcement officials from a number of jurisdictions and the Federal Bureau of Investigation began investigating the various incidents as well as the identity of "Dex".[5][4]

20.1 Technology

Pranknet participants initially used Skype to make their calls. As of 2009, Skype provided an uncontrolled registration system for users without proof of identity, making it difficult to trace and identify users.[8] After Skype began an internal investigation, Pranknet left Skype and briefly used Paltalk for its chats. However, Paltalk banned Pranknet after a February 2009 KFC incident. After Pranknet users were banned from Paltalk, the company was subjected to multiple DDoS attacks.[6] Beginning in 2009, members chatted before, during, and after each prank via Beyluxe Messenger, which is owned and operated outside North America. Audiences range from 40 to 200 people at any

given time.

Pranks that created sufficient havoc were posted on YouTube.[9] Updates were also provided through a Twitter account.[10]

20.2 Notable Pranknet incidents

In February 2009, "Dex" called a KFC restaurant in Manchester, New Hampshire. Posing as a manager from the corporate office, he persuaded employees to douse the building with fire suppression chemicals and to then proceed outside, remove all of their clothing and urinate on each other. He claimed the chemicals were caustic and this would render them inert.[10] When "Dex" posted the audio to YouTube he described it as "Epic KFC Prank Call (greatest ever)...dex successfully convinces the 3 female employees to undress fully nude outside and urinate on each other." Many months later "Dex", posing this time as an insurance adjuster called the same KFC and had the victims describe their experiences while Pranknet members listened.[6]

On February 10, "Dex" and a member called "DTA_Mike", posing as hotel front desk employees, called two separate guests at the Best Western in Shillington, Pennsylvania. Using the pretense of a ruptured gas line, the caller persuaded each guest to break a window and then throw the television out. "Dex" and his friend repeated the same stunt on February 19 with a Best Western in Santee, California.[6]

On April 30, a Pranknet member named "Rollin in the A" called Prejean's Restaurant in Lafayette, Louisiana posing as an official from the health department. This target was selected because the restaurant provided live video streaming of its dining area on their own website. The victim at this restaurant was told that Prejean's pork was tainted with the swine flu. "Rollin in the A" also told the manager to close the restaurant immediately and tell the customers (75 of them) that they may have eaten tainted food.[6]

On May 27, "Dex" called a Hampton Inn in York, Nebraska and tricked an employee into setting off the fire alarm. As guests made their way to the lobby, a second call was placed to the front desk. "Dex" claimed that, to avoid alleged fines, the fire department should not be called. Instead, the caller gave various bogus instructions to turn the alarm off, including going to a website that only displayed pornography. The next suggestion from the caller was to break the front windows of the hotel. A truck driver staying at the hotel volunteered, and under direction from "Dex", the man drove his semi-trailer truck into the front door.[11] Later that night, "Dex" tweeted: "I just pulled off the most epic prank. I had a hotel guest back his truck into the hotel front window (in the lobby), and break the window." The post was deleted in late July.[10]

On June 6, 2009, a prank was made on a Holiday Inn Express in Conway, Arkansas. The caller posed as a representative from the company that installed the hotel's fire sprinkler and claimed the system needed to be reset by pulling the fire alarm. Once the alarm was turned on, the clerk was told that the sprinklers would activate unless windows were broken.[12] The same day, the pranksters called a Comfort Suites in Gadsden, Alabama, persuading a clerk to pull a fire alarm; sprinklers were subsequently activated causing water damage.[13]

In July, a Pranknet member called a Hilton in Orlando, Florida and, purporting there to be a gas leak, convinced a family staying there to break windows with the lid for the toilet tank and throw their mattress out the window.[14] The incident cost $5,000 in damages.[10]

Also in July, a Pranknet caller informed two hotel guests that deadly spiders were about to infest their room. The caller was able to manipulate the couple into breaking their window with the tank lid from their toilet.[10]

On July 5, Pranknet members Powell and Markle called an Arby's in Baytown (where Powell lives) and talked a worker there into triggering the fire suppression system, causing an estimated $4,600 in damages. Powell failed in his attempts to get any windows broken.[6] Powell was later arrested and charged with criminal mischief for the incident.[15]

On July 20, Markle tricked a desk clerk at the Homewood Suites in Lexington, Kentucky into drinking another person's urine. The prank started with a call to a guest. The guest was told it was the front desk calling and that a prior guest had tested positive for Hepatitis C. The guest was then told there was a doctor on site and a simple urine test could determine if the guest was infected. The urine was to be brought to the front desk in a simple drinking glass. Switching roles, Markle then called the front desk alleging to be an employee of Martinelli's Cider. He told the clerk that a representative from the company would like to come downstairs with a sample of their new drink. The guest from the previous call then arrived and handed the clerk his urine. Markle then coaxed the woman to try it. He asked how

it tasted. "Horrible," she said. "That does not taste like cider. I'm not going to take another sip, that's horrible." Markle replied: "Well, I need to inform you of something, ma'am. I want you to understand that you just drank that man's urine."[6] In its investigation, the Lufkin Police Department's cyber crimes division requested a subpoena for Markle's Skype activities.[16] The police report classifies the Lexington incident as first-degree wanton endangerment, a Class D felony in Kentucky.[17] Markle was subsequently sentenced to a shock incarceration term of six months.[18]

Additionally, an employee at a Holiday Inn Express was persuaded by a Pranknet caller to set off a fire alarm, break windows, and set off sprinklers which flooded the building. Damages were estimated at $50,000.[9]

The Smoking Gun reported that Pranknet leader "Dex" was responsible for an October 21 hoax in which he phoned ESPN reporter Elizabeth Moreau, tricking her into breaking windows in her room at the Hilton Garden Inn in Gainesville, Florida. He then initiated a conference call with a front desk employee at the hotel, where he then claimed he was Moreau's boyfriend and that the damage was a result of them fighting, as well as making a number of vulgar statements.[19] As a result of the hoax, a Gainesville Police detective was assigned to the case.[19]

In November 2010, an elderly man staying at a Motel 6 in Spartanburg, South Carolina was tricked by a Pranknet member posing as a hotel administrator into destroying his television set and smashing mirrors in his room with a wrench to destroy hidden cameras supposedly left by a previous guest.[1] The man, told that there was a "midget" trapped in an adjoining room, was then tricked into destroying a sheetrock wall behind his room door, almost making his way through to the next room.[1] As one of the prankster's returned calls was heard by police and other guests who received prank calls soon called the front desk, the hotel did not hold the man accountable for the damages, but did ask him to leave.[1] The pranksters called back on March 11, 2011, persuading a guest to "disable" a sprinkler head by smashing it with a toilet lid to prevent a 'toxic gas' from entering the room.[20] According to TSG, "Motel 6 is a preferred target because Pranknet members can call directly into rooms without having to know a guest's name"[1] As of November 1, 2011, this is no longer possible. After police arrived to answer a 911 call placed by the motel manager, they declined to press charges against the victim but noted that other similar phone calls had been received at the motel.[1]

On December 5, 2010, two Pranknet members identified by *The Smoking Gun* collaborated to humiliate an Iraq War veteran, 22, at a Motel 6 in Amarillo, Texas. One, posing as the hotel receptionist, informed him that the prior occupant of his room had been diagnosed with "H1N1 flu virus", and transferred him to the other, posing as a physician, who over the course of half an hour directed him to induce vomiting, then to consume some of his own urine to "kill the incubation period", and finally to collect a stool sample in a pillowcase, which he was to bring to the front desk. A prankster then called the hotel's actual front desk, identifying himself by the guest's full name and claiming to be so angry with the service that he would leave a pillowcase full of feces at the front desk. The receptionist locked the door and called police, so the veteran returned to his room, where his conversation with police officers the receptionist had summoned became audible to the pranksters' followers. They finished by calling other visitors at the hotel describing aspects of the prank until the police were called again half an hour later. With voice electronically altered and posing as the mother of a boy making prank calls, one of the pranksters managed to convince police to put the victim back on the phone, who unknowingly recounted his experience to the pranksters.[21]

On January 9, 2011, a Holiday Inn in Omaha, Nebraska was targeted. Taking advantage of the ability to call guests of the hotel directly, the prankster pretended to be a Fire Department employee reading instructions from a computer checklist to prevent an explosion from a gas leak. These instructions included to "break the red glass vial in the sprinkler", leading to $115,000 in water damage in seven guest rooms and a conference room. The guest was also persuaded to rip a mirror from his wall to find the (nonexistent) shutoff valve.[22]

20.2.1   Phone and computer hijacking

Beginning in July 2009, "Dex" began hijacking phone numbers of U.S. businesses and had them forwarded to his Skype account. Claiming to be an authority from a particular business, he calls a phone company and claims they have no dial tone. He then requests that all calls be forwarded to the number he provides.[6]

On July 7, "Dex" took over incoming calls of the Olympic Game Farm in Port Angeles, Washington making obscene sexual comments to customers who called. On July 11, he repeated the stunt with the Fun 4 All amusement park in Chula Vista, California. On July 13 he took over incoming calls to a Best Western in Jacksonville, Florida for over 12 hours. In one interaction, a woman called to find out if her husband had arrived and was told first that he had been in an accident, and then that he was having sex with a man in his room and did not wish to be disturbed. On July 15, "Dex" controlled incoming calls to a Hilton Garden Inn in Tulsa, Oklahoma. He told people inquiring about a shuttle to take a cab and they'd be reimbursed. He told some callers the hotel had a swine flu outbreak and told other callers the

hotel was in the midst of a hostage situation.[6]

Talking hotel front desk clerks through a series of steps using TeamViewer, "Dex" has posed as a corporate headquarters IT supervisor and taken remote control of hotel computers.[6]

20.2.2   Craigslist abuse

Pranknet members frequently place Craigslist ads offering free tickets or items. Inquirers are bombarded with obscene sexual rants and racial epithets. A 12-year-old girl called about a free trampoline, and "Dex" told her not to get pregnant by a black man because "they have AIDS". Markle frequently calls women who are selling household items on the site. After getting the victim's home address, he then tells her he is on his way over to rape her and kill her children.[6]

20.3   Smoking Gun investigation

"Dex" and other Pranknet members had regularly taunted victims and others, saying they were untraceable.[6] In an interview with The Smoking Gun on June 17, 2009, "Dex" exhibited no worries about being tracked down or caught. In a July co-interview with Markle, he boasted: "It's too difficult to find me. I'm a ghost on the Internet. I do pretty much everything I can to keep anything out of my computer that would lead it back to my actual computer. I'm not a stupid individual, like I said."[6]

In June 2009, The Smoking Gun launched an investigation that lasted nearly two months and included travel to Windsor, Ontario and a stakeout outside Malik's mother's home. Smoking Gun editor William Bastone emailed "Dex", and during a Skype interview provided URLs on the Smoking Gun website. The URLs were unique; when Malik viewed them, it revealed his IP address and location.[23][24] The names, biographies and locations of Pranknet's founder "Dex" and a number of prolific members, and their other findings, were published on their website and provided to the FBI in August 2009.[11]

20.4   Members

According to crime reporting website The Smoking Gun, key members included:

- Tariq Malik, also known as Pranknet leader "Dex" (a tribute to the character Dexter Morgan, a fictional serial killer).[6] In an interview with The Globe and Mail, "Dex" denied he was Malik (but confirmed he is Canadian).[25]

- William Marquis, Pranknet's "second in command".[6] Known as Hempster, Marquis was previously convicted in 2004 for drunk driving and in 2005 for marijuana production.[6] CBC News attempted to interview Marquis regarding the Pranknet allegations. However, he did not answer his door.[5]

- James Markle, one of the group's most prolific callers. Markle was already a person of interest in a Lufkin Police investigation involving a phone call to a local McDonald's,[26] and was arrested for this subsequently.[27] The Smoking Gun had based the claim upon information from old MySpace and Facebook pages, and people from the area who identified Markle in photos.[28] The Smoking Gun also published official documents showing that Markle pled guilty to aggravated sexual assault of a child in 2005, serving two years in a juvenile detention facility for raping a 5-year-old girl and then threatening to kill her if she told anyone about the incident.[29] In an interview with *The Lufkin Daily News*, Markle denied that the person described on TSG was him, claiming instead it was another person called the Samoan Prankster.[26] He was charged with felonies in two separate states: for making a felony terroristic threat in the Lufkin McDonald's case and for terrorizing and criminal damage (both felonies) in a separate incident involving a Wendy's restaurant in Gretna, Louisiana.[30] He was later extradited to Louisiana as a result of the charges filed in the Gretna incident.[31] In December 2010, Markle was sentenced to 5 years imprisonment in Texas for the prank call to the Lufkin McDonald's.[32]

- Shawn Powell, previously imprisoned for indecency with a minor (for taking nude photos of an 8-year-old female relative), a felony that put him in custody for 13 months. He specialized in racist and threatening calls.[6] He was charged with criminal mischief for his part in a hoax call to the Baytown Arby's restaurant, resulting in the fire suppression system being activated and resulting in $1,350 worth of damage.[15]

- LeeAnn Jordan, who had used her PayPal account to receive international money transfers and to pay for Paltalk.[6]

A former member, Jericho Batsford, left the group in 2009 after the Conway, Arkansas incident, and contacted local FBI agents.[3] She told them she knew Dex's identity to be that of Malik[3] and that he was responsible for many incidents.[10] In response to her defection, Pranknet members have constantly harassed her home and her workplace via Skype and Beyluxe. Malik told members to be patient, that she would not answer the phone and let them get to her, and to instead "get her later on down the road, when she least expects it."[6] Batsford had participated in some phone pranks, but left when she witnessed members encouraging children under the age of 18 to make bomb threats.[3]

Officials in at least four U.S. States and six U.S. cities stated that they were considering charges against "Dex" and his possible extradition from Canada to face trial.[25]

20.5 References

[1] "Elderly Man Falls Victim To Motel 6 Prank". *The Smoking Gun*. 23 November 2010. Retrieved 23 November 2010.

[2] "Telephone Terrorist". The Smoking Gun. August 4, 2010. Retrieved 25 March 2013.

[3] Lamb, Joe (June 12, 2009), "CPD investigating prank call", *The Log Cabin Democrat*

[4] Hoyland, Christa (July 14, 2009), "FBI investigating incidents of QSR phone-in vandalism", *QSRweb*

[5] "Ontario man accused of mass online pranks", *CBC News*, August 6, 2009

[6] "Outing An Online Outlaw", *The Smoking Gun*, August 4, 2009

[7] Leyden, John (August 10, 2009), "Hotel prank call badboy tracked down to mum's flat", *The Register*

[8] Philippe BIONDI and Fabrice DESCLAUX, *Silver Needle in the Skype* (PDF), blackhat, retrieved 2009-08-09

[9] Leonard, Tom (July 15, 2009), "FBI probes PrankNET over thousands of dollars in damage caused to hotels and restaurants", *The Telegraph*

[10] Abrams, Joseph (July 14, 2009), "Online Pranksters Wreak Havoc at Hotels, Restaurants Nationwide", *Fox News*

[11] Wilkinson, Melanie (August 5, 2009), "Hotel prank unraveling, according to Court TV website", *York News-Times*

[12] Dickerson, Rachel Parker (August 7, 2009), "Web Site Unmasks Motel Prankster", *KATV*

[13] "Alabama Hotel Damaged In Phone Prank". The Smoking Gun. 2009-06-18.

[14] Beitsch, Rebecca; Edwards, Amy L. (July 9, 2009), "Pranksters strike: Indian River County deputy fooled into breaking hotel window with toilet tank", *Orlando Sentinel*

[15] "First Pranknet Arrest", *The Smoking Gun*, August 26, 2009

[16] Cook, Ashley (August 7, 2009), "Police expand investigation into Diboll man's activities", *Lufkin Daily News*

[17] Ulber, Emily (August 7, 2009), "Phone prank at south Lexington hotel might be linked to international ring", *Lexington Herald-Leader*

[18] "Felonious Phone Terrorist Admits, Apologizes For Heinous Hotel Urine Prank". The Smoking Gun. 2011-08-09.

[19] staff (25 October 2010). "Pranknet Boss Hoaxed ESPN Reporter | The Smoking Gun". *The Smoking Gun*. Retrieved 28 October 2010.

[20] "Stop Us If You've Heard This Before: Prank Caller Dials A Motel 6 Guest...". The Smoking Gun. 2011-03-11.

[21] "Vile Phone Prank Pulled On Iraq Vet". The Smoking Gun. 2014-12-14.

[22] "Hotel Prank Causes $115,000 In Damages". The Smoking Gun. 2011-01-15.

[23] Chen, Dalson (August 4, 2009), "Ontario man leader of notorious U.S. pranksters, website claims", *The Vancouver Sun*

[24] "Telephone Terrorist". *The Smoking Gun*. Retrieved 14 February 2011.

[25] Verma, Sonya (August 8, 2009), "Out-of-line pranksters take cover online", *The Globe and Mail*

[26] Cook, Ashley (August 6, 2009), "Diboll man alleged to be prankster says it's not him", *Lufkin Daily News*

[27] "Prank phone call caused $5,000 to McDonald's", *KTRE (Lufkin)*, September 9, 2009

[28] Phillips, Christel (August 7, 2009), "National Web site fingers Diboll teen as prankster", *KTRE*

[29] "Another Pranknet Child Molester", *The Smoking Gun*, August 6, 2009

[30] "Second Pranknet Member Arrested", *The Smoking Gun*, September 9, 2009

[31] Phillips, Christel (September 24, 2009), ""Prankster" Extradited", *KTRE (Lufkin)*

[32] "Degenerate Phone Prankster Receives Severe Dose Of Texas Justice", *The Smoking Gun*, December 2, 2010

20.6 External links

- Details, incident report and photos of the Conway, Arkansas incident

- Incident report of a Comfort Suites incident

- Orange County Sheriff Bulletin regarding pranks

Chapter 21

Pretext

A **pretext** (adj: **pretextual**) is an excuse to do something or say something that is not accurate. Pretexts may be based on a half-truth or developed in the context of a misleading fabrication. Pretexts have been used to conceal the true purpose or rationale behind actions and words.

In US law, a pretext usually describes false reasons that hide the true intentions or motivations for a legal action. If a party can establish a prima facie case for the proffered evidence, the opposing party must prove that the these reasons were "pretextual" or false. This can be accomplished by directly demonstrating that the motivations behind the presentation of evidence is false, or indirectly by evidence that the motivations are not "credible".[1] In *Griffith v. Schnitzer*, an employment discrimination case, a jury award was reversed by a Court of Appeals because the evidence was not sufficient that the defendant's reasons were "pretextual". That is, the defendant's evidence was either undisputed, or the plaintiff's was "irrelevant subjective assessments and opinions".[2]

A "pretextual" arrest by law enforcement officers is one carried out for illegal purposes such as to conduct an unjustified search and seizure.[3][4]

Marble Boat on Kunming Lake near Beijing.

As one example of pretext, in the 1880s, the Chinese government raised money on the pretext of modernizing the Chinese navy. Instead, these funds were diverted to repair a ship-shaped, two-story pavilion which had been originally constructed for the mother of the Qianlong Emperor. This pretext and the Marble Barge are famously linked with Empress Dowager Cixi. This architectural folly, known today as the Marble Boat (*Shifang*), is "moored" on Lake Kunming in what the empress renamed the "Garden for Cultivating Harmony" (*Yiheyuan*).[5]

Another example of pretext was demonstrated in the speeches of the Roman orator Cato the Elder (234-149 BC). For Cato, every public speech became a pretext for a comment about Carthage. The Roman statesman had come to believe that the prosperity of ancient Carthage represented an eventual and inevitable danger to Rome. In the Senate, Cato famously ended every speech by proclaiming his opinion that Carthage had to be destroyed (*Carthago delenda est*). This oft-repeated phrase was the ultimate conclusion of all logical argument in every oration, regardless of the subject of the speech. This pattern persisted until his death in 149, which was the year in which the Third Punic War began. In other words, any subject became a pretext for reminding his fellow senators of the dangers Carthage represented.[6]

21.1 Uses in warfare

The early years of Japan's Tokugawa shogunate were unsettled, with warring factions battling for power. The causes for the fighting were in part pretextural, but the outcome brought diminished armed conflicts after the Siege of Osaka in 1614-1615.

- **1614** (*Keichō 19*): The Shogun vanquished Hideyori and set fire to Osaka Castle, and then he returned for the winter to Edo.[7]

- **August 24, 1614** (*Keichō 19, 19th day of the 7th month*): A new bronze bell for the Hōkō-ji was cast

Temple bell at Hōkō-ji.

Inscription on bell at Hokoji in Kyoto

successfully ; but despite the dedication ceremony planning, Ieyasu forbade any further actions concerning the great bell:

> "[T]he tablet over the Daibutsu-den and the bell bore the inscription *"Kokka ankō"* (meaning "the country and the house, peace and tranquility"), and at this Tokugawa Ieyasu affect to take umbrage, alleging that it was intended as a curse on him for the character ⬚ (*an,* "peace") was placed between the two characters composing his own name ⬚⬚ (*"ka-kō",* "house tranquility") [suggesting subtly perhaps that peace could only be attained by Ieyasu's dismemberment?] ... This incident of the inscription was, of course, a mere pretext, but Ieyasu realized that he could not enjoy the power he had usurped as long as Hideyori lived, and consequently, although the latter more than once dis-

patched his *kerei* Katagiri Kastumoto to Sunpu Castle with profuse apologies, Ieyasu refused to be placated."[8]

- **October 18, 1614** (*Keichō 19, 25th day of the 10th month*): A strong earthquake shook Kyoto.[7]

- **1615** (*Keichō 20*): Osaka Summer Battle begins.

The next two-and-a-half centuries of Japanese history were comparatively peaceful under the successors of Tokugawa Ieyasu and the bakufu government he established.

21.1.1 United States

- During the War of 1812, US President James Madison was often accused of using impressment of American sailors by the Royal Navy as a pretext to invade Canada.

Main article: Pearl Harbor advance-knowledge debate

- Some have argued that United States President Franklin D. Roosevelt used the attack on Pearl Harbor by Japanese forces on December 7, 1941 as a pretext to enter World War II.[9] American soldiers and supplies had been assisting British and Soviet operations for almost a year by this point, and the United States had thus "chosen a side", but due to the political climate in the States at the time and some campaign promises made by Roosevelt that he would not send American boys to fight in foreign wars. Roosevelt could not declare war for fear of public backlash. The attack on Pearl Harbor united the American people's resolve against the Axis powers and created the bellicose atmosphere in which to declare war.

- Critics have accused United States President George W. Bush of using the September 11th, 2001 attacks and faulty intelligence about the existence of weapons of mass destruction as a pretext for the war in Iraq.[10]

21.2 Social engineering

Main article: Social engineering (security)

A type of social engineering called pretexting uses a pretext to elicit information fraudulently from a target. The pretext in this case includes research into the identity of a certain authorized person or personality type in order to establish legitimacy in the mind of the target.[11]

21.3 See also

- Plausible deniability
- Proximate cause
- Causes of the Franco-Prussian War

21.4 Notes

[1] "Pretext Law & Legal Definition". uslegal.com. Retrieved 13 March 2013.

[2] Defining "pretext" in discrimination cases by Karen Sutherland (2013)

[3] Criminal law - Pretextual arrests and alternatives to the objective tests by Robert D. Snook

[4] O'Day, Kathleen M. "Pretextual traffic stops: injustice for minority drivers". The University of Dayton School of Law. Retrieved 13 March 2013.

[5] Min, Anchee. (2007). *The Last Empress*, pp. 155-156;

[6] Hooper, William Davis *et al.* (1934). "Introduction," in Cato's *De Agricultura* (online version of Loeb edition).

[7] Titsingh, p. 410.

[8] Ponsonby-Fane, Richard. (1956). *Kyoto, the Old Capital of Japan*, p. 292; Titsingh, p. 410.

[9] Bernstein, Richard. "On Dec. 7, Did We Know We Knew?" *New York Times.* December 15, 1999.

[10] Borger, Julian. (2006). "Book says CIA tried to provoke Saddam to war," *The Guardian* (London). 7 September 2006.

[11] Federal Trade Commission (FTC): "Pretexting: Your Personal Information Revealed." February 2006.

21.5 References

- Bamford, James. (2004). *Pretext for War: 9/11, Iraq, and the Abuse of America's Intelligence Agencies.* New York: Doubleday Books. ISBN 978-0-385-50672-4; OCLC 55068034

- Cato, Marcus Porcius. *On Agriculture (De agricultura)* trans, William Davis Hooper and Harrison Boyd Ash. Cambridge: Harvard University Press. OCLC 230499252

- Isikoff, Michael and David Corn. 2006. *Hubris: The Inside Story of Spin, Scandal, and the Selling of the Iraq War* New York: Crown Publishers. ISBN 978-0-307-34681-0

- Min, Anchee. (2007). *The Last Empress.* New York: Houghton Mifflin Harcourt. ISBN 978-0-618-53146-2

- Ponsonby-Fane, Richard Arthur Brabazon. (1956). *Kyoto, the Old Capital of Japan,* Kyoto: Ponsonby Memorial Society.

- Stinnett Robert B. (2001). *Day of Deceit: The Truth about FDR and Pearl Harbor* New York: Simon & Schuster. ISBN 978-0-7432-0129-2

- Titsingh, Isaac. (1834). [Siyun-sai Rin-siyo/Hayashi Gahō, 1652], *Nipon o daï itsi ran; ou, Annales des empereurs du Japon.* Paris: Oriental Translation Fund of Great Britain and Ireland.

Chapter 22

Psychological subversion

Psychological subversion (PsychSub) is the name given by Susan Headley to a method of verbally manipulating people for information. It is similar in practice to so-called social engineering and pretexting, but has a more military focus to it. It was developed by Headley as an extension of knowledge she gained during hacking sessions with notorious early computer network hackers like Kevin Mitnick and Lewis de Payne.

22.1 Usage example

Headley often gave the following example[1] of the use of psychological subversion: Suppose the hacker needed access to a certain classified military computer called, say, IBAS. He would obtain the name of the base commander or other high-ranking official, gain access to the DNS network, (which is the separate military telephone network) and dial up the computer center he needed to reach, which was often in a secured facility. The person who answered the phone would usually be a low-ranking enlisted person, and the hacker would say something like, "This is Lieutenant Johanson, and General Robertson cannot access his IBAS account, and he'd like to know WHY?" This is all said in a very threatening tone of voice, clearly implying that if the general can't get into his account right away, there will be severe negative repercussions, most likely targeting the hapless person who answered the phone.

The hacker has the subject off guard and very defensive, wanting nothing more than to appease the irritated general as quickly as possible. The hacker then goes silent, giving the victim ample time to stammer into the phone and build up his fear level, while listening for clues from the victim as to how best to proceed. Eventually, the hacker suggests that the tech create a temporary account for the general, or change the general's password to that of the hacker's choice.

The hacker would then have gained access to a classified military computer. It is important to note that this technique would not work any more, in no small part thanks to Headley's teaching of the military agencies about such methods during the 1980s.

22.2 Scientific methodology

While pretexting methods and so-called social engineering are based on on-the-fly adaptations during a phone call made to the victim with very little pre-planning or forethought, the practice of PsychSub is based on the principles of NLP and practical psychology. The goal of the hacker or attacker who is using PsychSub is generally more complex and involves preparation, analysis of the situation, and careful thought about what exact words to use and the tone of voice in which to use them.

22.3 Classified thesis

Headley's thesis entitled "The Psychological Subversion of Trusted Systems" was classified by the DOD in 1984 and so far has not seen the light of day. As a result, further information about PsychSub is generally unavailable outside of Headley's own seminars on the subject during the 1980s at CIA technology and spycraft-type seminars such as Surveillance Expo.

22.4 References

[1] DEF CON III Archives

(1) Headley's talk at a hacker convention in Las Vegas

Chapter 23

Robin Sage

For the military training exercise, see United States Army Special Forces selection and training.

Robin Sage is a fictional American cyber threat analyst.

"Robin Sage" as she appeared on social networking pages.

She was created in December 2009 by Thomas Ryan, a controversial security specialist and white hat hacker from New York. Her name was taken from a training exercise of United States Army Special Forces.[1]

23.1 Fictional biography

According to Sage's social networking profiles, she is a 25-year-old "cyber threat analyst" at the Naval Network Warfare Command in Norfolk, Virginia. She graduated from MIT and had allegedly 10 years of work experience, despite her young age.[2] Ryan created several accounts under the name Sage on popular social networks like Facebook, LinkedIn, Twitter etc. and used those profiles to contact nearly 300 people, most of them security specialists, military personnel, staff at intelligence agencies and defense contractors.[1] Her pictures were taken from a pornography-related website in order to attract more attention.[2]

Despite the completely fake profile and no other real-life information, Sage was offered consulting work with notable companies Google and Lockheed Martin[2] and received dinner invitations by several of her male friends.[1]

Not everyone was fooled by Sage's profiles, though. Ryan admitted that his cover was already blown on the second day, when several of those she tried to befriend tried to verify her identity using the phone number he provided, checking email addresses outside the social networking sites or using the MIT alumni network to find her. Others recognized the fake identity of Sage based on her implausible profiles. Yet no central warning was issued about the profile, and users continued to connect with Sage despite warnings not to do so.[1]

23.2 Security problems revealed

Using those contacts, Ryan befriended men and women of all ages during a short time period between December 2009 and January 2010. Almost all of them were working for the United States military, government or companies (amongst the only organizations that did not befriend Sage were the CIA and the FBI[1]). Using these contacts, Ryan gained access to email addresses and bank accounts as well as learning the location of secret military units based on soldiers' Facebook photos and connections between different people and organizations.[2] She was also given private documents for review and was offered to speak at several conferences.[3]

23.3 "Getting in bed with Robin Sage"

Ryan presented his findings[4] as a speaker at the "Black Hat" conference in Las Vegas with a presentation he called "Getting in bed with Robin Sage".[2][3] He explained that his short experiment proves that seemingly harmless details shared via social networking pages can be harmful but also that many people entrusted with vital and sensitive information would share this information readily with third parties, provided they managed to capture their interest. He concluded that his findings could have compromised national security if a terrorist organization had employed similar tactics.[5]

23.4 References

[1] Waterman, Shaun (18 July 2010). "Fictitious femme fatale fooled cybersecurity". The Washington Times. Retrieved 3 August 2010.

[2] Jiménez, Camilo (2 August 2010). "Ein kurzes, heißes Leben" (in German). Süddeutsche Zeitung. Retrieved 3 August 2010.

[3] Goodchild, Joan (8 July 2010). "The Robin Sage experiment: Fake profile fools security pros". Network World. Retrieved 3 August 2010.

[4] Ryan, Thomas (July 2010). "Getting in Bed with Robin Sage." (PDF). Provide Security. Retrieved 25 August 2010.

[5] Batty, David (24 July 2010). "US security chiefs tricked in social networking experiment". The Guardian. Retrieved 3 August 2010.

Chapter 24

Rock Phish

Rock Phish is both a phishing toolkit and the entity that publishes the toolkit. Phishing is an email fraud method in which the perpetrator sends out legitimate-looking email in an attempt to gather personal and financial information from recipients.[1][2] The common information is that it is either a hacker or group of hackers, or a phishing tool kit, or that the same name is used for each.

24.1 Rock Phish Kit

In today's world, organizations that conduct any business online are aware of the various threats that they may be subject to. While basic threats such as phishing attacks, worms and trojans are familiar terms for any IT or security professional, traditional methods associated with fraudulent activity have evolved to new and advanced levels of complexity.

The Rock Phish toolkit enables non-technical users to easily create and implement phishing attacks. The kit works by configuring a single Web server as a host, with multiple domain name servers (DNS es) to host a variety of templates, each one of which closely resembles a different legitimate bank or business venture. Attackers can then launch multiple phishing attacks from the host, fooling customers and clients into responding to the professional, legitimate-looking email and entering their personal or financial data into the phisher's trap. Once harvested, credit card and banking information is channeled into a central server, the "Mother Ship," and sold through chat rooms to a dispersed network of money launderers that extract money from phishing victims' accounts.

24.2 Rock Phish Usage

F-Secure has created videos of the Rock Phish Kit in action on their blog.

Robert McMillan disputes the definition above, saying that "security experts" call such a description inaccurate.[2] He says *Rock Phish* is defined as a hacker or group of hackers stated to be behind "one-half of the phishing attacks being carried out these days." Because of the elusive nature of Rock Phish, the article reports Symantec as comparing it with the movie character Keyser Söze. VeriSign reports them as a group of Romanian origin.[1] In the April 2007 edition of PC World, in an article entitled "Online Criminals are Thriving even in the face of New Automated Defenses" calls *Rock Phish* "a single phishing gang". This report that calls them the Rock Phish gang comes from a research firm known as Gartner, supported by RSA.

Jeff Singleton of HackDefendr Security rebuts Robert McMillan's claim as invalid for the information presented on this page. The correct information of the hacking group called the Rock Phish Gang[3] in comparison with the type of attack via the kit which are also called Rock Phish are in fact different. The authors of the kit remain anonymous, Rock Phish has become the most popular phishing kit available online, with some estimates suggesting that the kit is used for half of all phishing attempts.

Independent of what definition is used, rock phishing is often used to refer to phishing attacks with some particular features. To minimize the effects of takedown, rock phishers work by registering a large number of domains, which are used to host scripting files that send and receive information from the perpetrator's main host. These types of attacks are hosted in such a way that they can be displayed on any compromised machine controlled by the perpetrators. Furthermore, advanced scripting set up by attackers allows the domains to move from ISP to ISP without any human intervention. Given that these types of online criminals have a deep knowledge of and experience in online exploitation, finding the source of and controlling damages done as a result of a rock phishing attack becomes extremely challenging.

An account of rock phishing tactics was presented at APWG eCrime '07.[4]

24.3 Rock Phishing History

It was in 2004 that we saw the genesis of the rock phish attack. The name stems from the first recorded attack in which attackers employed wild card DNS (domain name server) entries to create addresses that included the target's actual address as a sub-domain. For example, in the case of a site appearing as www.thebank.com.1.cn/thebank.html, "thebank.com" portion of the domain name is the "wild card", meaning its presence is purely superficial – it is not required in order for the phishing page to be displayed. "1.cn" is the registered domain name, "/thebank.html" is the phishing page, and the combination of "1.cn/thebank" will display the phishing page. This allows the perpetrators to make the wild card portion the legitimate domain name, so that it appears at first glance to be a valid folder path. The first rock phishing attacks contained the folder path "/rock", which led to the name of the attack as we know it today. To date, it is estimated that rock phishing has already cost businesses and consumers in excess of $100 million in damages, and it continues to grow.

Until this attack, phishing was becoming more pervasive, but was far from mainstream - in large part because free Web services only allowed for limited activities. More recently however, attackers have found a more surreptitious way to launch attacks through legitimate websites themselves by exploiting common vulnerabilities in the software running on the sites. Unlike popularized software applications that openly announce changes, automate updates and provide open access to programming tools, administrators often have to spend time seeking out Web software updates and security weaknesses. This delay in - or sometimes complete lack of – action provides ample opportunity for attackers to do considerable damage.

In addition, there has been a move to make website software more accessible to the non-tech user so they can create their own Web pages. The drop in the sophistication levels of the Web masters makes the risk of rock phishing higher – and the opportunity to catch these sites and shut them down in a timely manner much lower.

At the same time, perpetrators for their part have taken it upon themselves to become well-versed in Web server technology. These are not the typical casual hackers that typified the "phisher kings" of past years. These are highly sophisticated, well educated, highly coordinated teams of people with exceptional technology skills.

24.4 BCS OutLook

In simple terms a Rock phish requires ownership of multiples of domain names, which are normally nonsensical, e.g.

dio666.org. These are then constructed into spam email which creates the look and feel of a genuine communication. Underlying the Rock phish attack is the use of wildcard DNS, which is employed to resolve to variations of IP addresses, and then mapping them over to a dynamic gathering of compromised machines.[5]

24.5 References

[1] Compliance and Privacy (2006-12-15). "What is Rock Phish? And why is it important to know?". Compliance and Privacy. Retrieved 2006-12-15. Rock Phish is an individual or group of actors likely working out of Romania and nearby countries in the region. This group has been in operation since 2004 and is responsible for innovation in both spam and phishing attacks to date, such as pioneering image-spam (Ken Dunham, VeriSign)

[2] Robert McMillan (2006-12-12). "'Rock Phish' blamed for surge in phishing". InfoWorld. p. 2. Retrieved 2006-12-13. The first thing you need to know about Rock Phish is that nobody knows exactly who, or what, they are.

[3] Jeremy Kirk (2008-04-21). "'Rock Phish Gang' Adds Second Punch to Phishing Attacks.". IDG News Service. p. 1. Retrieved 2012-11-03. The Rock Phish gang surfaced around 2004, becoming well-known for its expertise in setting up phishing sites...

[4] Tyler Moore and Richard Clayton. "Examining the Impact of Website Take-down on Phishing." (PDF). *APWG eCrime Researcher's Summit, ACM Press, pp. 1-13*. Retrieved October 28, 2007.

[5] BCS March 2008 http://www.bcs.org/server.php?show=ConWebDoc.17968

Chapter 25

Rogue security software

Rogue security software is a form of malicious software and Internet fraud that misleads users into believing there is a virus on their computer, and manipulates them into paying money for a fake malware removal tool (that actually introduces malware to the computer). It is a form of scareware that manipulates users through fear, and a form of ransomware.[1] Rogue security software has become a growing and serious security threat in desktop computing in recent years (from 2008 on).[2]

25.1 Propagation

Rogue security software mainly relies on social engineering (fraud) to defeat the security built into modern operating system and browser software and install itself onto victims' computers.[2] A website may, for example, display a fictitious warning dialog stating that someone's machine is infected with a computer virus, and encourage them through manipulation to install or purchase scareware in the belief that they are purchasing genuine antivirus software.

Most have a Trojan horse component, which users are misled into installing. The Trojan may be disguised as:

- A browser plug-in or extension (typically toolbar)

- An image, screensaver or archive file attached to an e-mail message

- Multimedia codec required to play a certain video clip

- Software shared on peer-to-peer networks[3]

- A free online malware-scanning service[4]

Some rogue security software, however, propagate onto users' computers as drive-by downloads which exploit security vulnerabilities in web browsers, PDF viewers, or email clients to install themselves without any manual interaction.[3][5]

More recently, malware distributors have been utilizing SEO poisoning techniques by pushing infected URLs to the top of search engine results about recent news events.[6] People looking for articles on such events on a search engine may encounter results that, upon being clicked, are instead redirected through a series of sites[7] before arriving at a landing page that says that their machine is infected and pushes a download to a "trial" of the rogue program.[8][9] A 2010 study by Google found 11,000 domains hosting fake anti-virus software, accounting for 50% of all malware delivered via internet advertising.[10]

Cold-calling has also become a vector for distribution of this type of malware, with callers often claiming to be from "Microsoft Support" or another legitimate organization.[11]

25.2 Common Infection Vectors [12]

25.2.1 Black Hat SEO [13]

Black Hat search engine optimization (SEO) is a technique used to trick search engines into displaying malicious URLs in search results. The malicious webpages are filled with popular keywords in order to achieve a higher ranking in the search results. When the end user searches the web, one of these infected webpages is returned. Usually the most popular keywords from services such as Google Trends are used to generate webpages via PHP scripts placed on the compromised website. These PHP scripts will then monitor for search engine crawlers and feed them with especially crafted webpages that are then listed in the search results. Then, when the user searches for their keyword or images and clicks on the malicious link, they will be redirected to the Rogue security software payload.

25.2.2 Malvertising

Most websites usually employ third-party services for advertising on their webpages. If one of these advertising services is compromised,they may end up inadvertently infecting all of the websites using their service by showing advertising rogue security software.

25.2.3 Spam Campaigns

Spam messages that include malicious attachments, links to binaries and driveby download sites are another common mechanism for distributing Rogue security software. Spam emails are often sent with content associated with typical day-to-day activities such as parcel deliveries, or taxation documents, designed to entice users to click on links or run attachments. When users succumb to these kinds of social engineering tricks they are quickly infected either directly via the attachment, or indirectly via a malicious website. This is known as a driveby download. Usually in drive-by download attacks the malware is installed on the victim's machine without any interaction or awareness and occurs simply by visiting the website.

25.3 Operation

Once installed, the rogue security software may then attempt to entice the user into purchasing a service or additional software by:

- Alerting the user with the fake or simulated detection of malware or pornography.[14]

- Displaying an animation simulating a system crash and reboot.[2]

- Selectively disabling parts of the system to prevent the user from uninstalling the malware. Some may also prevent anti-malware programs from running, disable automatic system software updates and block access to websites of anti-malware vendors.[15]

- Installing actual malware onto the computer, then alerting the user after "detecting" them. This method is less common as the malware is likely to be detected by legitimate anti-malware programs.

- Altering system registries and security settings, then "alerting" the user.[16]

Developers of rogue security software may also entice people into purchasing their product by claiming to give a portion of their sales to a charitable cause. The rogue Green antivirus, for example, claims to donate $2 to an environmental care program for each sale made.[17]

Some rogue security software overlaps in function with scareware by also:

- Presenting offers to fix urgent performance problems or perform essential housekeeping on the computer.[14]

- Scaring the user by presenting authentic-looking pop-up warnings and security alerts, which may mimic actual system notices.[18] These are intended to use the trust that the user has in vendors of legitimate security software.[2]

Sanction by the FTC and the increasing effectiveness of anti-malware tools since 2006 have made it difficult for spyware and adware distribution networks—already complex to begin with[19]—to operate profitably.[20] Malware vendors have turned instead to the simpler, more profitable business model of rogue security software, which is targeted directly at users of desktop computers.[21]

Rogue security software is often distributed through highly lucrative affiliate networks, in which affiliates supplied with Trojan kits for the software are paid a fee for every successful installation, and a commission from any resulting purchases. The affiliates then become responsible for setting up infection vectors and distribution infrastructure for the software.[22] An investigation by security researchers into the Antivirus XP 2008 rogue security software found just such an affiliate network, in which members were grossing commissions upwards of $USD150,000 over 10 days, from tens of thousands of successful installations.[23]

25.4 Countermeasures

25.4.1 Private efforts

Law enforcement and legislation in all countries were very slow to react to the appearance of rogue security software even though it simply uses new technical means to carry out mainly old and well-established kinds of crimes. In contrast, several private initiatives providing discussion forums and lists of dangerous products were founded soon after the appearance of the first rogue security software. Some reputable vendors also began to provide lists of rogue security software, for example Kaspersky.[24] In 2005, the Anti-Spyware Coalition was founded, a coalition of anti-spyware software companies, academics, and consumer groups.

Many of the private initiatives were at first more or less informal discussions on general Internet forums, but some were started or even entirely carried out by individual people. The perhaps most famous and extensive one is the Spyware Warrior list of rogue/suspect antispyware products and websites by Eric Howes,[25] which has however not been updated since May 2007. The website recommends checking the following websites for new rogue anti-spyware programs, most of which are however not really new and are "simply re-branded clones and knockoffs of the same rogue applications that have been around for years"[26]

In December 2008, the US District Court for Maryland—at the request of the FTC—issued a restraining order against Innovative Marketing Inc, a Kiev-based firm producing and marketing the rogue security software products WinFixer, WinAntivirus, DriveCleaner, ErrorSafe, and XP Antivirus.[27] The company and its US-based web host, ByteHosting Internet Hosting Services LLC, had their assets frozen, were barred from using domain names associated with those products and any further advertisement or false representation.[28]

Law enforcement has also exerted pressure on banks to shut down merchant gateways involved in processing rogue security software purchases. In some cases, the high volume of credit card chargebacks generated by such purchases has also prompted processors to take action against rogue security software vendors.[29]

25.5 See also

- Anti-virus
- FraudTool
- List of rogue security software
- Scareware
- Technical support scam
- Winwebsec

25.6 References

[1] "Symantec Report on Rogue Security Software" (PDF). Symantec. 2009-10-28. Retrieved 2010-04-15.

[2] "Microsoft Security Intelligence Report volume 6 (July - December 2008)". Microsoft. 2009-04-08. p. 92. Retrieved 2009-05-02.

[3] Doshi, Nishant (2009-01-19), *Misleading Applications – Show Me The Money!*, Symantec, retrieved 2009-05-02

[4] Doshi, Nishant (2009-01-21), *Misleading Applications – Show Me The Money! (Part 2)*, Symantec, retrieved 2009-05-02

[5] "News Adobe Reader and Acrobat Vulnerability". blogs.adobe.com. Retrieved 25 November 2010.

[6] Vincentas (13 July 2013). "Rogue Security Software in Spy-WareLoop.com". Spyware Loop. Retrieved 24 July 2013.

[7] Chu, Kian; Hong, Choon (2009-09-30), *Samoa Earthquake News Leads To Rogue AV*, F-Secure, retrieved 2010-01-16

[8] Hines, Matthew (2009-10-08), *Malware Distributors Mastering News SEO*, eWeek, retrieved 2010-01-16

[9] Raywood, Dan (2010-01-15), *Rogue anti-virus prevalent on links that relate to Haiti earthquake, as donors encouraged to look carefully for genuine sites*, SC Magazine, retrieved 2010-01-16

[10] Moheeb Abu Rajab and Luca Ballard (2010-04-13). "The Nocebo Effect on the Web: An Analysis of Fake Anti-Virus Distribution" (PDF). Google. Retrieved 2010-11-18.

[11] "Warning over anti-virus cold-calls to UK internet users". BBC News. Retrieved 7 March 2012.

[12] "Sophos Fake Antivirus Journey from Trojan tpna" (PDF)., ctbalarmsinbirmingham.co.uk

[13] "Sophos Technical Papers - Sophos SEO Insights". *sophos.com.*

[14] *"Free Security Scan" Could Cost Time and Money*, Federal Trade Commission, 2008-12-10, retrieved 2009-05-02

[15] Vincentas (11 July 2013). "Rogue Security Software in Spy-WareLoop.com". Spyware Loop. Retrieved 28 July 2013.

[16] Vincentas (11 July 2013). "Rogue Anti-Spyware in Spy-WareLoop.com". Spyware Loop. Retrieved 28 July 2013.

[17] "Cantalktech.com". *cantalktech.com.*

[18] "SAP at a crossroads after losing $1.3B verdict". Yahoo! News. 24 November 2010. Retrieved 25 November 2010.

[19] *Testimony of Ari Schwartz on "Spyware"* (PDF), Senate Committee on Commerce, Science, and Transportation, 2005-05-11

[20] Leyden, John (2009-04-11). "Zango goes titsup: End of desktop adware market". The Register. Retrieved 2009-05-05.

[21] Cole, Dave (2006-07-03), *Deceptonomics: A Glance at The Misleading Application Business Model*, Symantec, retrieved 2009-05-02

[22] Doshi, Nishant (2009-01-27), *Misleading Applications – Show Me The Money! (Part 3)*, Symantec, retrieved 2009-05-02

[23] Stewart, Joe (2008-10-22), *Rogue Antivirus Dissected - Part 2*, SecureWorks

[24] Rogue security software

[25] "Spyware Warrior: Rogue/Suspect Anti-Spyware Products & Web Sites". *spywarewarrior.com.*

[26] "Virus, Spyware, & Malware Removal Guides". *BleepingComputer.*

[27] *Ex Parte Temporary Restraining Order RDB08CV3233* (PDF), United States District Court for the District of Maryland, 2008-12-03, retrieved 2009-05-02

[28] Lordan, Betsy (2008-12-10), *Court Halts Bogus Computer Scans*, Federal Trade Commission, retrieved 2009-05-02

[29] Krebs, Brian (2009-03-20), "Rogue Antivirus Distribution Network Dismantled", *Washington Post*, retrieved 2009-05-02

25.7   External links

- Howes, Eric L (2007-05-04), *Spyware Warrior: Rogue/Suspect Anti-Spyware Products & Web Sites*, retrieved 2009-05-02

- Mariani, Brian L (2011-05-20), *Fake malware scanners:*, retrieved 2011-05-20

Chapter 26

Romance scam

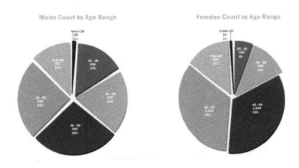

Gender and age demographics of victims of online romance scams in 2011.

A **romance scam** is a confidence trick involving feigned romantic intentions towards a victim, gaining their affection, and then using that goodwill to commit fraud. Fraudulent acts may involve access to the victims' money, bank accounts, credit cards, passports, e-mail accounts, or national identification numbers or by getting the victims to commit financial fraud on their behalf.[1]

26.1 Stolen images

Scammers post profiles, using stolen photographs of attractive persons, asking for others to contact them. This is often known as catfishing.[2] Letters are exchanged between the scammer and victim until the scammer feels they have groomed the victim enough to ask for money. This might be for requests for gas money or bus and airplane tickets to travel to visit the victim, medical expenses, education expenses etc. There is usually the promise that the fictitious character will one day join the victim in the victim's country. The scam usually ends when the victim realizes they are being scammed or stops sending money. Victims can be highly traumatized by this and are often very embarrassed and ashamed when they learn they have become a victim of a scam and that the romance was a farce.

In some cases, online dating services are themselves engaged in misrepresentation, displaying profiles which have been fabricated, which use personal information from users who have not agreed to be depicted on the site[3] or by presenting outdated or out-of-region profiles as current and local.

26.2 Internet

Scammers post profiles on dating websites,[4] social accounts, classified sites and even forums to groom new victims. Upon finding victims, scammers lure them to more private means of communication, (such as providing an e-mail address) to allow for fraud to occur.[1] The fraud typically involves the scammer acting as if they've quickly fallen for the victim so that when they have the opportunity to ask for money, the victim at that time has become too emotionally involved, and will have deep feelings of guilt if they decline the request for money from the scammer.

26.3 Common variations

Narratives used to extract money from the victims of romantic scams include the following:

- The scammer says their boss paid them in postal money orders. The scammer wants the mark to cash the money orders, and then wire money to the scammer. The forged money orders leave the banks to incur debts against the victims.[5]

- The scammer says they need the mark to send money to pay for a passport.[5]

- The scammer says they require money for flights to the victim's country because of being left there by a stepparent, or husband/wife, or because they are just tired of living in their country[6] and somehow never comes, or says that they are being held against their will by immigration authorities, who demand bribes.[7]

- The scammer says they have had gold bars or other valuables seized by customs and need to pay taxes to before they can recover them before joining the victim in his/her country[5]

- The scammer meets the victim on an online dating site, lives in a foreign country, falls in love, but needs money to join the victim in his/her country[5]

- The scammer says they are being held against their will for failure to pay a bill or requires money for hospital bills.[6]

- The scammer says they need the money to pay for the phone bills in order to continue communicating with the victim.[8]

- The scammer says they need the money for their or their parents' urgent medical treatment.[8]

- The scammer says they need the money to successfully graduate before they can visit the victim.[8]

- The scammer offers a job, often to people in a poor country, on payment of a registration fee. These are particularly common at African dating sites.[9]

- The scammer actually is employed directly or indirectly by a website, with a share of the victim's member or usage fees passed on to the scammer.[10]

26.3.1   Blackmail

Some romance scammers seek out a niche of various fetishes where they will find an obscure fetish and they will make the victim think that if they pay for the scammer's plane ticket that they will get to live out a sexual fantasy of theirs by having the scammer come to them to have sex. The scammers also like to entice victims to perform sexual acts on webcam. They then record their victims, play back the recorded images or videos to them and then extort money to prevent them from sending the recordings to friends, family, employers, often discovered via social media sites such as Facebook, Twitter etc.

26.3.2   Pro-daters

The pro-dater differs from the other scams in method of operation; a face-to-face meeting actually does take place in the scammer's country but is devoted solely into manipulating the mark into spending as much money as possible in relatively little time, with little or nothing in return. The scheme usually involves accomplices, such as an interpreter and a taxi driver, all of which must be paid by the victim at an inflated price. Everything is pre-arranged so

that the wealthy foreigner pays top dollar for accommodation, is taken not to an ordinary public café but to the most costly restaurant (usually some out-of-the-way place priced far above what locals would ever be willing to pay), and is manipulated into making various expensive purchases, including gifts such as electronics and fur coats.[11]

The vendors are typically part of the scheme. The mark leaves just as alone but poorer at the end of the trip. The merchandise is returned to the vendors, the pro-dater and the various accomplices pocket their respective cut of the take. As the pro-dater is eager to date again, the next date is immediately set up with the next wealthy foreigner.[12]

The supposed relationship goes no further, except to inundate the hapless mark with requests for more money after they return home.[13] Unlike a gold digger, who marries for money, a pro-dater is not necessarily single or available in real life.

26.3.3   419 scams

Another variation is the scammer has a need to marry in order to inherit millions of dollars of gold left by a father, uncle, or grandfather. The young woman will contact a victim and tell them of their plight of not being able to remove the gold from their country due to being unable to pay the duty or marriage taxes. The woman will be unable to inherit the fortune until she gets married. The marriage being a prequiste of the father, uncle or grandfather's will. The scammer keeps the victim believing that they are sincere, until they are able to build up enough rapport to ask for thousands of dollars to help bring the gold into the victim's country. The scammer will offer to fly to the victim's country to prove that they are a real person. The victim will send money for the flight. However when the victim goes to meet the scammer they never show up. The victim contacts the scammer to ask what happened. The scammer will provide an excuse such as not being able to get an exit visa, or illness of themselves or a family member. Scammers are very adept at knowing how to "play" their victims - sending love poems, sex games in emails, building up a "loving relationship" with many promises of "one day we will be married". Often photos of unknown African actresses will be used to lure the victim into believing they are talking to that person. Victims may be invited to travel to the scammer's country; in some cases the victims arrive with asked-for gift money for family members or bribes for corrupt officials, and then they are beaten and robbed or murdered.

26.3.4   Impersonation of soldiers

A rapidly growing technique scammers are using is to impersonate American military personnel. Scammers prefer to use the images, names and profiles of soldiers as this usually inspires confidence, trust and admiration in their female victims.[14] Also because military public relations often posts information on soldiers without mentioning their families or personal lives. Images are stolen from sites by organized internet crime gangs often operating out of Nigeria or Ghana. They tell their victims that they are lonely, looking to retire and settle down with a new love - but while they're deployed elsewhere, they concoct stories about needing special phones to communicate, supporting an orphanage with their own money, needing financial assistance because they can't access their own money in a combat zone, etc. The lies are too numerous and various to list them all. The scammer will say anything to get the victim to send money. And the money is always sent to a third party to be collected for the scammer. Sometimes the third party is real and sometimes they are fictitious as well. Funds sent by Western Union and MoneyGram do not have to be claimed by anyone showing identification if the sender sends money using a secret pass phrase and response and can be picked up anywhere in the world.[15]

26.4 SCAMwatch

SCAMwatch,[16] a website run by the Australian Competition and Consumer Commission (ACCC), provides information about how to recognise, avoid and report scams.[17]

In 2005 the ACCC and other agencies formed the Australasian Consumer Fraud Taskforce (ACFT). The site provides info about current scams, warning signs and staying safe.

26.5 Cultural references

- The Swedish film *Raskenstam* (1983; alternate title, *Casanova of Sweden*) is a fictionalized romantic comedy based on the true story of Swedish undertaker Gustaf Raskenstam,[18] who seduced over 100 women and convinced many to support his various projects financially.[19] He usually used newspaper contact ads, often with the headline "Sun and spring", which has become an idiomatic expression in Sweden. The film was directed by Gunnar Hellstrom, written by Hellstrom and Birgitta Stemberg, and executive produced by Hellstrom and Brian Wikstrom.[20]

- Several films and television episodes depict the story of Raymond Fernandez and Martha Beck, the American serial killer couple known as "The Lonely Hearts Killers", who are believed to have killed as many as 20 women during their murderous spree between 1947

and 1949. The pair met their unsuspecting victims through lonely hearts ads.

- *The Honeymoon Killers* (1969 film)
- *Deep Crimson* (1996 film)
- *Lonely Hearts* (2006 film)
- *Cold Case*: "Lonely Hearts" (season 4, episode 9), airdate November 19, 2006
- *Alleluia* (2014 film)

26.6 See also

- 419 scams

26.7 References

[1] "Online Romance Scams Continue To Grow," *KMBC*

[2] "catfishing - online dating scams".

[3] "Facebook info sharing created Zoosk.com dating profile for married woman". CBC News. 24 November 2014.

[4] "Love is lies". *http://gimletmedia.com*. Gimlet Media. Retrieved 20 February 2015. External link in |website= (help)

[5] "Seduced into scams: Online lovers often duped," *MSNBC*. 1.

[6] "International Financial Scams – Internet Dating, Inheritance, Work Permits, Overpayment, and Money-Laundering," *United States Department of State*

[7] "ROMANCE SCAMS," *US Diplomatic Mission in Ghana*

[8] "Russian women scams - and how to avoid them". Moscow Russia Insider's guide.

[9] "Nanny Scam Example - August 2010".

[10] "The mail-order bride boom - Fortune Tech". Tech.fortune.cnn.com. 2013-04-09. Retrieved 2014-01-01.

[11] "Nine Tips on How to Identify and Avoid Ukrainian Pro-Daters".

[12] "Romance Scam". *Romancescam*.

[13] "Tips how to recognize professional Asian pro-daters".

[14] Power, Julie (6 December 2014). "Love me don't: the West African online scam using US soldiers". *The Sydney Morning Herald*. Retrieved 6 December 2014.

[15] "Romance Scam". *Romancescam*.

[16] "ScamWatch Australia".

[17] "Dating and romance scams". ScamWatch Australia.

[18] "10 Most Bizarre Scams (That Actually Worked)".
      PopCrunch. August 12, 2010.

[19] Mannika, Eleanor. "*The New York Times* Movies: Raken-
      stam (1983)". *Rovi*. Retrieved July 11, 2014.

[20] "*Rackensam (1983): Production Credits*". *The New York
      Times*. Retrieved July 11, 2014.

26.8   External links

- Phishing at DMOZ

- Online Dating Scammers Using Stolen Images, CBS
  News February 11, 2009, retrieved July 7, 2011

- Recovery Scams, CupidScreen June 10, 2012, retrieved October 7, 2012

- www.RomanceScamsNow.com Major Anti-scammer
  information and resources website with over 100,000
  known scammer email addresses Large anti-scammer
  information and resources

- www.myrsai.com - RSA (romance scam awareness)
  International offer support and education for anyone
  who has been scammed or provide support and advice
  so you avoid being scammed

Chapter 27

Scam baiting

Scam baiting is a form of Internet vigilantism, where the vigilante poses as a potential victim to the scammer in order to waste their time and resources, gather information that will be of use to authorities, and publicly expose the scammer. It is primarily used to thwart advance-fee fraud scams and can be done out of a sense of civic duty (activism), as a form of amusement, or both. However, some of this scambaiting can involve racism[1] while there are other forms that document e.g. scammers tools and methods, warn potential victims, provide discussion forums, or take down fake websites.[2]

27.1 Methodology

A bait is very simply initiated, by answering a scam email, from a throwaway email account, i.e. one that is only used for baiting and untraceable back to the actual owner. The baiter then pretends to be receptive to the financial hook that the scammer is using.

The objectives of baiting are, in no particular order:

1. Keep the bait going as long as possible, thus costing the scammer time and energy.

2. Gather as much information as possible, so that the scammer can be personally identified and publicly exposed.

3. Ensure the scams, and any names used, are easily found by search-engine spiders, as a preventive strategy.

A popular method to accomplish the first objective is to ask the scammer to fill out made-up questionnaires, which is very time consuming. The idea is that when a scammer is preoccupied with a baiter who has no intention of falling victim to the scam, it prevents the scammer in question from conning genuine victims out of their money. Activists may bait scammers into taking long trips, encourage the use

poorly-made props, or teach English-language idioms that surreptitiously throw doubt upon the scam.[3]

Amusements that the baiter may gain from the interaction include fooling the scammer into falling for claims just as ludicrous as the ones that the scammer is using to defraud his victims. Baiters will often use joke names or references to Western popular culture which, while obviously ludicrous to a native or fluent English speaker, will go unnoticed by the scammer. Similarly baiters may introduce characters, and even plot-lines, from movies or television shows for comedic effect. It has also been known for the scammers themselves to adopt fake names that in their native culture would seem equally ludicrous. This reflects Western scambaiters using names from popular culture; in contrast Westerners would probably be unlikely to identify names that would be familiar with Nigerian or other West African popular culture.

27.2 Examples

In May 2004, a Something Awful forum poster asked for advice on how to deal with a bogus escrow scam from a buyer on eBay. Since the eBay auction was for an Apple PowerBook G4, another forum poster suggested that he construct a replica PowerBook out of cardboard. The buyer, who lived overseas, was forced to pay several hundred dollars to customs to claim the fake laptop.[4][5] A member of 419eater.com was able to convince a scammer to send him a wooden replica of a Commodore 64.[6]

In February 2011, the Belgian television show Basta portrayed, with hidden cameras, how a scammer was fooled during a meeting with baiters, raising the stakes by involving a one-armed man, two dwarves and a pony. Eventually, a police raid was faked, during which the baiters were arrested and the scammer went free, abandoning the money, and without any suspicion.[7]

In January 2014, members of the scambaiting website 419eater.com appeared in two segments of the Channel 4 show "Secrets of the Scammers". In the first segment scam-baiters persuaded a scammer to travel from London to a remote location in Cornwall by train and taxi to meet a victim (played by a baiter) and collect payment for a gold deal. In the second segment a female scammer met with two scam-baiters posing as victims in Trafalgar Square to pass them a fake check. This scammer was subsequently questioned by the police.[8]

27.3   See also

- Sting operation

- Internet vigilantism

27.4   References

[1] Nakamura, Lisa (2014). "'I WILL DO EVERYthing That Am Asked': Scambaiting, Digital Show-Space, and the Racial Violence of Social Media". *Journal of visual culture*: 258-273. Retrieved 2015-03-23.

[2] Zingerle, Andreas; Kronman, Linda (2013). "'Humiliating entertainment or social activism?': Analyzing Scambaiting Strategies Against Online Advance Fee Fraud": 352-355. Retrieved 2015-07-13.

[3] Cheng, Jacqui (2009-05-11). "Baiting Nigerian scammers for fun (not so much for profit)". *Ars Technica*. Retrieved 2015-12-26e. Check date values in: |access-date= (help)

[4] Rojas, Peter (2004-05-14). "Scamming the scammer". *Engadget*. Retrieved 2015-12-26.

[5] Roth, Wolf-Dieter (2004-05-28). "Wir basteln uns ein Apple G4 P-P-P-Powerbook". *Telepolis* (in German). Retrieved 2015-12-26.

[6] Madrigal, Alexis C. (2010-09-28). "How to Trick an Online Scammer Into Carving a Computer Out of Wood". *The Atlantic*. Retrieved 2015-12-26.

[7] Pest eens een internetfraudeur Basta on YouTube (in Dutch)

[8] Secrets of the Scammers on YouTube

27.5   External links

- Advanced fee fraud humor at DMOZ

Chapter 28

Scareware

Not to be confused with careware or shareware.

Scareware is a form of malicious software that uses social engineering to cause shock, anxiety, or the perception of a threat in order to manipulate users into buying unwanted software. Scareware is part of a class of malicious software that includes rogue security software, ransomware and other scam software with malicious payloads, which have limited or no benefit to users, and are pushed by unethical marketing practices. Some forms of spyware and adware also use scareware tactics.

A tactic frequently used by criminals involves convincing users that a virus has infected their computer, then suggesting that they download (and pay for) fake antivirus software to remove it.[1] Usually the virus is entirely fictional and the software is non-functional or malware itself.[2] According to the Anti-Phishing Working Group, the number of scareware packages in circulation rose from 2,850 to 9,287 in the second half of 2008.[3] In the first half of 2009, the APWG identified a 585% increase in scareware programs.[4]

The "scareware" label can also apply to any application or virus (not necessarily sold as above) which pranks users with intent to cause anxiety or panic.

28.1 Scam scareware

Internet Security bloggers/writers use the term "scareware" to describe software products that produce frivolous and alarming warnings or threat notices, most typically for fictitious or useless commercial firewall and registry cleaner software. This class of program tries to increase its perceived value by bombarding the user with constant warning messages that do not increase its effectiveness in any way. Software is packaged with a look and feel that mimics legitimate security software in order to deceive consumers.[5]

Some websites display pop-up advertisement windows or banners with text such as: "Your computer may be infected with harmful spyware programs.[6] Immediate removal may be required. To scan, click 'Yes' below." These websites can go as far as saying that a user's job, career, or marriage would be at risk.[7] Products using advertisements such as these are often considered scareware. Serious scareware applications qualify as rogue software.

In recent findings, some scareware is not affiliated with any other installed programs. A user can encounter a pop-up on a website indicating that their PC is infected.[8] In some scenarios, it is possible to become infected with scareware even if the user attempts to cancel the notification. These popups are especially designed to look like they come from the user's operating system when they are actually a webpage.

A 2010 study by Google found 11,000 domains hosting fake anti-virus software, accounting for 50% of all malware delivered via internet advertising.[9]

Starting on March 29, 2011, more than 1.5 million web sites around the world have been infected by the LizaMoon SQL injection attack spread by scareware.[10][11]

Research by Google discovered that scareware was using some of its servers to check for internet connectivity. The data suggested that up to a million machines were infected with scareware.[12] The company has placed a warning in the search results of users whose computers appear to be infected.

28.1.1 Spyware

Some forms of spyware also qualify as scareware because they change the user's desktop background, install icons in the computer's notification area (under Microsoft Windows), and generally make a nuisance of themselves, claiming that some kind of spyware has infected the user's computer and that the scareware application will help to remove the infection. In some cases, scareware trojans have replaced the desktop of the victim with large, yellow text reading "Warning! You have spyware!" or a box containing similar text, and have even forced the screensaver to change to "bugs" crawling across the screen. Winwebsec is

111

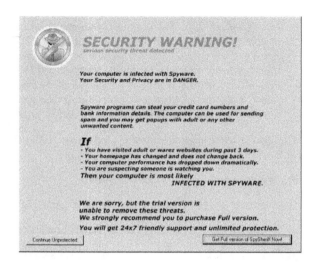

Dialog from SpySheriff, designed to scare users into installing the rogue software

the term usually used to address the malware that attacks the users of Windows operating system and produces fake claims similar to that of genuine anti-malware software.[13]

SpySheriff[14] exemplifies spyware/scareware: it purports to remove spyware, but is actually a piece of spyware itself, often accompanying SmitFraud infections. Other antispyware scareware may be promoted using a phishing scam.

Another example of scareware is Smart Fortress. This site scares people into thinking they have lots of viruses on their computer and asks them to buy the professional service.[15]

28.2 Uninstallation of security software

Another approach is to trick users into uninstalling legitimate antivirus software, such as Microsoft Security Essentials, or disabling their firewall.[16]

28.3 Legal action

In 2005, Microsoft and Washington State successfully sued Secure Computer (makers of Spyware Cleaner) for $1 million over charges of using scareware pop-ups.[17] Washington's attorney general has also brought lawsuits against Securelink Networks, High Falls Media, and the makers of Quick Shield.[18]

In October 2008, Microsoft and the Washington attorney general filed a lawsuit against two Texas firms, Branch Software and Alpha Red, producers of the Registry Cleaner XP scareware.[19] The lawsuit alleges that the company sent in-

cessant pop-ups resembling system warnings to consumers' personal computers stating "CRITICAL ERROR MESSAGE! - REGISTRY DAMAGED AND CORRUPTED", before instructing users to visit a web site to download Registry Cleaner XP at a cost of $39.95.

On December 2, 2008, the U.S. Federal Trade Commission ("FTC") filed a Complaint in federal court against Innovative Marketing, Inc., ByteHosting Internet Services, LLC, as well as individuals Sam Jain, Daniel Sundin, James Reno, Marc D'Souza, and Kristy Ross. The Complaint also listed Maurice D'Souza as a Relief Defendant, alleged that he held proceeds of wrongful conduct but not accusing him of violating any law. The FTC alleged that the other Defendants violated the FTC Act by deceptively marketing software, including WinFixer, WinAntivirus, DriveCleaner, ErrorSafe, and XP Antivirus. According to the complaint, the Defendants falsely represented that scans of a consumer's computer showed that it is had been compromised or infected and then offered to sell software to fix the alleged problems.[20][21][22]

28.4 Prank software

Another type of scareware involves software designed to literally scare the user through the use of unanticipated shocking images, sounds or video.

- An early program of this type is NightMare, a program distributed on the Fish Disks for the Amiga computer (Fish #448) in 1991. When NightMare executes, it lies dormant for an extended (and random) period of time, finally changing the entire screen of the computer to an image of a skull while playing a horrifying shriek on the audio channels.[23]

- Anxiety-based scareware puts users in situations where there are no positive outcomes. For example, a small program can present a dialog box saying "Erase everything on hard drive?" with two buttons, both labeled "OK". Regardless of which button is chosen, nothing is destroyed other than the user's composure.[24]

- This tactic was used in an advertisement campaign by Sir-Tech in 1997 to advertise *Virus: The Game*. When the file is run, a full screen representation of the desktop appears. The software then begins simulating deletion of the Windows folder. When this process is complete, a message is slowly typed on screen saying "Thank God this is only a game." A screen with the purchase information appears on screen and then returns to the desktop. No damage is done to the computer during the advertisement.

28.5 See also

- Ransomware

- Rogue security software

- Winwebsec

28.6 Notes

[1] "Millions tricked by 'scareware'". BBC News. 2009-10-19. Retrieved 2009-10-20.

[2] 'Scareware' scams trick searchers. BBC News (2009-03-23). Retrieved on 2009-03-23.

[3] "Scareware scammers adopt cold call tactics". The Register. 2009-04-10. Retrieved 2009-04-12.

[4] Phishing Activity Trends Report: 1st Half 2009

[5] John Leydon (2009-10-20). "Scareware Mr Bigs enjoy 'low risk' crime bonanza". The Register. Retrieved 2009-10-21.

[6] Carine Febre (2014-10-20). "Fake Warning Example". Carine Febre. Retrieved 2014-11-21.

[7] "Symantec Security Response: Misleading Applications". Symantec. 2007-08-31. Retrieved 2010-04-15.

[8] JM Hipolito (2009-06-04). "Air France Flight 447 Search Results Lead to Rogue Antivirus". Trend Micro. Retrieved 2009-06-06.

[9] Moheeb Abu Rajab and Luca Ballard (2010-04-13). "The Nocebo Effect on the Web: An Analysis of Fake Anti-Virus Distribution" (PDF). Google. Retrieved 2010-11-18.

[10] content.usatoday.com

[11] reuters.com

[12] "Google to Warn PC Virus Victims via Search Site". BBC News. 2011-07-21. Retrieved 2011-07-22.

[13] Vincentas (11 July 2013). "Scareware in Spy-WareLoop.com". Spyware Loop. Retrieved 27 July 2013.

[14] spywarewarrior.com filed under "Brave Sentry."

[15] "Smart Fortress 2012"

[16] theregister.co.uk

[17] Etengoff, Aharon (2008-09-29). "Washington and Microsoft target spammers". The Inquirer. Retrieved 2008-10-04.

[18] Tarun (2008-09-29). "Microsoft to sue scareware security vendors". *Lunarsoft*. Retrieved 2009-09-24. [...] the Washington attorney general (AG) [...] has also brought lawsuits against companies such as Securelink Networks and High Falls Media, and the makers of a product called Quick-Shield, all of whom were accused of marketing their products using deceptive techniques such as fake alert messages.

[19] "Fighting the scourge of scareware". BBC News. 2008-10-01. Retrieved 2008-10-02.

[20] "Win software". Federal Trade Commission.

[21] "Wanted by the FBI - SHAILESHKUMAR P. JAIN". FBI.

[22] "D'Souza Final Order" (PDF). Federal Trade Commission.

[23] Contents of disk #448. Amiga-stuff.com - see DISK 448.

[24] Dark Drive Prank

28.7 Further reading

- O'Dea, Hamish (2009-10-16). "The Modern Rogue – Malware With a Face". Australia: Microsoft.

28.8 External links

- Demonstration of scareware on YouTube

- The Case of the Unusable System

- Yes, that PC cleanup app you saw on TV at 3 a.m. is a waste

Chapter 29

Self-XSS

Self-XSS is a social engineering attack used to gain control of victims' web accounts, most commonly Facebook accounts.[1] In a self-XSS attack, the victim of the attack accidentally runs malicious code in his/her own web browser, thus exposing it to the attacker.[1]

29.1 Overview

Self-XSS operates by tricking users into copying and pasting malicious content into their browsers' web developer console.[1] Usually, the attacker posts a message that says by copying and running certain code, the user will be able to hack another user's account. In fact, the code allows the attacker to hijack the victim's account.[2]

29.2 History and mitigation

In the past, a very similar attack took place, in which users were tricked into pasting malicious JavaScript into their address bar. When browser vendors stopped this by preventing easily running JavaScript from the address bar,[3][4] attackers started using Self-XSS in its current form. Web browser vendors and web sites have taken steps to mitigate this attack. Mozilla Firefox[5] and Google Chrome[6] have both begun implementing safeguards to warn users about self-XSS attacks. Facebook and Google+ now display a warning message when users open the web developer console, and they link to pages explaining the attack in detail.[7][8]

29.3 Etymology

The "self" part of the name comes from the fact that the user is attacking him/herself. The "XSS" part of the name comes from the abbreviation for cross-site scripting, because both attacks result in malicious code running on a legitimate site.

However, the attacks don't have much else in common, because XSS is an attack against the website itself, whereas self-XSS is a social engineering attack against the user.[9]

29.4 References

[1] Scharr, Jill (July 28, 2014). "Facebook Scam Tricks Users Into Hacking Themselves". *Tom's Guide US*. Purch. Retrieved September 27, 2014.

[2] "Social Networking Security Threats". Sophos. n.d. Retrieved September 27, 2014.

[3] "Bug 656433 – Disallow javascript: and data: URLs entered into the location bar from inheriting the principal of the currently-loaded page". *Bugzilla*. Mozilla Foundation. May 11, 2011. Retrieved September 28, 2014.

[4] "Issue 82181: [Linux] Strip javascript: schema from pastes/drops to omnibox". *Google Code*. Google. May 10, 2011. Retrieved September 28, 2014.

[5] "Bug 994134 – Warn first-time users on pasting code into the console". *Bugzilla*. Mozilla Foundation. April 9, 2014. Retrieved September 28, 2014.

[6] "Issue 345205: DevTools: Combat self-XSS". *Google Code*. Google. May 10, 2011. Retrieved September 28, 2014.

[7] "What do Self-XSS scams look like?". *Facebook Help*. Facebook. July 11, 2014. Retrieved September 27, 2014.

[8] "What is Self-XSS?". *Facebook Help*. Facebook. July 15, 2014. Retrieved September 27, 2014.

[9] Ilascu, Ionut (July 28, 2014). "Hackers Trick Facebook Users into Self Cross-Site Scripting (XSS) Scam". *Softpedia*. SoftNews NET SRL. Retrieved September 27, 2014.

29.5 Further reading

- McCaney, Kevin (November 16, 2011). "4 ways to avoid the exploit in Facebook spam attack". *GCN*.

1105 Public Sector Media Group. Retrieved September 28, 2014.

Chapter 30

SMS phishing

In computing, **SMS phishing** or **smishing**[1] is a form of criminal activity using social engineering techniques. Phishing is the act of attempting to acquire personal information such as passwords and details by masquerading as a trustworthy entity in an electronic communication. Short Message Service (SMS) is the technology used for text messages on cell phones.[2]

SMS phishing uses cell phone text messages to deliver the *bait* to induce people to divulge their personal information.

On March 9, 2012, Walmart issued a fraud alert regarding a large number of scam texts that offered a nonexistent $1000 gift card as bait.[3]

30.1 References

[1] Vishing and smishing: The rise of social engineering fraud, BBC, Marie Keyworth, 2016-01-01

[2] SMS phishing article at ConsumerAffairs.com

[3] Fraud Alert

Chapter 31

Social Hacking

Social hacking describes the act of attempting to manipulate outcomes of social behaviour through orchestrated actions. The general function of social hacking is to gain access to restricted information or to a physical space without proper permission. Most often, social hacking attacks are achieved by impersonating an individual or group who is directly or indirectly known to the victims or by representing an individual or group in a position of authority.[1] This is done through pre-meditated research and planning to gain victims' confidence. Social hackers take great measures to present overtones of familiarity and trustworthiness to elicit confidential or personal information.[2] Social hacking is most commonly associated as a component of "social engineering".

Although the practice involves exercising control over human behaviour rather than computers, the term "social hacking" is also used in reference to online behaviour and increasingly, social media activity. The technique can be used in multiple ways that affect public perception and conversely, increase public awareness of social hacking activity. However, while awareness helps reduce the volume of hacks being carried out, technology has allowed for attack tools to become more sophisticated.

31.1   Social Hacking Techniques

Carrying out a social hacking attack involves looking for weaknesses in user behaviour that can be exploited through seemingly legitimate means.[3] Three popular methods of attack include dumpster diving, role playing, and spearphishing.

31.1.1   Dumpster Diving

Sifting through garbage is a popular tactic for social hackers to recover information about the habits, activities, and interactions of organizations and individuals. Information retrieved from discarded property allows social hackers to create effective profiles of their targets. Personal contact information such as employee titles and phone numbers can be appropriated from discarded phone books or directories and used to gain further technical information such as login data and security passwords. Another advantageous find for social hackers is discarded hardware, especially hard drives that have not properly been scrubbed clean and still contain private and accurate information about corporations or individuals.[4] Since surfing through people's curbside garbage is not a criminal offence and does not require a warrant, it is a rich resource for social hackers, as well as a legally accessible one. Dumpster diving can yield fruitful, albeit smelly results for information seekers such as private investigators, stalkers, nosy neighbours, and the police.

31.1.2   Roleplaying

Establishing trust by fooling people into believing in the legitimacy of a false character is one of the main tenets of social hacking. Adopting a false personality or impersonating a known figure to trick victims into sharing personal details can be done in person or via phone conversation.

In person

By posing as third party maintenance workers in an office building, medical practitioners in a hospital, or one of many other forms, social hackers can get past security personnel and other employees undetected. In both examples, uniform apparel is associated with specific job functions, giving people reason to trust impersonators. A more complicated manoeuver would involve a longer planning cycle, such as taking up employment inside an organization that is being targeted for an attack.

In the movie Ocean's Eleven, a sophisticated crew of con artists plot an elaborate heist to rob three popular Las Vegas casinos by assimilating themselves in the everyday activities of the casinos' operations. Although the heist is executed in less than a day, the planning cycle is long and notably fastidious. An imperative function of the attack is to present credibility in the roles being impersonated, to which attention to detail is inevitably required.

Tailgating

Tailgating is the act of following someone into a restricted space, such as an office building or an academic institution. Third party maintenance workers, or medical personnel, as mentioned above, often have limited cause to justify their credibility because of their appearances. Similar to role playing, tailgating functions around the assumption of familiarity and trust.[5] People are less likely to react suspiciously to anyone who appears to fit in to the surrounding environment, and will be even less liable to question individuals who don't call attention to themselves. Following behind someone in an unassuming fashion may even eliminate the need to establish a rapport with authorized personnel.

31.1.3   Spear Phishing

Online social hacks include "spear phishing" in which hackers scam their victims into releasing sensitive information about themselves or their organization. Hackers will target individuals within specific organizations by sending emails that appear to come from trusted sources including senior officials within the organization who hold positions of authority. To appear convincing, a social hacker's email message has to establish a tone of familiarity that belies any suspicion from its recipient. The email is designed to put forth a request for information that ties logically to the person sending it.[6] Often, company employees will fall prey to these emails and share personal information such as phone numbers or passwords, thinking that the information transfer is taking place in a secure environment. In more sinister scenarios, the emails from hackers may be embedded with malware that infects victims' computers without their knowledge and secretly transfers private data directly to hackers.[7]

A successful example of spear phishing was highly publicized in the news media in January 2014, when Target, a U.S.-based retailer, experienced a security breach that allowed hackers to steal customers' credit card and personal data information.[8] Later, it was revealed that the cyber criminals were able to access Target's financial and personal data files by targeting a third party mechanical company that had access to Target's network credentials. The social implications of such a high profile social hack affect Target's popularity as a retailer, but also consumers' trust and loyalty towards the brand.

31.2   Security

Although Target may not have been slacking in its security, the hackers were able to infiltrate Target's network indirectly, by identifying a third party company with by access to Target's credentials. The social hack was in defrauding employees of the third party to divulge sensitive information, while the cybercrime was conducted by means of a malware infected email phishing attack.[9] The need for vigilant online security is highlighted by cyber-attacks against corporations like Target as well as other global businesses and high-traffic websites. Even small websites are vulnerable to attacks, specifically because their security protection is presumed to be low.[10] In Target's case, the third party mechanical company had inadequate security software which left them open to a malware attack.[11]

In a similar incident, Yahoo Mail also announced in January 2014 that their system had been hacked and a number of user email accounts had been accessed.[12] While the origin of the cause was unclear, poor security was again at the centre of the trouble. In both cases, large corporations with assumed understanding of security policies were compromised. Also in both cases, consumer data was stolen.[13]

In a study by Orgill et al., an observation is made that "it is important that each person responsible for computer security ask if their system is vulnerable to attacks by social engineers, and if so, how can the effect of a social engineering attack be mitigated."[14] Using strong passwords[15] is one simple and easy method that assists in such mitigation, as is using reliable and effective anti-virus software. Other preventative measures include using different logins for services used, frequently monitoring accounts and personal data, as well as being alert to the difference between a request for help and a phishing attempt from strangers.[16]

31.3   Ethical Hacking

To counter security breaches at the hands of social hackers as well as technical hackers, companies employ security professionals, known as ethical hackers, or more popularly, white hat hackers, to attempt to break into their systems in the same manner that social hackers would employ. Ethical hackers will leverage the same tools methods as hackers with criminal intent but with legitimate objectives. Ethical hackers evaluate security strengths and weaknesses and provide corrective options. Ethical hacking is also known as penetration testing, intrusion testing and red teaming.[17]

31.4 Impacting Social Media

The internet affords social hackers the ability to populate content spaces without detection of suspicious behaviour. Social hacking can also occur in environments where user-generated content is prevalent. This includes the opportunity to influence opinion polls and even to skew data beyond a point of validity. Social hacking can also be used to provide favourable reviews e.g. on product websites. It can also be used to counter negative feedback with an influx of positive responses e.g. on blog or news article comment sections. Social hacking can cause damage to the online profile of a person or a brand by the simple act of accessing information that is openly available through social media channels.[18]

31.5 Technology Appropriation

Technology appropriation can be perceived as a type of social hacking in that it involves social manipulation of a technology. It describes the effort of users to make sense of a technology within their own contexts beyond adopting its intended use. When this happens, the use of the technology can change. Adaptation of a technology can incorporate reinterpretation of its function and meaning, to the effect that the technology itself can take on a new role. Appropriation accentuates that the user adjusts the technology for his own best practice, while adaptation advises that the use sometimes changes in general.[19]

31.6 Social Enterprise

Social hacking is also affiliated with social enterprise. Social enterprise can be represented in the form of for-profit or non-profit organizations that encourage socially responsible business strategies for long-term environmental and human well-being. The concept of socially hacking new enterprises within the existing capitalist structure is a human endeavour that encourages people to re-evaluate the social systems that we are accustomed to, in order to identify the problems that are not being addressed.[20] New enterprises can then be created to replace the old with systems that reinforce sustainability and regenerative growth.

31.7 See also

- Certified Social Engineering Prevention Specialist (CSEPS)
- Cyberheist

- Internet Security Awareness Training
- IT risk
- Penetration test
- Phishing
- SocialHacks.net
- Piggybacking (security)
- SMiShing
- Vishing

31.8 References

[1] http://www.cwu.edu/~{}tiddr/Courses/Archive/ ACCT565/WebQuests/04SocialEngineering/ 04SocialEngineeringWebQuest.pdf

[2] Hodson, Steve (August 13, 2008). "Never Mind Social Media, How About Social Hacking?". Mashable.

[3] http://www.computerweekly.com/tip/ Social-hacking-The-easy-way-to-breach-network-security

[4] http://www.cwu.edu/~{}tiddr/Courses/Archive/ ACCT565/WebQuests/04SocialEngineering/ 04SocialEngineeringWebQuest.pdf

[5] http://www.pcworld.com/article/182180/top_5_social_ engineering_exploit_techniques.html

[6] http://www.techradar.com/news/internet/ phishing-just-got-personal-avoiding-the-social-media-trap-1224150

[7] http://searchsecurity.techtarget.com/definition/ spear-phishing

[8] http://www.huffingtonpost.com/2014/02/12/target-hack_ n_4775640.html

[9] http://krebsonsecurity.com/2014/02/ email-attack-on-vendor-set-up-breach-at-target/

[10] http://thenextweb.com/dd/2014/04/02/ stop-social-hackers-before-attack/

[11] http://krebsonsecurity.com/2014/02/ email-attack-on-vendor-set-up-breach-at-target/

[12] http://www.forbes.com/sites/jameslyne/2014/01/31/ yahoo-hacked-and-how-to-protect-your-passwords/

[13] http://www.biztechmagazine.com/article/2014/01/ snapchats-data-breach-should-be-wake-call-startups

[14] http://dl.acm.org/citation.cfm?id=1029577/

[15] http://gcn.com/Articles/2012/05/23/
Military-dating-hack-government-social-media-risks.
aspx?Page=2

[16] http://lifehacker.com/5933296/
how-can-i-protect-against-hackers-who-use-sneaky-social-engineering-techniques-to-get-into-my-accounts

[17] http://dx.doi.org.myaccess.library.utoronto.ca/10.5120/
229-380

[18] http://www.usatoday.com/story/
tech/columnist/2014/01/02/
snapchat-breach-new-tech-economy-john-shinal-usa-today/
4250487/

[19] http://www.igi-   global.com/dictionary/
technology-appropriation/29492   http:
//www.creativeapplications.net/reviews/
appropriating-interaction-technologies-social-hacking-at-itp/

[20] http://www.theguardian.com/
social-enterprise-network/gallery/2014/feb/21/
from-afripads-to-zamalasha-social-enterprise-stories-from-africa-in-pictures/
print

- Morrison, Dan. "The System is Failing, Hack the System". TheGuardian.com. Retrieved January 15, 2014.

- "Types of Social Engineering". National Plant Diagnostic Network.

- Beck, Rochelle. "Hack Capitalism".

Chapter 32

Social jacking

Social jacking is malicious technique tricking the users for clicking vulnerable buttons or compromise them by showing false appearing pages, it is a mixture of click jacking technique to breach browser security and social engineering. It may be also referred as User interface disguising method, it is a variant of click jacking method.

32.1 Technique

The original page or vulnerable page is loaded using iframe tag, after that all the unnecessary contents in that webpage displayed in iframe is removed by placing white background div tag elements by using absolute positioning property using css, thus all unnecessary information in the displayed vulnerable page is removed and only buttons or links are alone made visible to the user, more over some additional social engineering messages like click the below button so get access or get reward is displayed above the iframe tag, so the user is made to click the visible button without knowing what happens when he clicks the button.

32.2 Examples

- Suppose the user has logged into his web based email, now we send a link to the user for the tricked webpage, the user clicks the link and the tricked or specially crafted webpage is loaded, the loaded webpage has an iframe tag through which the users web based email inbox is loaded and we hide all the unnecessary information in the loaded webpage and make only the "delete all" button in the inbox page to be visible, now we add the text above iframe saying some messages which makes the user to click the delete all button, now when the user clicks the delete all button his all mails got deleted .

32.3 Prevention

Prevention of these methods is quite tough, its up to the user by identifying and analyzing the webpages and he should not click any anonymous links or buttons .

32.4 Implementation

Social jacking can be easily implemented using Google Web Toolkit, where we can design the webpage using wysiwyg GUI builder and drag white background colored panel over the iframe window thus hiding the unnecessary information, while revealing the vulnerable buttons alone.

32.5 See also

- Social engineering
- Clickjacking
- Browser security
- Internet safety
- Internet security
- Cross-site scripting
- Phishing

32.6 References

Chapter 33

Tabnabbing

Tabnabbing is a computer exploit and phishing attack, which persuades users to submit their login details and passwords to popular websites by impersonating those sites and convincing the user that the site is genuine. The attack's name was coined in early 2010 by Aza Raskin, a security researcher and design expert.[1][2] The attack takes advantage of user trust and inattention to detail in regard to tabs, and the ability of modern web pages to rewrite tabs and their contents a long time after the page is loaded. Tabnabbing operates in reverse of most phishing attacks in that it doesn't ask users to click on an obfuscated link but instead loads a fake page in one of the open tabs in your browser.[3]

The exploit employs scripts to rewrite a page of average interest with an impersonation of a well-known website, when left unattended for some time. A user who returns after a while and sees the rewritten page may be induced to believe the page is legitimate and enter their login, password and other details that will be used for improper purposes. The attack can be made more likely to succeed if the script checks for well known Web sites the user has loaded in the past or in other tabs, and loads a simulation of the same sites. This attack can be done even if JavaScript is disabled, using the "meta refresh" meta element, an HTML attribute used for page redirection that causes a reload of a specified new page after a given time interval.[4]

The NoScript extension for Mozilla Firefox defends both from the JavaScript-based and from the scriptless attack, based on meta refresh, by preventing inactive tabs from changing the location of the page.[5]

33.1   Example

"It can detect that you're logged into Citibank right now and Citibank has been training you to log into your account every 15 minutes because it logs you out for better security. It's like being hit by the wrong end of the sword.", said Aza Raskin.[6]

33.2   See also

- Phishing

- Hacker (computer security)

33.3   References

[1] Claburn, Thomas (2010-05-25). "Tabnapping attack makes phishing easy". Information Week. Retrieved 2012-02-19.

[2] "Aza Raskin's original tabnabbing disclosure". Azarask.in. 2010-05-25. Retrieved 2012-02-19.

[3] Christina Warren 164 (2010-05-25). "New Type of Phishing Attack Goes After Your Browser Tabs". Mashable.com. Retrieved 2012-02-19.

[4] Adler, Eitan (2010-05-30). "Eitan Adler's thoughts: Tabnabbing Without Javascript". Blog.eitanadler.com. Retrieved 2012-02-19.

[5] "NoScript 1.9.9.81 changelog announcing specific tabnapping protection". Noscript.net. Retrieved 2012-02-19.

[6] Magid, Larry (2010-06-11). "Tabnabbing: Like phishing within browser". News.cnet.com. Retrieved 2012-02-19.

33.4   External links

- "Devious New Phishing Tactic Targets Tabs". Krebson security. 2010-05. Check date values in: |date= (help)

122

Chapter 34

Trojan horse (computing)

For other uses, see Trojan horse (disambiguation).

A **Trojan Horse**, or **Trojan**, in computing is any malicious computer program which misrepresents itself to appear useful, routine, or interesting in order to persuade a victim to install it. The term is derived from the Ancient Greek story of the wooden horse that was used to help Greek troops invade the city of Troy by stealth.[1][2][3][4][5]

Trojans are generally spread by some form of social engineering, for example where a user is duped into executing an e-mail attachment disguised to be unsuspicious, (e.g., a routine form to be filled in), or by drive-by download. Although their payload can be anything, many moderns forms act as a backdoor, contacting a controller which can then have unauthorized access to the affected computer.[6] While Trojans and backdoors are not easily detectable by themselves, computers may appear to run slower due to heavy processor or network usage.

Unlike computer viruses and worms, Trojans generally do not attempt to inject themselves into other files or otherwise propagate themselves.[7]

34.1 Purpose and uses

If installed or run with elevated privileges a Trojan will generally have unlimited access. What it does with this power depends on the motives of the attacker.

34.1.1 Destructive

- Crashing the computer or device.
- Modification or deletion of files.
- Data corruption.
- Formatting disks, destroying all contents.
- Spread malware across the network.

- Spy on user activities and access sensitive information.[8]

34.1.2 Use of resources or identity

- Use of the machine as part of a botnet (e.g. to perform automated spamming or to distribute Denial-of-service attacks)
- Using computer resources for mining cryptocurrencies [9]
- Using the infected computer as proxy for illegal activities and/or attacks on other computers.
- Infecting other connected devices on the network.

34.1.3 Money theft, ransom

- Electronic money theft
- Installing ransomware such as CryptoLocker

34.1.4 Data theft

- Data theft, including for industrial espionage
- User passwords or payment card information
- User personally identifiable information
- Trade secrets

34.1.5 Spying, surveilance or stalking

- Keystroke logging
- Watching the user's screen
- Viewing the user's webcam
- Controlling the computer system remotely

123

Trojan horses in this way may require interaction with a malicious controller (not necessarily distributing the Trojan horse) to fulfill their purpose. It is possible for those involved with Trojans to scan computers on a network to locate any with a Trojan horse installed, which the hacker can then control. .[10]

Some Trojans take advantage of a security flaw in older versions of Internet Explorer and Google Chrome to use the host computer as an anonymizer proxy to effectively hide Internet usage,[11] enabling the controller to use the Internet for illegal purposes while all potentially incriminating evidence indicates the infected computer or its IP address. The host's computer may or may not show the internet history of the sites viewed using the computer as a proxy. The first generation of anonymizer Trojan horses tended to leave their tracks in the page view histories of the host computer. Later generations of the Trojan horse tend to "cover" their tracks more efficiently. Several versions of Sub7 have been widely circulated in the US and Europe and became the most widely distributed examples of this type of Trojan horse.[10]

In German-speaking countries, spyware used or made by the government is sometimes called *govware*. Govware is typically a trojan horse software used to intercept communications from the target computer. Some countries like Switzerland and Germany have a legal framework governing the use of such software.[12][13] Examples of govware trojans include the Swiss MiniPanzer and MegaPanzer[14] and the German "state trojan" nicknamed R2D2.[12]

Due to the popularity of botnets among hackers and the availability of advertising services that permit authors to violate their users' privacy, Trojan horses are becoming more common. According to a survey conducted by BitDefender from January to June 2009, "Trojan-type malware is on the rise, accounting for 83-percent of the global malware detected in the world." Trojans have a relationship with worms, as they spread with the help given by worms and travel across the internet with them.[15] BitDefender has stated that approximately 15% of computers are members of a botnet, usually recruited by a Trojan infection.[16]

34.2   Notable examples

34.2.1   Private and Governmental

- FinFisher - Lench IT solutions / Gamma International

- DaVinci / Galileo RCS - HT S.r.l. (*hacking team*)

- 0zapftis / r2d2 StaatsTrojaner - DigiTask

- TAO QUANTUM/FOXACID - NSA

- Magic Lantern - FBI

- WARRIOR PRIDE - GCHQ

34.2.2   Publicly available

- Netbus - 1998 (published)

- Sub7 - 1999 (published)

- Back Orifice - 1998 (published)

- Beast - 2002 (published)

- Bifrost Trojan - 2004 (published)

- DarkComet - 2008 (published)

- Blackhole exploit kit - 2012 (published)

- Gh0st RAT - 2009 (published)

- MegaPanzer BundesTrojaner - 2009 (published)

34.2.3   Detected by security researchers

- Zeus - 2007 (discovered)

- Flashback Trojan - 2011 (discovered)

- ZeroAccess - 2011 (discovered)

- Koobface - 2008 (discovered)

- Vundo - 2009 (discovered)

- Meredrop - 2010 (discovered)

- Coreflood - 2010 (discovered)

34.3   See also

- Computer security

- Remote administration

- Remote administration software

- Cyber spying

- Dancing pigs

- Exploit (computer security)

- Industrial espionage

- Malware

- Principle of least privilege

- Privacy-invasive software

- Reverse connection

- Rogue security software

- Social engineering (security)

- Spam

- Spyware

- Timeline of computer viruses and worms

34.4 References

- Carnegie Mellon University (1999): "CERT Advisory CA-1999-02 Trojan Horses", ЎЦ

[1] Landwehr, C. E; A. R Bull; J. P McDermott; W. S Choi (1993). *A taxonomy of computer program security flaws, with examples.* DTIC Document. Retrieved 2012-04-05.

[2] "Trojan Horse Definition". Retrieved 2012-04-05.

[3] "Trojan horse". *Webopedia.* Retrieved 2012-04-05.

[4] "What is Trojan horse? - Definition from Whatis.com". Retrieved 2012-04-05.

[5] "Trojan Horse: [coined By MIT-hacker-turned-NSA-spook Dan Edwards] N.". Retrieved 2012-04-05.

[6] "What is the difference between viruses, worms, and Trojans?". Symantec Corporation. Retrieved 2009-01-10.

[7] "VIRUS-L/comp.virus Frequently Asked Questions (FAQ) v2.00 (Question B3: What is a Trojan Horse?)". 9 October 1995. Retrieved 2012-09-13.

[8] "Hackers, Spyware and Trojans – What You Need to Know". Comodo. Retrieved September 5, 2015.

[9] Robert McMillan (2013): Trojan Turns Your PC Into Bitcoin Mining Slave, Retrieved on 2015-02-01

[10] Jamie Crapanzano (2003): "Deconstructing SubSeven, the Trojan Horse of Choice", SANS Institute, Retrieved on 2009-06-11

[11] Vincentas (11 July 2013). "Trojan Horse in SpyWareLoop.com". Spyware Loop. Retrieved 28 July 2013.

[12] Basil Cupa, Trojan Horse Resurrected: On the Legality of the Use of Government Spyware (Govware), LISS 2013, pp. 419-428

[13] "Dokument nicht gefunden!". Federal Department of Justice and Police. Archived from the original on May 6, 2013.

[14] "Swiss coder publicises government spy Trojan - Techworld.com". News.techworld.com. Retrieved 2014-01-26.

[15] BitDefender.com Malware and Spam Survey

[16] Datta, Ganesh. "What are Trojans?". *SecurAid.*

34.5 External links

- Trojan Horses at DMOZ

Chapter 35

Website spoofing

Website spoofing is the act of creating a website, as a hoax, with the intention of misleading readers that the website has been created by a different person or organization. Normally, the spoof website will adopt the design of the target website and sometimes has a similar URL.[1] A more sophisticated attack results in an attacker creating a "shadow copy" of the World Wide Web by having all of the victim's traffic go through the attacker's machine, causing the attacker to obtain the victim's sensitive information.[2]

Another technique is to use a 'cloaked' URL.[3] By using domain forwarding, or inserting control characters, the URL can appear to be genuine while concealing the address of the actual website.

The objective may be fraudulent, often associated with phishing or e-mail spoofing, or to criticize or make fun of the person or body whose website the spoofed site purports to represent. Because the purpose is often malicious, "spoof" (an expression whose base meaning is innocent parody) is a poor term for this activity so that more accountable organisations such as government departments and banks tend to avoid it, preferring more explicit descriptors such as "fraudulent" or "phishing".[4]

As an example of the use of this technique to parody an organisation, in November 2006 two spoof websites, www.msfirefox.com and www.msfirefox.net, were produced claiming that Microsoft had bought Firefox and released Microsoft Firefox 2007.[5]

35.1   See also

- Email spoofing

- Hoax

- Spoofing attack

- Referer spoofing

35.2   References

[1] "Spoof website will stay online", BBC News, 29 July 2004

[2] http://www.cs.princeton.edu/sip/pub/spoofing.pdf

[3] Anti-Phishing Technology", Aaron Emigh, Radix Labs, 19 January 2005

[4] See e.g.   or

[5] "Fake Sites Insist Microsoft Bought Firefox", Gregg Keizer, InformationWeek, 9 November 2006

Chapter 36

Whitemail

Whitemail, coined as an opposite to blackmail, has several meanings.

36.1 Economics

See also: Economics, Mergers and Acquisitions, Microeconomics, Takeover and Industrial organization

In economics, whitemail is an anti-takeover arrangement in which the target company will sell significantly discounted stock to a friendly third party. In return, the target company helps thwart takeover attempts, by

1. raising the acquisition price of the raider

2. diluting the hostile bidder's number of shares

3. increasing the aggregate stock holdings of the company

36.2 Social culture

Whitemail can also be considered as legally compensating someone for doing their job in a manner benefiting the payer. For example, if a person gives a maître d' a $20 bill in order to secure a table more quickly than other patrons who had arrived earlier, this could be considered whitemail. It is merely a compensatory incentive for someone to do their job quicker, better, or in a manner more advantageous to the payer. It can be considered a bribe, depending on the person being offered the incentive and the action the incentive is intended to influence.

36.3 Fiction

In Terry Pratchett's Discworld universe, whitemail is an *anti-crime*. Whitemail is the threat of revealing a person's good deeds for purposes of ruining the person's reputation (e.g. as a gangster).

36.4 Fundraising

In fundraising, whitemail is a donation received without a response form, coupon, statement, or other source identification, so it cannot be attributed to any particular fundraising campaign. These donations often come in generic, white-colored envelopes.

36.5 E-mail

See also: Identity theft, Anonymous remailer and Whitelists

1) Automated inbound fax and letter handling: Whitemail can used to refer to the automated handling of inbound faxes and letters as customer requests to, and at, service and reception desks. For example, KANA Whitemail uses this terminology and is a provider of software to integrate Customer Relations Management (CRM) systems with email clients.

2) White listed email: Whitemail can be used as a term to denote email that is sent through a white listed email service (e.g. iContact, Constant Contact, Get Response, and others). This type of email usually requires mailing list approval or double opt-in by the email recipients. This has a higher deliverability than normal direct email lists and is usually used for the delivery of newsletters or other regular information distributed to clients or subscribers.

3) Anonymous email: Whitemail was an anonymous mailer hosted on biomatic.org. It would allow any visitor to send e-mail messages to any address at no cost and with no registra-

tion required, simply using the site's interface. Whitemail even allowed its users to provide any e-mail address (their own, somebody else's or one that does not exist) that would then appear to the recipient as the message's origin. The Whitemail service was removed from the site at version 3 in 2004

36.6 References

36.7 External links

- "Whitemail". Retrieved 2006-12-07.

Chapter 37

Wifiphisher

"**Wifiphisher**" is a security tool that mounts fast automated phishing attacks against WPA networks in order to obtain the secret passphrase. It is a social engineering attack that unlike other methods it does not include any bruteforcing. It is an easy way for obtaining WPA credentials.[1] [2]

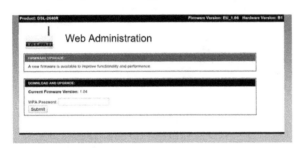

wifiphisher

37.1 Scenario

WiFiPhisher tool uses "Evil Twin" attack scenario. Same as Evil Twin, the tool first creates a phony wireless Access Point (AP) masquerade itself as the legitimate WiFi AP. It then directs a denial of service (DoS) attack against the legitimate WiFi access point, or creates RF interference around it that disconnects wireless users of the connection and prompts users to inspect available networks. Once disconnected from the legitimate WiFi access point, the tool then force offline computers and devices to automatically reconnects to the evil twin, allowing the hacker to intercept all the traffic to that device. The technique is also known as AP Phishing, WiFi Phishing, Hotspotter, or Honeypot AP. These kind of attacks make use of phony access points with faked login pages to capture user's WiFi credentials, credit card numbers, launch man-in-the-middle attacks, or infect wireless hosts. As soon as the victim requests any web page from the internet, WifiPhisher tool will serve the victim a realistic fake router configuration looking page that will ask for WPA password confirmation due to a router firmware upgrade. The tool, thus, could be used by hackers and cy-bercriminals to generate further phishing and man-in-the-middle attacks against connected users.

37.2 Requirements

- Kali Linux.

- Two wireless network interfaces, one capable of injection

37.3 Phases

37.3.1 Phase 1-Victim is being deauthenticated from her access point

Further information: Wi-Fi deauthentication attack

Wifiphisher continuously jams all of the target access point's wifi devices within range by sending 802.11 deauthentication frames to the client from the access point, to the access point from the client, and to the broadcast address as well.

37.3.2 Phase 2-Victim joins a rogue access point

Wifiphisher sniffs the area and copies the target access point's settings. It then creates a rogue wireless access point that is modeled on the target. It also sets up a NAT/DHCP server and forwards the right ports. Consequently, because of the jamming, clients will start connecting to the rogue access point. After this phase, the victim is MiTMed.

37.3.3 Phase 3-Victim is being served a realistic router config-looking page

wifiphisher employs a minimal web server that responds to HTTP & HTTPS requests. As soon as the victim requests a page from the Internet, wifiphisher will respond with a realistic fake page that asks for WPA password confirmation due to a router firmware upgrade.

37.4 Usage

37.5 References

[1] AU-KBC Research centre, Madras Institute of Technology, Anna University. S.Sibi, Chakkaravarthy. "Wifiphisher".

[2] Veltech Research & Development, Veltech University. Dr.Udaya, Baskaran; E, Kamalanaban; Dr.P, Visu; Dr.P, Sarasu; K.A.Varun, Kumar; A, Harish; A, Aravind; Sushmitha, Chalapathy. "Wifiphisher". *http://www. veltechuniv.edu.in/"*.

-
-
-
-

Chapter 38

WOT Services

For the cryptography term, see Web of trust.

WOT Services, Ltd is a Finnish company that runs the partly crowdsourced Internet website reputation rating tool **WOT (Web of Trust)**. The installed WOT browser add-on, available for Firefox, Google Chrome and Internet Explorer, shows its users the reputations of websites, which are calculated through a combination of user ratings and data from other sources. To generate revenue WOT licenses the use of its reputation database to other businesses.

38.1 History

WOT was founded in 2006 by Sami Tolvanen and Timo Ala-Kleemola, who wrote the WOT software as post-graduates at the Tampere University of Technology in Finland. They launched the service officially in 2007, with serial entrepreneur and angel investor Esa Suurio as CEO. In November 2009 Suurio moved on to his next endeavor.

In 2009 MySQL founder Michael Widenius invested in WOT and became a member of the board of directors.[1]

The company has partnered with Facebook, hpHosts, LegitScript, Mail.ru, Panda Security, Phishtank, GlobalSign and TRUSTe.[2][3][4][5][6]

In November 2013 WOT surpassed 100 million downloads.[7]

38.2 The rating tool

According to the company information the WOT software computes the measure of trust the rating users have in websites, combined with data from, among others, Google Safe Browsing. The WOT browser add-on is available for all major operating systems and browsers. To view or submit ratings, no subscription is required. To be able to write comments on score cards and in the forum, one needs to be registered.

The add-on sends user ratings to the WOT site, and it determines how the computed results are displayed, depending on user's settings. For instance, when visiting a poorly rated site, a warning screen may pop up, or only a red icon in the user's browser tool-bar is shown. Color-coded icons are also shown next to external links on the pages of leading search engines, on email services, on social network sites, and on Wikipedia.

Ratings are cast by secret ballot. They can be given in the categories "trustworthiness" and "child safety". To specify at least one reason for a rating is mandatory, via multiple choice in the rating interface.

The user rating system is meritocratic; the weight of a rating is algorithmically calculated for each user individually.

38.3 Reviews

The New York Times and the Washington Post made mention of WOT[8][9][10] and the add-on was mentioned and reviewed by the trade press and download sites. The reviewers opinions vary from good to excellent, though some critical remarks were made.

PC Magazine's Neil Rubenking concluded "Web of Trust's protection is free, and it doesn't impact browsing speed; it's well worth trying out". However, on the minus side he found several clearly adult sites unrated and he wished WOT would also rate sponsored search results, like its main competitors do.[11]

PC World's Preston Gralla concluded: "Try WOT (Web of Trust), an excellent--and free--browser add-on that offers protection", and Rick Broida wrote in an article "I also highly recommend Web of Trust, a free browser plug-in that shows you if Web links are safe--before you click them".[12][13]

Softpedia reviewer Ionut Ilascu wrote: "The reliability of the service has grown in the past years, despite voices accusing it of being exactly the opposite of what it should be, and proof is the collaboration with Facebook, Opera and Mail.ru Group.", concluding "As a service, WOT (Web of Trust) may be viewed as biased, but the latest developments in balancing the user opinion in order to provide relevant information point to the contrary. The extension is non-obtrusive but still has room for improvements.".[14]

38.4 Lawsuits

In 2011 a lawsuit in Florida, USA against WOT and some of its forum members, demanding to remove ratings and comments, was dismissed with prejudice. In Germany some preliminary injunctions were issued by courts, to delete feedback.[15]

38.5 See also

- McAfee SiteAdvisor

- Norton Safe Web

- Website Reputation Ratings

38.6 References

[1] Modine, Austin (17 February 2009). "The Register - MySQL daddy juices Finnish security firm". Retrieved 21 December 2014.

[2] "Facebook Security - Keeping You Safe from Scams and Spam". 12 May 2011. Retrieved 31 May 2014.

[3] "Mail.Ru Group Launches New Browser Featuring Web of Trust Safe-Surfing Technology" (Press release). Rocket Science PR. 8 August 2012.

[4] Schaffhauser, Dian (11 August 2009). "The Journal - Panda Security, Against Intuition Offer Free 'Web of Trust' Browser Addon". Retrieved 31 May 2014.

[5] "Friends of PhishTank". Retrieved 31 May 2014.

[6] "GlobalSign - GlobalSign Partners with Web of Trust to Provide Reputation Data in the Website Passport". 15 March 2012. Retrieved 18 December 2014.

[7] "Web of Trust hits 100 million Downloads Milestone". 12 November 2013. Retrieved 28 January 2015.

[8] Richmond, Riva (19 May 2010). "New York Times - Five Ways to Keep Online Criminals at Bay". Retrieved 21 December 2014.

[9] Krebs, Brian (29 July 2008). "Washington Post - Three Quarters of Malicious Web Sites Are Hacked". Retrieved 21 December 2014.

[10] Bell, Melissa (13 May 2011). "Washington Post - After big news stories, watch out for social media viruses". Retrieved 21 December 2014.

[11] Rubenking, Neil J. (Aug 13, 2009). "PC Magazine - Web of Trust Review and Rating". Retrieved 17 May 2011.

[12] Gralla, Preston (26 April 2009). "PCWorld - Say WOT? Web of Trust Rates Web Site Safety". Retrieved 21 December 2014.

[13] Broida, Rick (4 January 2010). "PCWorld - Make Your New PC Hassle-Free, Part 3: Keep It Secure". Retrieved 21 December 2014.

[14] Ilascu, Ionut (26 September 2013). "Softpedia - Web of Trust Review". Retrieved 21 December 2014.

[15] "WOT Wins Lawsuit In The US". ArcticStartup. 13 December 2011. Retrieved 22 December 2011.

38.7 Text and image sources, contributors, and licenses

38.7.1 Text

- **Social engineering (security)** *Source:* https://en.wikipedia.org/wiki/Social_engineering_(security)?oldid=700473923 *Contributors:* Kpjas, The Anome, ChangChienFu, Frecklefoot, Olrick, SGBailey, Mdebets, Rossami, Netsnipe, Kaihsu, Uriber, Ventura, Dcoetzee, Daniel Quinlan, WhisperToMe, Khym Chanur, Jerzy, Robbot, Academic Challenger, Jfire, Alerante, Leonard G., Chinasaur, AlistairMcMillan, Brockert, Matt Crypto, Mckaysalisbury, Beland, IGEL, Apotheon, Cynical, Gscshoyru, TonyW, Chmod007, D6, Jkl, Discospinster, Rich Farmbrough, Pmsyyz, Arnold-Reinhold, MeltBanana, Xezbeth, Bender235, ESkog, Fenice, EDGE, Chuayw2000, Smalljim, Brutulf, Ddddan, Bjornar, Guy Harris, Mac Davis, NTK, Wtmitchell, Rebroad, Knowledge Seeker, Omphaloscope, WolFStaR, RainbowOfLight, Kleinheero, Nuno Tavares, Woohookitty, Mindmatrix, Moitio, Pol098, Dionyziz, Waldir, Xiong Chiamiov, Gettingtoit, Rjwilmsi, Coemgenus, Chipuni, Vary, Teemu Maki~enwiki, Syced, G Clark, RobertG, Ground Zero, DuFF, DevastatorIIC, Intgr, Bmicomp, Benlisquare, Lukeonia1, Roboto de Ajvol, YurikBot, Beagle2, Hydrargyrum, Gaius Cornelius, Rsrikanth05, Kimchi.sg, TheMandarin, Dialectric, Thesloth, Joelr31, Dmoss, Tony1, Deku-shrub, Tomisti, Studiosonic, CWenger, LeonardoRob0t, JDspeeder1, John Broughton, Dravir, KnightRider~enwiki, SmackBot, Elonka, McGeddon, Unyoyega, Cutter, Lord Matt, Shabda, Gilliam, Evilandi, Da nuke, Lexlex, Nbarth, Abaddon314159, Midnightcomm, Aldaron, Cybercobra, EVula, Virgil Vaduva, DMacks, Pgillman, Evlekis, Ksharkawi~enwiki, Tmchk, SashatoBot, Srikeit, Nafango2, Gizzakk, Othtim, Ehheh, Lamename3000, Phoenixrod, Courcelles, J Cricket, Chovain, Tawkerbot2, Cryptic C62, Aaa111, Lioux, Thepatriots, Cumulus Clouds, MeekMark, Penbat, Equendil, Gogo Dodo, Jlmorgan, Dancter, Shirulashem, Doug Weller, Mhw1986, Nuwewsco, Omicronpersei8, Tunheim, PKT, Thijs!bot, Ann F, RobotII, RevolverOcelotX, Paquitotrek, Chrisdab, TXiKi, Nick Number, Dawnseeker2000, Oreo Priest, I already forgot, AntiVandalBot, WinBot, Majorly, Seaphoto, Gdo01, Oddity-, Alphachimpbot, Dougher, Arsenikk, MER-C, Ph.eyes, Primarscources, Jay1279, Dp76764, VoABot II, Rohasnagpal, Starschreck, Heqwm, CliffC, Jim.henderson, AlexJTaylor, Einsteininmyownmind, RJBurkhart3, Tgeairn, Myredroom, Javawizard, Anton Khorev, Princess Tiswas, Liangent, Salliesatt, Sesquiped, (jarbarf), RenniePet, Adamdaley, KylieTastic, TopGun, Mzanger, Black Walnut, Fskrc1, 28bytes, Wilku997, MenasimBot, Emergentchaos, Philip Trueman, NoticeBored, Jockpereira, JhsBot, BwDraco, Greswik, Haseo9999, Tsnapp, Chahax, Edkollin, Sue Rangell, Michael Frind, Hmwith, Eric1608, SieBot, Trackinfo, Malcolmxl5, Sephiroth storm, Ronald S. Davis, Bentogoa, Jojalozzo, Faradayplank, Dddenton, Lightmouse, DavidDW, Svick, HaploTR, Fishnet37222, Jumpropekids, ClueBot, Wshepp, GBYehuda, Zarkthehackeralliance, Mild Bill Hiccup, Johnbourscheid, Takeaway, Alexbot, Socrates2008, Ngebendi, Sjoerdat13, Corporeality, DarthTaper, DanielPharos, ChiuMan, Thingg, Versus22, Katanada, Anon126, XLinkBot, Ost316, Richard-of-Earth, WikHead, Lobro~enwiki, Rosenny, Proflevy, Thipburg, Namzie11, Addbot, WeatherFug, Johnisnotafreak, MrOllie, Download, CarsracBot, Buster7, West.andrew.g, OlEnglish, Frehley, Luckas-bot, Quadrescence, Yobot, Fizyxnrd, Nirvana888, Inemanja, Vanish user s8jswe823rnfscu8sejhr4, AnomieBOT, XL2D, DaedalusInfinity, Tucoxn, JackieBot, Jeff Muscato, Materialscientist, ArthurBot, Quebec99, The Firewall, JmCor, Xqbot, Crzer07, RibotBOT, Pradameinhoff, InfoSecPro, Thehelpfulbot, FrescoBot, Zomgoogle, Seeoven, KuroiShiroi, Overloggingon, DivineAlpha, Pinethicket, Borninlyoko, Bmclaughlin9, RedBot, Katheder, Full-date unlinking bot, Mns556, JMMING, Lotje, Arkelweis, Skakkle, Tbhotch, Noommos, EmausBot, John of Reading, Bbarmada, Mugg1991, Wikipelli, K6ka, Pro translator, Frankfusco, H I T L E R37, Donner60, ColinGreenlees, ChuispastonBot, Pastore Italy, Usg.usss, Ebehn, Keavon, ClueBot NG, Jack Greenmaven, Beyondwithinitself, Augustalex, Widr, Oddbodz, Helpful Pixie Bot, Terminated Joker, BG19bot, MusikAnimal, Faraz Davani, Thisisnotausernameyaitis, Doctorwho321, Several Pending, Pratyya Ghosh, Buffped, Jncc21, IjonTichyIjonTichy, Mogism, Frosty, Ekips39, Yamaha5, Blythwood, Star767, Northwind Arrow, Iratez, Wayweary, SylviaSawires, LiaJohnson, TandonAman, SEgouge, KH-1, ChamithN, Jdiggs45, Darianpearson, Sanjeetkashyap, Hannahmaryfresia, Johntame, Jablestech, Seattlehackerspace and Anonymous: 499

- **419eater.com** *Source:* https://en.wikipedia.org/wiki/419eater.com?oldid=656918064 *Contributors:* Bryan Derksen, SimonP, Modemac, Booyabazooka, Wwwwolf, Bueller 007, Darkwind, WhisperToMe, VeryVerily, Chrism, MykReeve, Oberiko, Phil Sandifer, Hillel, Poccil, Mark Zinthefer, Rich Farmbrough, Paul August, Night Gyr, WegianWarrior, Jnestorius, Reinyday, Luckyluke, Kedge~enwiki, Scott5114, Kenyon, Sander Marechal, RussBot, Kerowren, Gaius Cornelius, Bgrainger, Sturmovik, SmackBot, TheBilly, McGeddon, Filius Rosadis, Bluebot, Can't sleep, clown will eat me, Frap, Xyzzyplugh, Downwards, Savidan, Theelectricchild, Scientizzle, Zhadov, Neil916, AntiVandalBot, Genericus, MECU, Athanatis, Jarbury, The Sanctuary Sparrow, CliffC, Archolman, UnitedStatesian, Panfakes, Leejnd, Escape Orbit, ElizaDoolittle419, Neweaver, DumZiBoT, XLinkBot, Yobot, AnomieBOT, Calamity Lotta, Vof1960, Tedtheman-bi gal, Shiver419, RjwilmsiBot, DASHBot, Sonic12228, Kinkreet, BattyBot, DerekSmythe, Limefrost Spiral, AJScambaiter and Anonymous: 74

- **Clickjacking** *Source:* https://en.wikipedia.org/wiki/Clickjacking?oldid=701607708 *Contributors:* Julesd, Chealer, Nurg, Cloud200, Rchandra, Ary29, Mormegil, Tristan Schmelcher, Stesmo, Chmeee, Dismas, Woohookitty, Mindmatrix, Daira Hopwood, NoamNelke, Rjwilmsi, Bgwhite, ChrisBoyle, Deku-shrub, Rwalker, SmackBot, Rtc, C.Fred, Martylunsford, Mistress Selina Kyle, Netpagz, Kuru, Eastlaw, H4l9k, Safalra, Chad.hutchins, Andrew Clark, Widefox, Guy Macon, Mathfreq, Eliz81, Dc197, Tarunbk, JavierMC, Kitzur, Regnareb, Curb Safe Charmer, Amegghiuvirdura, WikiLaurent, Wikiold1, Shoebhakim, Doloco, XLinkBot, Duncan, Avoided, MystBot, Jabberwoch, Sweeper tamonten, Addbot, PatrickFlaherty, MrOllie, Farmercarlos, Exor674, 84user, Luckas-bot, Yobot, Dhaun, AnomieBOT, Happyrabbit, MichaelCoates, IllestFlip, SassoBot, Affinemesh94464, Shlominar, X7q, Haeinous, CousinJohn, RjwilmsiBot, DexDor, Offnfopt, Dwvisser, Timtempleton, Dewritech, Peaceray, 15turnsm, ZéroBot, H3llBot, Mark Martinec, Petrb, ClueBot NG, Crazymonkey1123, Helpful Pixie Bot, BG19bot, Deepanker70, BattyBot, Cimorcus, Cyberbot II, ChrisGualtieri, Dr Dinosaur IV, Ruby Murray, Dedobl1, Saectar, Abdf882c25e08d9ba219fe33f17591fe, ToonLucas22, ACookieBreak, Teddylev, Neermuzic and Anonymous: 85

- **Cyber spying** *Source:* https://en.wikipedia.org/wiki/Cyber_spying?oldid=699417911 *Contributors:* Rjwilmsi, Siddhant, Icedog, Mmernex, Rtc, Midway, TAnthony, Atulsnischal, Fconaway, Huzzlet the bot, Adamdaley, Olegwiki, Moonraker12, ترجمان05, SimonTrew, Jusdafax, XLinkBot, Addbot, Ironholds, Suwa, Xqbot, PabloCastellano, Jersey92, HamburgerRadio, Citation bot 1, Gjcarter, Lotje, RjwilmsiBot, Sabres87, H3llBot, EneMsty12, Lousterawesome, Zabanio, Davidiad, TheLurkerMan, BattyBot, Isaidnoway, Hmainsbot1, S.zahiri, Madtee, Dannyruthe, Coreyemotela, ICPSGWU, Sharanyanaveen and Anonymous: 18

- **Cyber-collection** *Source:* https://en.wikipedia.org/wiki/Cyber-collection?oldid=620051643 *Contributors:* Tabletop, Chris the speller, BilCat, Keith D, Bookbrad, Kazemita1, ChrisGualtieri, TheBlueCanoe, Madmoron, Madtee, Lorryspacy and Anonymous: 2

- **Cyberwarfare** *Source:* https://en.wikipedia.org/wiki/Cyberwarfare?oldid=699709357 *Contributors:* The Anome, Edward, Paul A, Conti, Tpbradbury, Jredmond, Donreed, Nurg, Ancheta Wis, Tom harrison, Gracefool, Utcursch, Slowking Man, Beland, AndrewKeenanRichardson, Orange Goblin, Openfly, Rich Farmbrough, Wikiacc, Kzzl, Pk2000, TheMile, Devil Master, Bobo192, Giraffedata, Obradovic Goran, YDZ,

Dominic, H2g2bob, Johntex, Bobrayner, Richard Arthur Norton (1958-), Woohookitty, Mindmatrix, Rbcwa, JeffUK, Plrk, Paxsimius, BD2412, Rjwilmsi, Friejose, Qqqqqq, Nihiltres, Vsion, Lmatt, Chobot, Benlisquare, Bgwhite, Wavelength, RussBot, WritersCramp, ONEder Boy, Neil.steiner, Neurotoxic, Deku-shrub, Eclipsed, Kal-El, Intershark, Gregzeng, Arthur Rubin, Geoffrey.landis, Katieh5584, SmackBot, Mmernex, Rtc, McGeddon, C.Fred, Chris the speller, Bluebot, H2ppyme, Snori, Mordantkitten, Frap, Radagast83, Abmac, Uriel-238, Daveschroeder, Ohconfucius, WngLdr34, Mathiasrex, Robofish, NYCJosh, Hvn0413, Hu12, Levineps, Iridescent, Kencf0618, Joseph Solis in Australia, Octane, Quodfui, CmdrObot, Ale jrb, Zarex, TVC 15, Neelix, NathanDahlin, Old port, Bobblehead, Hcobb, Nick Number, Alphachimpbot, NByz, Res2216firestar, Turgidson, MER-C, SiobhanHansa, Geniac, Magioladitis, Bongwarrior, Flayer, Buckshot06, XMog, Esanchez7587, Bytecount, Hbent, Atulsnischal, Sjjupadhyay~enwiki, CommonsDelinker, KTo288, Billy Pilgrim, Teh dave, Maurice Carbonaro, Public Menace, Hodja Nasreddin, Octopus-Hands, Andareed, Tukkek, Hillock65, Jevansen, TopGun, Tkgd2007, Ashcroftgm, Fences and windows, Pmedema, WazzaMan, Saibod, LeaveSleaves, Rsnbrgr, Staka, Falcon8765, B.L.A.Z.E, Oth, Kevinfromhk, Boulainvilliers, Kbrose, Moonriddengirl, Rockstone35, BStarky, Flyer22 Reborn, Avaarga, WannabeAmatureHistorian, Oxymoron83, Skinny87, Jericho347, Dillard421, RJ CG, Deciwill, Martarius, Chessy999, Niceguyedc, Trivialist, MasterXC, Gordon Ecker, Nymf, Bvlax2005, Rhododendrites, Arjayay, Light show, DumZiBoT, Kgcoleman, Emdarraj, XLinkBot, Avoided, Scostigan, Jaanusele, Addbot, AkhtaBot, StereotypicalWizard, Spy-Ops, Green Squares, Blaylockjam10, Golf2232, 5 albert square, Myk60640, Lightbot, Jarble, Goodmanjoon, Suwa, आशीष भटनागर, Luckas-bot, Yobot, Tohd8BohaithuGh1, Bruce404, Waqashsn, Millinski, AnomieBOT, Apollo1758, FeelSunny, 1exec1, Bsimmons666, Jim1138, Mbeimcik, Ulric1313, Materialscientist, Aneah, ArthurBot, Xqbot, Sionus, Capricorn42, Dondiw, DJWolfy, Alexander Mclean, Wdl1961, BritishWatcher, Miguelito Vieira, Irvick, Peace2keeper, Crzer07, Pradameinhoff, What9999999333, Howsa12, Gordonrox24, Vihelik, Tanagram, FrescoBot, Sidna, Stanszyk, Remdarraj, Jersey92, Deadhorseflogging, HamburgerRadio, Pinethicket, I dream of horses, RedBot, Rochdalehornet, Full-date unlinking bot, Xeworlebi, Utility Monster, NFSreloaded, Jonkerz, Lotje, Collegeofgolf, Oliver H, Remiked, Woodlot, Jfmantis, RjwilmsiBot, TjBot, VernoWhitney, Lopifalko, Techhead7890, 09lamin, EmausBot, John of Reading, Ghostofnemo, SoAuthentic, Hirsutism, Kaiser1935, Rail88, GoingBatty, P@ddington, Cybercitizen123, Cowfman, Wikipelli, 7th sojourn, Unmourned, Sabres87, ZéroBot, Prayerfortheworld, EneMsty12, Cymru.lass, Erianna, Quantumor, Quite vivid blur, GermanJoe, Joesolo13, Pastore Italy, Boundto, Zabanio, Cat10001a, Paddingtonbaer, Pymansorl, ClueBot NG, Antrim Kate, Satellizer, Rawkage, BrekekekexKoaxKoax, Rezabot, Helpful Pixie Bot, Dukes08, BG19bot, M0rphzone, Paganinip, Donzae, Utkal Ranjan Sahoo, Cyyfann, Jassy pal, Jayadevp13, Cyberbot II, Khazar2, Jabotito48, Mogism, Freshjane0, Dileepp89, Hellowns, Pahlevun, SFK2, That1guy77, Dhruvpubby, Kennethgeers, Madtee, Tentinator, Reziebear, TheJoeAlt, Newuser2013, Rmjl, Wikiuser13, Reacher1989, Beastlymac, CFlaherty, Fixture, CrowJU2, Monkbot, Cybersecurity101, Arsonhussy99, Betyd, S166865h, ICPSGWU, ChamithN, Kashifs294, TheCoffeeAddict, Rubbish computer, LCEwald, BlakeTS, Prinsgezinde, Nøkkenbuer, Alainsfeir2, RoadWarrior445 and Anonymous: 236

- **Domain name scams** *Source:* https://en.wikipedia.org/wiki/Domain_name_scams?oldid=689195285 *Contributors:* CesarB, Cyp, Charles Matthews, Topbanana, Edcolins, Jareha, Rich Farmbrough, Pearle, Woohookitty, Allen3, BD2412, Rjwilmsi, Bubba73, NawlinWiki, Hm2k, Groyolo, Amalthea, SmackBot, Dweller, Bluebot, Rkinch, Skabraham, Streamline~enwiki, GDallimore, Joshrowe, DumbBOT, Mojo Hand, Funandtrvl, Venus Copernicus, Clarafury, Mild Bill Hiccup, Subversive.sound, Stevenh123, Cst17, Tassedethe, Peridon, Yobot, AnomieBOT, 90, Materialscientist, E0steven, FoxBot, Tbhotch, EmausBot, Noloader, Helpful Pixie Bot, Calabe1992, Hojo5415, AndreiMincov, BattyBot, Cyberbot II, ChrisGualtieri, Raging439, Reatlas, Epicgenius, Jodosma, Claursen, Grand'mere Eugene, Hellotoday44, Domainnametalk12, Jcaudle and Anonymous: 25

- **Fakesysdef (malware)** *Source:* https://en.wikipedia.org/wiki/Fakesysdef_(malware)?oldid=662064163 *Contributors:* Daranz, Woohookitty, Bgwhite, Wavelength, Adavidb, Jdaloner, AnomieBOT, FrescoBot, Lotje, Josve05a, Antiqueight, SealAndBear, Sourov0000, cb and Anonymous: 1

- **Gh0st RAT** *Source:* https://en.wikipedia.org/wiki/Gh0st_RAT?oldid=697048359 *Contributors:* Dratman, Sukiari, Rjwilmsi, XP1, Skizzik, Mr. Vernon, Loadmaster, DumbBOT, Atulsnischal, Editor437, Flyer22 Reborn, Thingg, SlubGlub, Citation bot 1, Pinethicket, RjwilmsiBot, CharlieEchoTango, ClueBot NG, Lowercase sigmabot, Yejianfei, Kaartic and Anonymous: 14

- **In-session phishing** *Source:* https://en.wikipedia.org/wiki/In-session_phishing?oldid=686906069 *Contributors:* The Anome, FlaBot, SmackBot, Frap, Addbot, Erik9, FrescoBot, Tinton5, Tbhotch, Zollerriia, Securetier, Ego White Tray, Dan3697, Epicgenius, ErinEliza123 and Anonymous: 5

- **List of rogue security software** *Source:* https://en.wikipedia.org/wiki/List_of_rogue_security_software?oldid=700408902 *Contributors:* Discospinster, Smalljim, Lawrence King, Jobu, Chris the speller, Chris55, Fayenatic london, Geniac, Michael Goodyear, Kevinmon, Hbent, Drm310, Ignatzmice, Bonadea, Deor, Malcolmxl5, RJaguar3, France3470, Blanchardb, Socrates2008, Donsity, XLinkBot, NellieBly, Ben Ben, Lacrymocéphale, AnomieBOT, Addihockey10, James1011R, Stars1408, HamburgerRadio, Deadrat, Lotje, Punkofthedeath, John of Reading, TuneyLoon, Somebody500, Kunal0315, Rspence1234, WiiRocks566, Squady7, Roambassador, Zalchmen, ClueBot NG, Salmon92, Candlestick21, Guitarheroman202, Korrawit, Egg Centric, Asintro, Meltdown627, HappyLogolover2011, Fbacchin, Toxicgas1, Tonyjkent, Mark Arsten, Retireduser455656, Mikeshinobi1, BattyBot, Eduardofeld, Tangaling, Caaaake, EagerToddler39, Croberts pcd, Epicgenius, Froglich, Darth Occulus, Comp.arch, Vilmatech, OliviawithZiZi, Tonygoodmen, Bustedbrain16, Dsprc, Mamoth55, Heavy Punch, A8v, JackDaniels11, Zoethecomputergal, Rye Giggs, Jerodlycett, Acivon6791, PcSecAndy, Hfdhsdfhysfgadfgsadf, Dominic Hoe, Microsoftantivirus, EnigmaLord515 and Anonymous: 83

- **Lottery scam** *Source:* https://en.wikipedia.org/wiki/Lottery_scam?oldid=698945533 *Contributors:* Edward, Boud, Pnm, Gisle~enwiki, WhisperToMe, Bearcat, Psychonaut, HangingCurve, Antandrus, Beland, Cow, Chris Howard, Mormegil, Rich Farmbrough, Selphie, Alansohn, Saga City, Geraldshields11, Tomash, SmthManly, Commander, Bgwhite, Strecken, WayneRay, Grafen, Scamdex, McGeddon, Gilliam, Thumperward, A. B., Britmax, Kuru, BillFlis, Hu12, CJBot, Gogo Dodo, Studerby, Alucard (Dr.), Dancter, Thijs!bot, Marek69, Barek, MER-C, SiobhanHansa, Glen, MartinBot, CommonsDelinker, J.delanoy, Bonadea, Funandtrvl, Wws.info, Born2x, Drewshaker, Bfpage, Antonio Lopez, Tombomp, Zragon, EBC2000, Andise1, Krisroe, S.Tarikh, HumphreyW, XLinkBot, Ost316, Addbot, Willking1979, PlumCrumbleAndCustard, Mike5053, AnomieBOT, Hairhorn, Shoowak, GrouchoBot, Qiik, LittleWink, Lotje, Arviandgee, Pablo.peinado, Thomas97531, Jon Unheard, Feakins, Polisher of Cobwebs, Papg2010, Crashed74, ClueBot NG, Tracytarg, Cyberbot II, Cobalion254, Rlbeers, JNMBBB, Juhuyuta, Abhishekryan147, Akka1965, Some Gadget Geek, Aswin96, Mohamed riad abdelnaser and Anonymous: 59

- **Man-in-the-browser** *Source:* https://en.wikipedia.org/wiki/Man-in-the-browser?oldid=701445177 *Contributors:* Moxfyre, Mindmatrix, Kmg90, BD2412, Rjwilmsi, Arthur Rubin, Frap, Mistress Selina Kyle, RomanSpa, Alaibot, Utopiah, Widefox, AndreasWittenstein, Froid,

Monkeyjunky, Sunderland06, Remember the dot, Qu3a, Funandtrvl, Flopster2, Calliopejen1, SimonTrew, JL-Bot, Aua, DanielPharos, Pmd-golden, Addbot, AnomieBOT, Grolltech, ErikvanB, Gsgriffin, ZéroBot, Erianna, Donner60, John Smith 104668, Pastore Italy, ClueBot NG, Organ feaster, MeanMotherJr, Zhaofeng Li, Cyberbot II, Fmcarthy, ZovianLord, Prigaleutji and Anonymous: 25

- **New_Utopia** *Source:* https://en.wikipedia.org/wiki/New_Utopia?oldid=641441467 *Contributors:* Ubiquity, Zanimum, Cyde, Gene Poole, Alex756, Vanished user 5zariu3jisj0j4irj, Ww, Maximus Rex, VeryVerily, Francs2000, Owen, Phil Boswell, Kizor, Postdlf, Dhodges, Djinn112, PenguiN42, Quarl, Ihavenolife, OwenBlacker, Touchon, Solitude, Pjacobi, Sunborn, Jpgordon, Enric Naval, L33tminion, Pearle, Alphaboi867, Hu, IJzeren Jan, Vortexentity, KriZe, Firsfron, MacRusgail, Drumguy8800, Xoloz, Grafen, Chick Bowen, Danlaycock, Black Falcon, Georgewilliamherbert, GraemeL, SV Resolution, Kingboyk, FrozenPurpleCube, DocendoDiscimus, SmackBot, Elonka, Johnski, Alligators1974, Cybercobra, Kotjze, Panchitaville, Barry m, JzG, GMcGath, ChrisCork, Cydebot, PaperTruths, Nicodemous~enwiki, CommonsDelinker, Wikihonduras, MuzikJunky, Gene93k, Mild Bill Hiccup, JeffVegas21, Good Olfactory, Airplaneman, Yobot, PureBliss, SassoBot, Bhardwaz, Full-date unlinking bot, Blanes, ClueBot NG, Tonjeidea, RoadRangerX, Nicodemous44, Vycl1994 and Anonymous: 43

- **Advance-fee scam** *Source:* https://en.wikipedia.org/wiki/Advance-fee_scam?oldid=700526426 *Contributors:* AxelBoldt, Magnus Manske, Derek Ross, Brion VIBBER, The Anome, Tarquin, Malcolm Farmer, Eclecticology, Rmhermen, PierreAbbat, Fubar Obfusco, Detritus, Camembert, Modemac, Steverapaport, Edward, Ubiquity, Michael Hardy, Eivind, Booyabazooka, Isomorphic, Liftarn, Wwwwolf, AlexR, Tregoweth, Ihcoyc, Ams80, Ahoerstemeier, Arwel Parry, Kingturtle, Julesd, KTDykes, Vzbs34, Netsnipe, Alex756, Schneelocke, Timwi, Dcoetzee, Paul Stansifer, Teresag, WhisperToMe, Radiojon, Imc, LMB, Mackensen, Khym Chanur, AaronSw, Bloodshedder, Pakaran, Frazzydee, Shantavira, Denelson83, Thorn~enwiki, Hankwang, ChrisO~enwiki, Chris 73, Jredmond, RedWolf, Donreed, Yelyos, JosephBarillari, Lowellian, ThwartedEfforts, Clngre, Texture, Auric, Gidonb, Bkell, David Edgar, PBP, Pengo, Mlk, Desplesda, Ferkelparade, Brian Kendig, HangingCurve, Mark Richards, Pashute, Muzzle, Duncharris, Bob McDob, Pascal666, Falcon Kirtaran, Costyn, Bobblewik, Wmahan, MarkSweep, Quarl, Jossi, DragonflySixtyseven, Bodnotbod, Ary29, Sam Hocevar, Nerd65536, Creidieki, Rgrg, Sonett72, Grunt, Lacrimosus, Mike Rosoft, Wanted, Mjec, DanielCristofani, Wfaulk, JTN, Arcataroger, Mark Zinthefer, Discospinster, ElTyrant, Rich Farmbrough, FT2, D-Notice, Browolf, WegianWarrior, Kbh3rd, JoeSmack, Hapsiainen, Kaszeta, Izalithium, El C, Aude, Coolcaesar, Xed, Perfecto, Causa sui, Arancaytar, Rpresser, Bobo192, NetBot, Reinyday, Shenme, Fremsley, Davis21Wylie, Jerryseinfeld, Aquillion, Kjkolb, Ghoseb, Towel401, Orzetto, Gary, Anthony Appleyard, Eleland, Walter Görlitz, Interiot, Inky, Babajobu, Jlascar, Andrewpmk, Ricky81682, Sade, Edeans, Robert Mercer, Metron4, Adam Katz, Cromwellt, Saga City, Evil Monkey, Tony Sidaway, Drat, Danthemankhan, LFaraone, Deathphoenix, Algocu, Richard Weil, Kay Dekker, SmthManly, Preost, Woohookitty, Mindmatrix, Kyle Maxwell, RHaworth, Rhys Llwyd, Madmardigan53, Localh77, LoopZilla, SimonFr, Mkb218, Pol098, WadeSimMiser, Pogue, Takatam, Damicatz, Isnow, Cornince, Waldir, Stevey7788, Yoghurt, Graham87, Kalmia, BD2412, Haikupoet, Dpv, Dubkiller, Rjwilmsi, Sander Marechal, WCFrancis, Commander, Chrisabraham, RiseAbove, MZMcBride, Quietust, Jehochman, Frenchman113, Brighterorange, Sango123, W3bbo, Yamamoto Ichiro, ColinJF, Ageo020, Ian Pitchford, Bedawyn~enwiki, Stoph, StephanCom, Loggie, Frob, Avalyn, Bennie Noakes, Twisto, Igordebraga, Stephen Compall, Digitalme, Gwernol, YurikBot, Wavelength, AlexP~enwiki, Hairy Dude, RussBot, Robert A West, H.b.~enwiki, Alinush, WayneRay, Calicore, Gaius Cornelius, CambridgeBayWeather, Wimt, GeeJo, TheMandarin, NawlinWiki, Wiki alf, Dialectric, Welsh, Tomroes~enwiki, BirgitteSB, Aaron Brenneman, Bgrainger, Scs, Vlad, Asarelah, Jeremy Visser, CLW, User27091, Saric, Secant1, Morcheeba, Gorgonzilla, SFGiants, Nikkimaria, Closedmouth, Abune, Th1rt3en, Vert~enwiki, BorgQueen, Petri Krohn, Doctorbob, MStraw, Spliffy, David Biddulph, ViperSnake151, Kungfuadam, Svelyka, RJO, Knowledgeum, Entheta, Borisbaran, AndrewWTaylor, Scamdex, Veinor, Biyibandele, A bit iffy, SmackBot, Swiss Banker, Melchoir, McGeddon, Bigbluefish, Piroteknix, WilyD, Adrian232, Verne Equinox, PizzaMargherita, Stifle, Iph, Fishhead, Nil Einne, Shai-kun, Filius Rosadis, Gilliam, Buck Mulligan, Leamanc, Dhbarr, Durova, Larsroe, Artoftransformation, Bluebot, Jprg1966, Thumperward, Jeekc, Christopher denman, PrimeHunter, Wackymax, Robocoder, TheFeds, SquarePeg, Farry, Zephyrad, Colonies Chris, A. B., Freshmeat, Emurphy42, Hgrosser, Famspear, Can't sleep, clown will eat me, TheMacAttack, Nlapierre, Heapchk, Chlewbot, OrphanBot, Nixeagle, Drleftover, Rrburke, GRuban, Metageek, Grover cleveland, E. Sn0 =31337=, Downtown dan seattle, Downwards, Savidan, Valenciano, TedE, Luzaire, 419baiter, Doodle77, Bobjuch, Johnkirkby, Manderr, Serein (renamed because of SUL), Gryffon, JzG, Calvados~enwiki, Khazar, John, Vgy7ujm, BurnDownBabylon, Christina Preston, JohnI, Flamingblur, Credmond, Azate, Loadmaster, BillFlis, Lampman, Bkd, Dbo789, Waggers, Jdng, Etafly, Hu12, Corvi, Iridescent, 293.xx.xxx.xx, Isibingo, Joseph Solis in Australia, Blakegripling ph, GMcGath, Marysunshine, Phoenixrod, Courcelles, Linkspamremover, Pontificake, Bubbha, Joshuagross, ChrisCork, SkyWalker, Macca7174, Rnickel, CmdrObot, Ivan Pozdeev, Jayunderscorezero, Amy lee is my god, BeenAroundAWhile, Picaroon, JohnCD, Mushrom, Zyxoas, Gannett, ShelfSkewed, Maima, Acabtp, Shultz IV, Penbat, CJBot, Inzy, ExTechOp, Cydebot, Abeg92, AniMate, A876, Gogo Dodo, Heff01, Alucard (Dr.), Damouns, Joewein, Kozuch, Gonzo fan2007, Tarmulane, Omicronpersei8, Tornados28, Fyedernoggersnodden, Thijs!bot, Nowshining, Keraunos, Headbomb, I do not exist, Squilax, Abut, Grahamdubya, E. Ripley, Benqish, MinnesotanConfederacy, Natalie Erin, AntiVandalBot, Akradecki, Shirt58, Vertrag, Czj, Aruffo, Julia Rossi, Ed629, Silver seren, Lonn.daniel, Damelch, Mahhag, Salgueiro~enwiki, Chadjj, Richiez, Thomaskibu, Barek, MER-C, Tech2blog, Operatorhere, Workaphobia, Godcast, Geniac, Bongwarrior, Dugdale, Soiazabel, LordHedgie, Astragale, Spellmaster, Somearemoreequal, Mysteryquest, CapnPrep, WLU, .V., Chrisandvicky, Kayau, Thefifthdoctor, Tracer9999, Dontdoit, Flowanda, MartinBot, Grandia01, CliffC, Naohiro19, Gamma2delta, Nativebreed, CoBritis, Kateshortforbob, Brinkie, ACJJ, J.delanoy, ESLachance, Wa3frp, SooperJoo, Bluebiru, RoyBatty42, Barts1a, Dispenser, Gthb, Silas S. Brown, Naniwako, Kristindorsett, Coppertwig, Mike Sorensen, NewEnglandYankee, Rdkr, SJP, Ukt-zero, Garet300, Butnotthehippo, Donmike10, DMCer, Rexparry sydney, RJASE1, DraxusD, RadioTheodric, Rohaandg, Signalhead, Vranak, Hellno2, Wws.info, Superherongpogi, Andrewmonks, FireWeed, DOHC Holiday, Johnny Au, Holme053, Cadby Waydell Bainbrydge, Fences and windows, Dom Kaos, Scamorama, Philip Trueman, Marknagel, Behemothing, TXiKiBoT, Jkeene, Spallen, Technopat, Ragemanchoo, NPrice, Michendo, MannyJane, Qxz, Liko81, Aryattack, Katyism, Kitty's little helper, Hne123, Homergreg, Martin451, ^demonBot2, Noformation, Bearian, Wiae, TheCleanUpCrew, Billgdiaz, Goinggreat, Netglobalbooks, Enigmaman, Summortus, Nicknackrussian, Falcon8765, Enviroboy, The Last Melon, Michael Frind, Logan, Poor Poor Pitiful Me, Foxmajik, Stupid47, Drewice, Bfpage, Aviara, SieBot, MuzikJunky, Leerutherford, Beatrice002, Ostap R, Euryalus, Juanpedromartinezdecastilloruiz, Grieferhate, This, that and the other, STPgroup, Mikehcg, Duplicity, ReadQT, BlueAzure, DorTheScripter, Flyer22 Reborn, Arbor to SJ, Darkaxel, Doctorfluffy, Jack1956, Lightmouse, BrokeTheInterweb, Dillard421, Zragon, Smoothpyrogen, Brettdykes, EBC2000, Ajk91, Florentino floro, JL-Bot, Zappa san, Martarius, ClueBot, Immblueversion, Binksternet, Lenaforsgren, Libraryg, Emmanuel2012, Nnemo, Orbit.love, Supertouch, Drmies, Trivialist, William Ortiz, MrKIA11, Auntof6, Mr. Laser Beam, Gu1dry, Bonap, Jusdafax, Tryptamine dreamer, Jenalex, Ajisekanla, KnightStrider, Julierogier, Siboniwe, FWatcher, S.Tarikh, Blackwasp01, Thehelpfulone, Jtle515, I8189720, DumZiBoT, Marsh Tracy, XLinkBot, Little Mountain 5, Mull1979, Lilaspastia, Spoonkymonkey, Lemchesvej, Jackass91418, Addbot, Sidewinder, Willking1979, Dr Special, AVand, Flyingmonkeyairlines, Blechnic, Dmgmem, Dloseke, Scientus, Krietns, Dyadron, Download, Zamte, Chzz, JamesJBloom, Tassedethe, Pillwords, Evildeathmath, Lightbot, OlEnglish, Latroba, Gail, Dreamsmith,

ShootinPutin109, Elgreggo11, Ben Ben, Cqmgeorgian, Yobot, 2D, Fraudwatchers org, THEN WHO WAS PHONE?, Exp man, Lerichard, AnomieBOT, Kristen Eriksen, Rubinbot, Mr.Grave, Piano non troppo, Flopsy Mopsy and Cottonmouth, Michaelkirschner, Materialscientist, Citation bot, Kittybye, James500, LilHelpa, Xqbot, Transity, Romancescam, Nasnema, Junkcops, Tad Lincoln, Jmundo, Anonymous from the 21st century, Mark Schierbecker, RibotBOT, Mathias419, Amaury, Huybau, Rfgrgrg, Piosystems, Tramlanluan, RetiredWikipedian789, Capstan capstan, Hillsbro, FrescoBot, Shipnerd62962, Tunapul, Kwiki, Metaphysicalangst, Louperibot, PigFlu Oink, LittleWink, Calmer Waters, Suppart, Btilm, Nigerianspam, Brizzygrl, Latios, Пахатов Дмитрий, Isaacvsgottfried, Abw1987, Trappist the monk, HelenOnline, Lotje, RandomBlackDude, Reaper Eternal, Greggganders, KirstnF, RjwilmsiBot, ElPeste, Burstinghead, DASHBot, AndrewAfresh, John of Reading, Harrywiganboy, Wiki.Tango.Foxtrot, Mcaldwell42, Dewritech, GoingBatty, Mtnphotoman, Active Banana, Gimmetoo, Tommy2010, Kayusyussuf, AvicBot, Ida Shaw, Jenks24, Midnightauthor, Babytweety10982, H3llBot, Gremlinsa, Cherylwaller, FiReSTaRT, XxDestinyxX, Wingman4l7, Gparyani, Rcsprinter123, Wikipedian192, Motanu02, Yaturi3, ResidentAnthropologist, Whoop whoop pull up, ClueBot NG, Gareth Griffith-Jones, Jack Greenmaven, MelbourneStar, Shadeyon, Loginnigol, Xqrt923, Stream1, Hrritage9384, Widr, CasualVisitor, Harsimaja, Helpful Pixie Bot, Josephmate, Jamie Tubers, Ramaksoud2000, Nfiliposi, Myuphrid, BG19bot, Archrith, Mythpage88, Eruditescholar, Harizotoh9, 419team, MrAmazingAwesomeness, Applesandapples, BattyBot, Eduardofeld, Fraulein451, ChrisGualtieri, DerekSmythe, Klaustheviking, Brianwilfred, Itbeso, MDT109, SternComradeLoyalFascist, IjonTichyIjonTichy, Koopatrev, Waqob, Chow, Hmainsbot1, ThisCatHasClaws, Mogism, Viewmont Viking, Jlenney, ProfessorTofty, BDE1982, Me, Myself, and I are Here, Vanischenu from public computers, MarchOrDie, Epicgenius, Zxzn, Polychose, 69.76.50.211 ip, Kap 7, Tentinator, Obercc, WikiFraud419, EvergreenFir, Hoppeduppeanut, Froglich, BenStein69, Nickg82, YarLucebith, Furjo, Lemonsdrops, Beneficii, Sofia Lucifairy, JohnPhillipBrown, AKS.9955, Agyemang143, Scam protecters, Polemicista, Oiyarbepsy, KH-1, Tullyvallin, WhiteHawkWiki, Julietdeltalima, JamianMM, FourViolas, DiffuseGoose, TheWirelyWire, Austinclive, Chriswx817, Ugoegbuchulam, OliverDFW, Matterington, Spadde, Simikay and Anonymous: 946

- **Operation Newscaster** *Source:* https://en.wikipedia.org/wiki/Operation_Newscaster?oldid=684587034 *Contributors:* Egsan Bacon, Fuddle, John of Reading, Klbrain, Pahlevun, DoomCult and Anonymous: 1

- **Patched (malware)** *Source:* https://en.wikipedia.org/wiki/Patched_(malware)?oldid=653633961 *Contributors:* Bgwhite, Nick Number and SealAndBear

- **PayPal** *Source:* https://en.wikipedia.org/wiki/PayPal?oldid=700155259 *Contributors:* Steffen, Nv8200pa, Pne, Gary, CyberSkull, Matthew Platts, Bayle Shanks, Syrthiss, SmackBot, McGeddon, Aaron of Mpls, TimBentley, Victoria h, Frap, Clorox, Britmax, CmdrObot, Ultimus, Dawnseeker2000, Jeffjordan, JMyrleFuller, Huey45, Funandtrvl, Wysprgr2005, SiemEik, Lightbot, AnomieBOT, Neurolysis, Randomcrumb, Khazar2, Rupert loup and Anonymous: 18

- **Phishing** *Source:* https://en.wikipedia.org/wiki/Phishing?oldid=701038244 *Contributors:* Eloquence, The Anome, Tim Chambers, Arvindn, Fubar Obfusco, William Avery, Shii, David spector, Frecklefoot, Edward, Nealmcb, Patrick, Olrick, Michael Hardy, Fred Bauder, Lousyd, Tannin, Ixfd64, Gojomo, Tregoweth, CesarB, Mkweise, Ahoerstemeier, Julesd, Jonathan Chang, Pratyeka, Nikai, Netsnipe, Scott, GCarty, Schneelocke, Janko, WhisperToMe, Zoicon5, Tpbradbury, Kaare, David Shay, Nv8200pa, K1Bond007, ZeWrestler, SEWilco, Raul654, Pakaran, MrWeeble, Pollinator, Jeffq, Saqib (usurped)~enwiki, Paul W, Hankwang, Kizor, Chris 73, Moncrief, Postdlf, Danutz, Academic Challenger, Flauto Dolce, Meelar, Auric, Jondel, Andrew Levine, Vikreykja, Asn, Isopropyl, Sjl, Centrx, Smjg, DocWatson42, Hylaride, Mintleaf~enwiki, Nichalp, Inter, Ævar Arnfjörð Bjarmason, Brian Kendig, Muke, Bkonrad, Wikibob, Matt Crypto, SWAdair, DÅ,ugosz, Bobblewik, Ragib, OverlordQ, Catdude, PDH, Maximaximax, TheListener, Nickptar, TonyW, Neutrality, Klemen Kocjancic, Mmj, Chmod007, EagleOne, Chron, Rolandg, Ta bu shi da yu, Mormegil, Rfl, Monkeyman, Poccil, Sparky the Seventh Chaos, Ocon, DanielCD, JTN, A-giau, RossPatterson, Discospinster, Rich Farmbrough, Rhobite, Sladen, Vsmith, R.123, Browolf, Paul August, Unixslug, Bender235, CanisRufus, El C, Kiand, Lycurgus, Chroot, Art LaPella, RoyBoy, Dalf, One-dimensional Tangent, Perfecto, Alxndr, Grick, Bobo192, Exmachina~enwiki, Smalljim, Scott Ritchie, Jerryseinfeld, Novakyu, Cunningham, Minghong, Wrs1864, Sam Korn, Pearle, Iolar~enwiki, Poli, ClementSeveillac, Knucmo2, Phils, Storm Rider, Alansohn, Digiplaya, Anthony Appleyard, Chuck Adams, JohnAlbertRigali, ABCD, RoySmith, Redfarmer, Bart133, Snowolf, Kelson Vibber, Wtmitchell, G026r, Omphaloscope, Vuo, Deathphoenix, SteinbDJ, Grnch, Blaxthos, Richwales, RyanGerbil10, Brookie, Dtobias, CaptainMike, Firsfron, OwenX, Mindmatrix, Scriberius, LOL, Simon Shek, Scjessey, Mhoulden, Daniel Wright, Wocky, Scootey, Frankie1969, Wayward, Matthew Platts, Zhen-Xjell, Palica, Dysepsion, Fleetham, Graham87, Marskell, MC MasterChef, David Levy, JIP, Josh Parris, Ryan Norton, Tbird20d, Dearsina, Rjwilmsi, Jake Wartenberg, Jivecat, Commander, Carbonite, SMC, Ligulem, Jehochman, Brighterorange, Rmatney, FlaBot, Directorblue, SchuminWeb, RobertG, Intersofia, Master Thief Garrett, Who, SouthernNights, Mark83, RexNL, Thenowhereman, Intgr, Chobot, Scosco62, Nagytibi, Bornhj, DVdm, Bgwhite, Cactus.man, Tylerwillis, EvilZak, The Rambling Man, YurikBot, Wavelength, Borgx, Kinneyboy90, I need a name, Phantomsteve, Ikester, Conscious, Taejo, Mgway, Bhny, Splash, Zigamorph, Chaser, Akamad, Ori Livneh, Stephenb, Archelon, Mithridates, Debroglie, Gaius Cornelius, CambridgeBayWeather, Rsrikanth05, Pseudomonas, Rabasolo, Jaremfan, Finbarr Saunders, NawlinWiki, Rick Norwood, Hm2k, Wiki alf, Janke, Johann Wolfgang, AlMac, Janarius, RazorICE, Robchurch, Joelr31, Robert McClenon, PhilipO, DanBri, AlbertR, Tony1, Alex43223, Zwobot, FlyingPenguins, LarryMac, EEMIV, Deku-shrub, DeadEyeArrow, Bota47, Zzuuzz, Ali K, Lt-wiki-bot, Gorgonzilla, Ka-Ping Yee, Reyk, StealthFox, Fram, JLaTondre, Fedkad, David Biddulph, 7Train, Allens, Groyolo, That Guy, From That Show!, Chris Chittleborough, Alextrevelian 006, Veinor, SmackBot, KnowledgeOfSelf, Sanjay ach, The Monster, Unyoyega, Pgk, Vald, KelleyCook, Doc Strange, AKismet, 42istheanswer, ImaginaryFriend, Adam murgittroyd, Macintosh User, Gilliam, Julian Diamond, Betacommand, Andy M. Wang, Lakshmin, Chris the speller, Telempe, BabuBhatt, SchfiftyThree, Hibernian, Jerome Charles Potts, Mark7-2, Lexlex, Jnavas, Nintendude, Anabus, Can't sleep, clown will eat me, Gabr~enwiki, AussieLegend, Ismail ngr, Frap, Webrunner69, Chlewbot, KaiserbBot, MBlume, JonHarder, Dskushwaha, Rrburke, Mugaliens, Cocopopz2005, Jmlk17, Hateless, Dwchin, Nakon, Jbergquist, Govvy, Kendrick7, Petrichor, Sigma 7, Ligulembot, Intelliot, Risker, Juux, Nishkid64, Harryboyles, Kuru, ManiF, Bjankuloski06en~enwiki, Nagle, Castleinthesky, Shattered, Ckatz, 3210, Douglas Ryan VanBenthuysen, Wildwik, Slakr, Stwalkerster, Beetstra, Optimale, George The Dragon, Emurph, BrockF5, HoodedHound, Manifestation, Mtford, Keycard, Lee Carre, Nathanrdotcom, SimonD, Ant honey, Alan.ca, WilliamJE, Joseph Solis in Australia, Igoldste, IamTheWalrus, Courcelles, Linkspamremover, J Cricket, Tawkerbot2, Cnd, Porterjoh, TheHerbalGerbil, CWY2190, KnightLago, Bhxinfected, Jesse Viviano, MarsRover, WeggeBot, Neelix, Timtrent, Colostomyexplosion, CJBot, Equendil, AndrewHowse, NotAnotherAliGFan, Lightblade, Byziden, Harmonk, MC10, DavidForthoffer, SunDog, Vanished user vjhsduheuiui4t5hjri, Gogo Dodo, Travelbird, Tomasic, Colin Keigher, Ksangani, Otto4711, ST47, Alucard (Dr.), Dancter, Roymstat, Tawkerbot4, The snare, Chrislk02, Kozuch, Omicronpersei8, Spamlart, Michaelorgan, Gimmetrow, Thijs!bot, Epbr123, Oktober42, Cain Mosni, Andyjsmith, Nonagonal Spider, Oliver202, John254, Gerry Ashton, Horologium, Z10x, Leon7, NigelR, Dawnseeker2000, I already forgot, Mentifisto, KrakatoaKatie, Anti-VandalBot, Luna Santin, Widefox, EmeryD, Oducado, Just Chilling, Credema, Spencer, Captainspalding, Wayiran, Jenny Wong, Ronaldgray, Storkk, Canadian-Bacon, DOSGuy, JAnDbot, Jacobratkiewicz, Lamather, MER-C, CosineKitty, Epeefleche, Inks.LWC, Dafphee, Symode09,

Yuhaian, Greensburger, GGreeneVa, PhilKnight, WolfmanSF, Shoejar, Bongwarrior, VoABot II, 1995hoo, Mike5906, Gboweswhitton, Dfense, JamesBWatson, Sdhonda, Tedickey, Nyttend, Zyschqual, Homunq, Rohasnagpal, Nposs, DerHexer, JaGa, Zgadot, SquidSK, Gjd001, Martin-Bot, CliffC, Lisamh, Jeannealcid, John Millikin, Rhlitonjua, Roastytoast, Bemsor, CommonsDelinker, No more anonymous editing, Einstein-inmyownmind, Lilac Soul, EdBever, Tgeairn, J.delanoy, Kimse, Bigzig91090, Paul1953h, Herbythyme, 72Dino, Hodja Nasreddin, Laurus-nobilis, Passgo, Hooksbooks, Vineetcoolguy, AntiSpamBot, RenniePet, Ronchristie, NewEnglandYankee, SJP, Kraftlos, Vindi293, Ponguru, Sanjeevchris, Cmichael, Atropos235, Juliancolton, Inomyabcs, Remember the dot, DorganBot, Treisijs, TopGun, Sbanker, Lcawte, Jarry1250, Funandtrvl, Lwalt, Kelaos, Lights, Vranak, X!, Sergivs-en, Deor, VolkovBot, Morenooso, Safemariner, Butwhatdoiknow, Kyle the bot, Bsroiaadn, Aesopos, Profilepitstop, Philip Trueman, Amh library, TXiKiBoT, Oshwah, GimmeBot, Anonymous Dissident, ElinorD, GcSwRhIc, Olly150, Vanished user ikijeirw34iuaeolaseriffic, TwilligToves, Lradrama, Wpedzich, Bodybagger, ITurtle, Michaeldsuarez, Dirkbb, Ryco01, Lamro, Randybandy, Nicknackrussian, Salaamhuq, Falcon8765, Digita, Generic9, Insanity Incarnate, Alcmaeonid, Monty845, LittleBenW, Allebor-goBot, Michael Frind, Legoktm, Tayquan, Biscuittin, JonnyJD, Yngvarr, SieBot, Ergateesuk, YourEyesOnly, Dawn Bard, Matthew Yeager, Kkrouni, Yintan, Duplicity, Bentogoa, Happysailor, Flyer22 Reborn, Oda Mari, Man It's So Loud In Here, Arbor to SJ, Surreptitious Evil, Henke37, Pyroknight28, Antonio Lopez, Lightmouse, Alex.muller, CrazytalesPublic, OKBot, Lakers3021, Zragon, Markus-jakobsson, C'est moi, Anchor Link Bot, 🀀🀀🀀🀀~enwiki, WikiLaurent, Redfoot, Tomheinan, Daven29, Pinkadelica, Dolphin51, Treekids, Denisarona, Mat-tKeegan, Tuntable, Boudville, TheCatalyst31, ImageRemovalBot, SallyForth123, Martarius, ClueBot, Josang, Muhammadsb1, Kai-Hendrik, GorillaWarfare, The Thing That Should Not Be, Plastikspork, Unbuttered Parsnip, Jotag14, Pwitham, ColinHelvensteijn, Jobeard, Drmies, Mh-jackson, SuperHamster, JTBX, Magicheader, Ferwerto, Niceguyedc, Dylan620, Piledhigheranddeeper, Trivialist, Rprpr, Jliford, Mspraveen, RozMW, Joshdaman111, Mkativerata, Excirial, Socrates2008, Resoru, PixelBot, Gtstricky, Aftiggerintel, Lartoven, Mralokkp, Rhododen-drites, Sun Creator, NuclearWarfare, Cenarium, Sjoerdat13, Iohannes Animosus, Aquillyne, Bnefriends, Fattyjwoods, CMW275, Citricsquid, Peskeyplum, Thingg, Aitias, Versus22, PotentialDanger, PCHS-NJROTC, MelonBot, Stevenrasnick, Berean Hunter, Johnuniq, Apparition11, Katester1100, DumZiBoT, Alchemist Jack, XLinkBot, Jed 20012, Sigrulfr, Rror, Nepenthes, Freeworld4, Avoided, ZEUHUD, Mitch Ames, WikHead, Dnvrfantj, RyanCross, Blackrabbit99, HexaChord, Addbot, Xp54321, Proofreader77, WeatherFug, G J Lee, Wiseguy2tri, Mrkoww, Lets Enjoy Life, D0762, CanadianLinuxUser, Fluffernutter, CactusWriter, MrOllie, Pie Fan, Cambalachero, Bassbonerocks, Chzz, Debresser, AnnaFrance, Favonian, SpBot, LinkFA-Bot, Jasper Deng, CuteHappyBrute, Pillwords, Ps-Dionysius, Tide rolls, 1RadicalOne~enwiki, Luckas Blade, Gail, LuK3, Joyson Konkani, Electrosaurus, Legobot, Publicly Visible, Luckas-bot, Yobot, Stronginthepost, Fereve1980, Barek Oco-rah, Andrewtc, Freikorp, Aparicio99, THEN WHO WAS PHONE?, Bookwormrwt, Iangfc, Eamonster, Securus, AnomieBOT, OllieGeorge, Whittlepedia, Jim1138, Piano non troppo, AdjustShift, Past-times, Kingpin13, Glenfarclas, Flewis, Materialscientist, ArthurBot, LovesMacs, Xqbot, JimVC3, Capricorn42, Sampayu, BurntSynapse, Southboundon5, Buggss, Inferno, Lord of Penguins, Oddityoverseer13, GrouchoBot, RibotBOT, Pradameinhoff, Mrbakerfield, Sophus Bie, InfoSecPro, PM800, Sesu Prime, Ms dos mode, Valentino76, FrescoBot, Ryryrules100, א תומר., Griffind3, MikePeterson2008, Mommy2mack08, Qfissler, Jersey92, DivineAlpha, Stressy, HamburgerRadio, Citation bot 1, Bob-mack89x, Pinethicket, Elockid, ZonedoutWeb, Ngyikp, RedBot, OMGWEEGEE2, YetAnotherAuthor, Footwarrior, B-Machine, Plasticspork, OnlineSafetyTeam, Abc518, Blast73, Seinucep, LCE1506, Mns556, Mikazagreat, Lotje, Vrenator, Clarkcj12, Abdullah000, Reaper Eternal, Himugk, Minimac, Digitalee, .::Icy Fire Lord::., Mean as custard, RjwilmsiBot, Iceflame2539, Bento00, Offnfopt, Deagle AP, EmausBot, Wik-itanvirBot, Snow storm in Eastern Asia, Dewritech, GoingBatty, RA0808, Slightsmile, Tommy2010, TuHan-Bot, Wikipelli, Dcirovic, K6ka, John Cline, Fæ, Bollyjeff, Imgoutham, Ziva 89, The Nut, H3llBot, Zap Rowsdower, Pomyo is a man, Divineale, TyA, Δ, L Kensington, Dan-muz, Ready, Donner60, Senctisn, Bancrofttech, Cimp3, DASHBotAV, ClueBot NG, Twat1234567890, Manubot, LogX, This lousy T-shirt, Jogeed, Amr.rs, Mideal, Muon, Mesoderm, Key2503, OAnimosity, Sudhanshu15, Vjhamilton, Lowercase sigmabot, BG19bot, Hz.tiang, The Mark of the Beast, Hallows AG, Frze, Ajay.gautam.ip, Contentasaurus, Mark Arsten, Xtrenity, Dumbtube, Félix Wolf, Kdeathlord1, KScarfone, Wfjones55, Pikachu Bros., Sincec793, Kellieebee, Nookof90, Mdann52, Bhargav jhaveri, Gypsumwolf, Khazar2, Superkc, Dexbot, Rollbacker, Mr. Guye, Killhi12, TwoMartiniTuesday, Dailyfrauds, Pete Mahen, Frosty, Grseko, Faizan, Epicgenius, Polychose, Melonkelon, QuantifiedElf, Amsterdad, BlueRidiculous, Babitaarora, CobraBanker, Andrew.c.manson, D Eaketts, Qed237, Pst9, Golopotw, WikiJuggernaut, Njol, Nable-Com, SillyEditor, Dashawn888, 19tchs, Powermelon, Monkbot, Horseless Headman, Fine.tuna, AKS.9955, Kamilesgay97, Joeleoj123, Amey mahale, Gcsfl, Biblioworm, Minkoychoi, Essayjeans, Nclkatze, KH-1, Ammanabajwa, ChamithN, WikiGopi, AnyFree, Shinydiscoball, Lout-phichristopher, Lime02lime, TeaLover1996, Lawligator, Greenmow, Billyriobr, Destor918, ToonLucas22, Jennifer1122, Kwayflompy, Pdjw, Emiliuso, Notnot9, Supdiop, Prinsgezinde, KasparBot, Kelecharte, Ujjwal Sahay, Anarchyte, Piyush Golani, 236benderavenue, Trusted Bank, Indianprogrammer.in, Boybless, Pencilsharper, Matthews david, CLCStudent, Sroates, Ryster3103, Synkarae, Herusantoeso and Anonymous: 1242

- **Pranknet** *Source:* https://en.wikipedia.org/wiki/Pranknet?oldid=686251959 *Contributors:* Skysmith, Auric, FT2, Deathawk, NTK, Gerald-shields11, Nightscream, Flarn2006, Wavelength, Jreinstedler, JDspeeder1, SmackBot, Acdx, Gobonobo, Melicans, Nick Number, Rgoodermote, Skier Dude, Falcon8765, Laval, Work permit, Crash Underride, CutOffTies, Sfan00 IMG, ClueBot, Uncle Milty, Trivialist, RenamedUser jaskldjslak901, Wnt, Stickee, Good Olfactory, SaintHammett, Legobot, Thomasxstewart, Retro00064, AnomieBOT, Jim1138, Gensanders, Multixfer, Erik9bot, Meishern, Citation bot 1, Skyerise, Ouellette, Yanitor, Unimatrixzeroone, 420MuNkEy, Mwikiuser, RydiaRealm, Dian-naa, Jasonbe49, Disrupts, Balph Eubank, GoingBatty, Qrsdogg, Johnmark2000, Pillowsack, Fæ, Deepakmrl, Orange Suede Sofa, Peter Karlsen, ClueBot NG, Hey07979, Charles2940, Helpful Pixie Bot, DBigXray, Maxmidnight, 133719807aa, ULTRASTAR123, RightfulDex, CamelCase, Zwoc-RennisX and Anonymous: 68

- **Pretext** *Source:* https://en.wikipedia.org/wiki/Pretext?oldid=698587329 *Contributors:* LordAmeth, Bobrayner, Vegaswikian, Street Scholar, SmackBot, McGeddon, Lds, Hmains, Lexlex, Da Vynci, 16@r, Lioux, Chrisdab, Magioladitis, Pikolas, DandyDan2007, VolkovBot, Luminum, Enkyo2, Addbot, Gongshow, John of Reading, Faceless Enemy, ZéroBot, Helpful Pixie Bot, Faraz Davani, Wodrow, SaintAloysius, Star767 and Anonymous: 15

- **Psychological subversion** *Source:* https://en.wikipedia.org/wiki/Psychological_subversion?oldid=601708041 *Contributors:* Woohookitty, Btyner, Josh Parris, RussBot, SmackBot, McGeddon, Frap, Clicketyclack, Penbat, Phatom87, Galaxiana, Darklilac, R'n'B, DumZiBoT, Queen-momcat, Gabriel1907, DrilBot, Star767 and Anonymous: 5

- **Robin Sage** *Source:* https://en.wikipedia.org/wiki/Robin_Sage?oldid=694700501 *Contributors:* Zaui, AJim, SoWhy, Mike R, DragonflySix-tyseven, Rich Farmbrough, Art LaPella, Woohookitty, Vegaswikian, Chris the speller, Ben Moore, Warrenfish, Buckshot06, NuclearWarfare, C628, Addbot, Vegaswikian1, Xqbot, Westley Turner, Northsidewoman, Pastore Italy, NCnomad and Anonymous: 7

- **Rock Phish** *Source:* https://en.wikipedia.org/wiki/Rock_Phish?oldid=619487837 *Contributors:* ZeWrestler, Chowbok, PatrickFisher, Blank-Verse, BD2412, Rjwilmsi, RussBot, SmackBot, Chris the speller, Bluebot, Timtrent, Phatom87, Credema, Alekjds, Funandtrvl, PRSnell, Pxma,

FrescoBot, HamburgerRadio, DaveDaytona, H3llBot, KScarfone, ChrisGualtieri, Khazar2, Hackdefendr and Anonymous: 16

- **Rogue security software** *Source:* https://en.wikipedia.org/wiki/Rogue_security_software?oldid=699309888 *Contributors:* Fubar Obfusco, Julesd, WhisperToMe, Mazin07, Senthil, Nurg, Jfire, Vsmith, Bender235, Cwolfsheep, Charonn0, Espoo, Anthony Appleyard, Ron Ritzman, Woohookitty, RHaworth, MyFavoriteMartin, JIP, Rjwilmsi, Koavf, Quietust, Bubba73, Kri, Aussie Evil, NawlinWiki, FlyingPenguins, Real decimic, Nailbiter, Kevin, SmackBot, Jasy jatere, SmackEater, Ohnoitsjamie, RocketMaster, Chris the speller, Improbcat, Trimzulu, JonHarder, Azumanga1, Nakon, Dreadstar, Kukini, Fanx, Cableguytk, Green Giant, JHunterJ, Peyre, TheFarix, Blakegripling ph, RekishiEJ, Cryptic C62, FatalError, Fredvries, CmdrObot, Ivan Pozdeev, Jackzhp, Iuio, Greystork, Davidnason, Sadaphal, DevinCook, Poowis, Jesse Viviano, Seven of Nine, Gogo Dodo, Ameliorate!, Satori Son, Malleus Fatuorum, Nonagonal Spider, Dalahäst, Pogogunner, Obiwankenobi, AjaaniSherisu, Barek, Mark Grant, Geniac, Rhodilee, VoABot II, WikiMax, Michael Goodyear, Schumi555, Inclusivedisjunction, Gwern, CliffC, Falazure, R'n'B, CommonsDelinker, .1337., Pharaoh of the Wizards, Skier Dude, AppleMacReporter, Chaosraiden, TanookiMario257, Talon Kelson, Bonadea, VolkovBot, N3cr0m4nc3r, Philip Trueman, Jart351, Kok3388, Haseo9999, Synthebot, LittleBenW, AlleborgoBot, PedroDaGr8, Raiden X, Malcolmxl5, IHateMalware, Sephiroth storm, Flyer22 Reborn, EwanMclean2005, Es101, Phykyloman~enwiki, Jessejaksin, ClueBot, Chuckbronson45, LizardJr8, Chiazwhiz, Regardless143, Excirial, Socrates2008, Anon lynx, NuclearWarfare, Purplewowies, Autoplayer, Htfiddler, DanielPharos, Callinus, SF007, DumZiBoT, Mikon8er, Ginnrelay, Sigrulfr, Wikiuser100, Jennysue, Texasrexbobcat, Addbot, Xp54321, Trapped34, Flo 1, Smithereen, GastonRabbit, Yobot, Tohd8BohaithuGh1, Marvel Freak, Jponiato, KieranC15, SilverEyePro, Killiondude, Obersachsebot, CPU01, Jeffrey Mall, Junkcops, 吱吱吱, A1a33, S0aasdf2sf, КоЯп, BubbleDude22, AndrewCrogonklol, Pre-Cautioned Watcher, Beaconblack, Uvula!, Fastguy397, WPANI, Stars1408, ObbySnadles, HamburgerRadio, Citation bot 1, MaxwellHerme, ASCMSEM1, Jacobdead, Σ, Starbox, MichaelRivers, Deadrat, Lotje, CenSorShot, Kanzler31, Born2bgratis, Spyware exspert, Sky17565292, Ebe123, Progprog, Techguy197, Kunal0315, Napeyga, Champion, Dlowe2224, Ego White Tray, DClason93, Kldukes, Rich Smith, Skylar130, Helpful Pixie Bot, Kinaro, IlSignoreDeiPC, Terryforsdyke, Meatsgains, JC.Torpey, HybridBiology, Farqad, Tangaling, Zeeyanwiki, Codename Lisa, Webclient101, Kephir, Soda drinker, Sourov0000, MasterONEz, Marufseu, PersistedUser, Revantteotia, Logonemeri, Keni and Anonymous: 262

- **Romance scam** *Source:* https://en.wikipedia.org/wiki/Romance_scam?oldid=697531712 *Contributors:* The Anome, Ahoerstemeier, WhisperToMe, Mboverload, MBisanz, Mbloore, Guthrie, Carbenium, Czolgolz, Killing Vector, Pol098, Jeff3000, Wikiklrsc, Johan Lont, LordKenTheGreat, Strecken, Sus scrofa, Splintercellguy, RussBot, Icarus3, NawlinWiki, Complainer, Grafen, Robertetaylor, Moe Epsilon, Syrthiss, NeOak, SONORAMA, Toddgee, Back ache, SmackBot, Ybelov, Nil Einne, Gilliam, Ohnoitsjamie, TimBentley, Fuzzform, Robocoder, BIL, Willy turner, Slakr, Hu12, Audiosmurf, CmdrObot, BeenAroundAWhile, Ajbrowe, Lee-Lee 44, Travelbird, Manfroze, PKT, BetacommandBot, Biruitorul, Turkeyphant, JustAGal, Ebde, Dreaded Walrus, Thomaskibu, Barek, Strayalleycatz, TheEditrix2, Geniac, Magioladitis, Froid, Anaxial, Verdatum, Mike.lifeguard, Silver923, Rdkr, MKoltnow, Bonadea, S (usurped also), Pleasantville, Mwhitty, Goinggreat, NinjaRobotPirate, Poor Poor Pitiful Me, Swliv, Hattes, Whiteghost.ink, Zragon, ClueBot, Twenora86, Fiveiambline, Ndenison, Trivialist, WrthThRisk, Poet Note, Alexbot, NuclearWarfare, Ngebendi, Mlaffs, Stalek, Jcmcc450, XLinkBot, Addbot, FokkerTISM, Fluffernutter, Lindert, MrOllie, Download, Lightbot, Luckas-bot, Yobot, Jonvanhelsing, Exp man, Againme, Edwinsummers, Magog the Ogre, AnomieBOT, Rubinbot, Romancescambaiter, Paranormal Skeptic, Ircuser25, Sole Flounder, Xqbot, Romancescam, Activecommunity, Pietro morrizio, Thafriendbill, Unveiled, Icarei, Xfactor2000, Bobmack89x, SpaceFlight89, Greenskinorc, Lotje, Fakers2go, Szegedi László, Dewritech, Mtnphotoman, Fæ, Neun-x, Elena-rd, Miraline, ClueBot NG, MelbourneStar, Widr, Helpful Pixie Bot, Brunette2cute4u, BG19bot, Annadaviduk, StrangeApparition2011, Warsilver, Dominicwatkins, MeanMotherJr, K7L, Lugia2453, Darthgorgoroth, Blaua, GhanaGoldScam, Cupidscreen, Mdzhang, Flat Out, Entyre, Sofia Lucifairy, Hesdave, Zubbyj, Agyemang143 and Anonymous: 131

- **Scam baiting** *Source:* https://en.wikipedia.org/wiki/Scam_baiting?oldid=701350349 *Contributors:* Damian Yerrick, Fubar Obfusco, Modemac, Ronabop, Haakon, CatherineMunro, Amcaja, Paul Stansifer, WhisperToMe, VeryVerily, Onebyone, Denelson83, Dale Arnett, ChrisO~enwiki, Texture, DocWatson42, Karn, Ich, KirbyMeister, WhiteDragon, Schmiddy, Dbachmann, WegianWarrior, MBisanz, Perfecto, JRM, Revolutionary, Shred, Gargaj, BRW, Drat, SmthManly, Gmaxwell, DrMel, Woohookitty, Stevey7788, Mandarax, Yoghurt, Graham87, Deltabeignet, Cuchullain, BD2412, Xorkl000, Rjwilmsi, Sander Marechal, Ligulem, Capsela, Riki, Idaltu, Metropolitan90, Agamemnon2, Hairy Dude, Mike Young, The Hokkaido Crow, Aaron Brenneman, Fantusta, ChuckEye, Secant1, Zzuuzz, Kestenbaum, Penelope D, Sturmovik, Bob Hu, Nishantp, Entheta, That Guy, From That Show!, KnightRider~enwiki, SmackBot, WilyD, PizzaMargherita, Stifle, RedSpruce, The Rhymesmith, Tyciol, KiloByte, Apeloverage, Can't sleep, clown will eat me, TheMacAttack, Brentonstrine, Jbhood, Yoink23, Nekrorider, Savidan, 419baiter, Christina Preston, JoshuaZ, Latinata, Godfrey Daniel, Phatpat88, Pabobfin, Dreftymac, Twas Now, Linkspamremover, JayHenry, Pontificake, Winston Spencer, CBM, Fair Deal, Alucard (Dr.), Clovis Sangrail, Cloudysky2003, Omicronpersei8, Zhadov, Akimbomidget, I already forgot, RBowden, Darklilac, Hullubulloo, Mark87, JoeBrennan, Geniac, Magioladitis, CheMechanical, Brother Francis, .V., Thefifthdoctor, MartinBot, CliffC, Archolman, Davesf, Thmgroup, SooperJoo, Cvitullo, Ukt-zero, DMCer, Funandtrvl, Liko81, Pfluffy, Wenli, NinjaRobotPirate, Baseball Bugs, Zragon, ClueBot, William Ortiz, Auntof6, Bonap, TheRedPenOfDoom, Correctionpatrol4, Thingg, Dziewa, Anon126, XLinkBot, Addbot, Krietns, Tide rolls, Yobot, KamikazeBot, Mkwan79, Rjanag, Mann jess, Calamity Lotta, Pinethicket, A8UDI, Tbhotch, Johngalt592, Danrilor, Scambaiting, Motanu02, Ego White Tray, ClueBot NG, Bubo virginianus, Alexzarach, Nfiliposi, Nemesis64, AJScambaiter, HalinaZakowicz, Wheredidninjago, Ugoegbuchulam, Amas419, VutonQ and Anonymous: 168

- **Scareware** *Source:* https://en.wikipedia.org/wiki/Scareware?oldid=700730683 *Contributors:* Edward, Andres, Nurg, Xanzzibar, Ebear422, Grm wnr, Andrewferrier, Evice, CanisRufus, Kappa, TheParanoidOne, Jivlain, Kgrr, Mandarax, NeonMerlin, Robert A West, Nentuaby, SmackBot, C.Fred, Robocoder, Breno, Goodnightmush, Sabertooth, Uruiamme, Prolog, Barek, TheOtherSiguy, AlmostReadytoFly, Michael Goodyear, Maurice Carbonaro, DoubleZeta, SovereignGFC, VolkovBot, Fences and windows, TXiKiBoT, Darkrevenger, Jamelan, The Seventh Taylor, Thisismyrofl, LittleBenW, Logan, Moonriddengirl, Alexbot, Socrates2008, Callinus, Mikon8er, Nathan Johnson, ErkinBatu, MystBot, Addbot, Zellfaze, Sillyfolkboy, GastonRabbit, Megaman en m, Luckas-bot, Yobot, UltraMagnus, Metalhead94, Xqbot, Vanished user oweironvoweiuo0239u49regt8j3849hjtowiefj234, 吱吱吱, Cantons-de-l'Est, Tabledhote, FrescoBot, LucienBOT, Haein45, HamburgerRadio, Anonymous07921, Winterst, Starbox, Train2104, Deadrat, Jonkerz, Lotje, Teenboi001, Chris Rocen, WikitanvirBot, Angrytoast, Illogicalpie, Pooh110andco, ZéroBot, Fæ, The Nut, Wabbott9, Staszek Lem, Taistelu-Jaska, DASHBotAV, Roambassador, ClueBot NG, Vibhijain, Northamerica1000, Mccallister8, Flexo013, Security Shield, Farqad, Codename Lisa, Mogism, Sourov0000, 069952497a, Mannir muhammad and Anonymous: 70

- **Self-XSS** *Source:* https://en.wikipedia.org/wiki/Self-XSS?oldid=680227119 *Contributors:* Frap, Anupam, WereSpielChequers, Cosmo0, Unbuttered Parsnip, C628, 23W, Jakec, Jackmcbarn, Piperpet and Anonymous: 6

- **SMS phishing** *Source:* https://en.wikipedia.org/wiki/SMS_phishing?oldid=698189960 *Contributors:* Dimadick, Dave6, DragonflySixtyseven, O'Dea, Nibblus, Stardust8212, Fedkad, SmackBot, McGeddon, Unforgettableid, Ohnoitsjamie, Amalas, A876, Widefox, CliffC, Dominic7848,

Glacialfox, Kelvinruttman, Eduardofeld, Tutelary, Niraj.adyyyy, Th4n3r, Hsr.rautela, Adhithyan15, Cyberbot II, ChrisGualtieri, MadGuy7023, JayMyers-NJITWILL, Ghostman1947, Rezonansowy, SoledadKabocha, Djairhorn, Lugia2453, JoshLyman2012, Jc86035, Siravneetsingh, Soda drinker, Discuss-Dubious, Sourov0000, Cablewoman, Bugzeeolboy, NimaBoscarino, RootSword, Dave Braunschweig, Epicgenius, CatBall-Sack, Eyesnore, Gaman0091, DavidLeighEllis, Ugog Nizdast, Khabir123, Kushay titanium, Someone not using his real name, Manish2911, Oranjelo100, Dannyruthe, Sathishguru, STH235SilverLover, Joseph 0515, Marp pro, Rkpayne, Monkbot, Sidharta.mallick, Filedelinkerbot, Abcdfeghtys, Laura J. Pyle, Biblioworm, TerryAlex, Classofthewise, Earthquake58, ChamithN, HamadPervaiz, Eteethan, Helpguy77, Box-OfChickens, TQuentin, KasparBot, Ceannlann gorm, James the king12, JeremiahY, TeacherWikipedia, OldMcdonald12345, Drakeblair08, Kurousagi, Majneeds2chill, Vansockslayer, Aditya3929, User0071987, Bradley!90432754, Pa19602030fu, Voidcub and Anonymous: 1178

- **Website spoofing** *Source:* https://en.wikipedia.org/wiki/Website_spoofing?oldid=689117687 *Contributors:* Mindmatrix, McGeddon, Rmosler2100, Blakegripling ph, Qwyrxian, Smile a While, Deipnosophista, Seaphoto, Just Chilling, JAnDbot, Nthep, Magioladitis, Stephen-chou0722, K0rana, Sbanker, Croxley, AlasdairGreen27, Kent Pete, Addbot, Fieldday-sunday, Keylock191, Yobot, AnomieBOT, LilHelpa, Alph Bot, Sp0eedy, Maheshwaranvs, ClueBot NG, BG19bot, George8211, Richgrim, Harris.teitelbaum, Kschwartz95, Tarwets, Kylelf, MXocrossIIB, L sun 123, Dickscawed and Anonymous: 32

- **Whitemail** *Source:* https://en.wikipedia.org/wiki/Whitemail?oldid=653504655 *Contributors:* B4hand, Kev, Auric, John Vandenberg, Radell, Hairy Dude, Barefootguru, Dlyons493, Wikipeditor, Serendipodous, SmackBot, KMcD, McGeddon, StephenJMuir, Commander Keane bot, Cy-debot, Chrislk02, Mattisse, Heroeswithmetaphors, MarshBot, Tqbf, Funandtrvl, Nikthestunned, Malone67, Tpb, Addbot, AndrewHZ, Dcun010, Gtx44 and Anonymous: 6

- **Wifiphisher** *Source:* https://en.wikipedia.org/wiki/Wifiphisher?oldid=680894963 *Contributors:* Brianhe, Deku-shrub, Lakun.patra and Harishmfs

- **WOT Services** *Source:* https://en.wikipedia.org/wiki/WOT_Services?oldid=688265119 *Contributors:* Jm34harvey, Andrewman327, Finlay McWalter, Bkell, Xanzzibar, Alan Liefting, Byap, Wtmitchell, Feezo, Woohookitty, Rjwilmsi, Master Thief Garrett, Ian.hawdon, DVdm, Kollision, Skydot, Gaius Cornelius, GeoffCapp, Waryklingon, Arthur Rubin, SmackBot, J.smith, JzG, ShakingSpirit, Blakegripling ph, IanOfNorwich, Skybon, Kozuch, PamD, Faigl.ladislav, Widefox, Seaphoto, Danger, SiobhanHansa, Gert7, Magioladitis, Froid, Cander0000, Dbiel, ErikHSommer.dk, Markuswinter, VolkovBot, Eddie mars, Gillyweed, Way29, Baseball Bugs, Hello71, Samker, Maralia, Martarius, Frmorrison, Trivialist, EhJJ, DanielPharos, Dank, Burner0718, UKWikiGuy, XLinkBot, Totlmstr, Addbot, Xp54321, Debsalmi, ConCompS, WeatherFug, Oisjfw, Kartano, KamikazeBot, Samtar, AnomieBOT, Zoombus, Scootzer99, S0aasdf2sf, GrouchoBot, Securityadvisor, Freedomstarcat, Lordalpha1, Fellowedmonton, Oneforfortytwo, HamburgerRadio, FranklinPiat, Retired user 0001, HoworHow, Dinamik-bot, Cenkdemir, Stefanie079, RjwilmsiBot, DexDor, WikitanvirBot, Cmavr8, Wikipelli, ZéroBot, WikiManOne, R3velate, AutoGeek, Oskar1984, JenniBee, Crabel, ClueBot NG, Eleanor213, Helpful Pixie Bot, Knox490, Meego's Keeper, Imho1979, Hannes1983, Convello, Thegreatgrabber, Achowat, Cyan.aqua, YFdyh-bot, Sorgoz, Cerabot~enwiki, Abigail.gutierrez, Jdturbo, Mcharvat90, MWill72, Elaqueate, ScrapIronIV and Anonymous: 80

38.7.2 Images

- **File:Ambox_important.svg** *Source:* https://upload.wikimedia.org/wikipedia/commons/b/b4/Ambox_important.svg *License:* Public domain *Contributors:* Own work, based off of Image:Ambox scales.svg *Original artist:* Dsmurat (talk · contribs)

- **File:Ambox_rewrite.svg** *Source:* https://upload.wikimedia.org/wikipedia/commons/1/1c/Ambox_rewrite.svg *License:* Public domain *Contributors:* self-made in Inkscape *Original artist:* penubag

- **File:Clicking_Upload_button_on_abovetopsecret_triggers_clickjacking_warning_on_NoScript_141128-cropped.png** *Source:* https://upload.wikimedia.org/wikipedia/commons/7/7c/Clicking_Upload_button_on_abovetopsecret_triggers_clickjacking_warning_on_NoScript_141128-cropped.png *License:* CC0 *Contributors:* self *Original artist:* <https://noscript.net/ + self>

- **File:Commons-logo.svg** *Source:* https://upload.wikimedia.org/wikipedia/en/4/4a/Commons-logo.svg *License:* CC-BY-SA-3.0 *Contributors:* ? *Original artist:* ?

- **File:Computer-aj_aj_ashton_01.svg** *Source:* https://upload.wikimedia.org/wikipedia/commons/d/d7/Desktop_computer_clipart_-_Yellow_theme.svg *License:* CC0 *Contributors:* https://openclipart.org/detail/105871/computeraj-aj-ashton-01 *Original artist:* AJ from openclipart.org

- **File:Crystal_Clear_app_browser.png** *Source:* https://upload.wikimedia.org/wikipedia/commons/f/fe/Crystal_Clear_app_browser.png *License:* LGPL *Contributors:* All Crystal icons were posted by the author as LGPL on kde-look *Original artist:* Everaldo Coelho and YellowIcon

- **File:Crystal_Clear_app_kedit.svg** *Source:* https://upload.wikimedia.org/wikipedia/commons/e/e8/Crystal_Clear_app_kedit.svg *License:* LGPL *Contributors:* Sabine MINICONI *Original artist:* Sabine MINICONI

- **File:Crystal_Clear_device_cdrom_unmount.png** *Source:* https://upload.wikimedia.org/wikipedia/commons/1/10/Crystal_Clear_device_cdrom_unmount.png *License:* LGPL *Contributors:* All Crystal Clear icons were posted by the author as LGPL on kde-look; *Original artist:* Everaldo Coelho and YellowIcon;

- **File:Edit-clear.svg** *Source:* https://upload.wikimedia.org/wikipedia/en/f/f2/Edit-clear.svg *License:* Public domain *Contributors:* The *Tango! Desktop Project. Original artist:*
  The people from the Tango! project. And according to the meta-data in the file, specifically: "Andreas Nilsson, and Jakub Steiner (although minimally)."

- **File:Emoji_u1f4f1.svg** *Source:* https://upload.wikimedia.org/wikipedia/commons/1/17/Emoji_u1f4f1.svg *License:* Apache License 2.0 *Contributors:* https://code.google.com/p/noto/ *Original artist:* Google

- **File:Example_of_Domain_Slamming_phishing_email_by_Network_Solutions.png** *Source:* https://upload.wikimedia.org/wikipedia/commons/b/bd/Example_of_Domain_Slamming_phishing_email_by_Network_Solutions.png *License:* CC BY-SA 3.0 *Contributors:* Screen capture from my Inbox
  Previously published: None *Original artist:* Noloader

- **File:Fbi_duquesne.jpg** *Source:* https://upload.wikimedia.org/wikipedia/commons/0/07/Fbi_duquesne.jpg *License:* Public domain *Contributors:* ? *Original artist:* ?

- **File:Firefox_2.0.0.1_Phising_Alert.png** *Source:* https://upload.wikimedia.org/wikipedia/commons/6/68/Firefox_2.0.0.1_Phising_Alert.png *License:* CC-BY-SA-3.0 *Contributors:* No machine-readable source provided. Own work assumed (based on copyright claims). *Original artist:* No machine-readable author provided. KErosEnE~commonswiki assumed (based on copyright claims).

- **File:Flag_of_Iran.svg** *Source:* https://upload.wikimedia.org/wikipedia/commons/c/ca/Flag_of_Iran.svg *License:* Public domain *Contributors:* URL http://www.isiri.org/portal/files/std/1.htm and an English translation / interpretation at URL http://flagspot.net/flags/ir'.html *Original artist:* Various

- **File:Folder_Hexagonal_Icon.svg** *Source:* https://upload.wikimedia.org/wikipedia/en/4/48/Folder_Hexagonal_Icon.svg *License:* Cc-by-sa-3.0 *Contributors:* ? *Original artist:* ?

- **File:Hokoji-Bell-M1767.jpg** *Source:* https://upload.wikimedia.org/wikipedia/commons/7/74/Hokoji-Bell-M1767.jpg *License:* Public domain *Contributors:* No machine-readable source provided. Own work assumed (based on copyright claims). *Original artist:* No machine-readable author provided. Fg2 assumed (based on copyright claims).

- **File:Hokoji-BellDetail-M1767.jpg** *Source:* https://upload.wikimedia.org/wikipedia/commons/c/c9/Hokoji-BellDetail-M1767.jpg *License:* Public domain *Contributors:* Own work *Original artist:* Fg2

- **File:Internet_map_1024_-_transparent,_inverted.png** *Source:* https://upload.wikimedia.org/wikipedia/commons/3/3f/Internet_map_1024_-_transparent%2C_inverted.png *License:* CC BY 2.5 *Contributors:* Originally from the English Wikipedia; description page is/was here. *Original artist:* The Opte Project

- **File:Logo_sociology.svg** *Source:* https://upload.wikimedia.org/wikipedia/commons/a/a6/Logo_sociology.svg *License:* Public domain *Contributors:* Own work *Original artist:* Tomeq183

- **File:Marbleboot.jpg** *Source:* https://upload.wikimedia.org/wikipedia/commons/4/49/Marbleboot.jpg *License:* CC-BY-SA-3.0 *Contributors:* Own work *Original artist:* Rolf Müller (User:Rolfmueller)

- **File:Merge-arrow.svg** *Source:* https://upload.wikimedia.org/wikipedia/commons/a/aa/Merge-arrow.svg *License:* Public domain *Contributors:* ? *Original artist:* ?

- **File:Merge-arrows.svg** *Source:* https://upload.wikimedia.org/wikipedia/commons/5/52/Merge-arrows.svg *License:* Public domain *Contributors:* ? *Original artist:* ?

- **File:Mergefrom.svg** *Source:* https://upload.wikimedia.org/wikipedia/commons/0/0f/Mergefrom.svg *License:* Public domain *Contributors:* ? *Original artist:* ?

- **File:Monitor_padlock.svg** *Source:* https://upload.wikimedia.org/wikipedia/commons/7/73/Monitor_padlock.svg *License:* CC BY-SA 3.0 *Contributors:* Transferred from en.wikipedia; transferred to Commons by User:Logan using CommonsHelper. *Original artist:* Lunarbunny (talk). Original uploader was Lunarbunny at en.wikipedia

- **File:NewsOnAir.org.jpg** *Source:* https://upload.wikimedia.org/wikipedia/en/d/dd/NewsOnAir.org.jpg *License:* Fair use *Contributors:* http://www.hotforsecurity.com/wp-content/uploads/2014/05/newsonair.jpeg *Original artist:* ?

- **File:Newscaster.jpg** *Source:* https://upload.wikimedia.org/wikipedia/en/8/8c/Newscaster.jpg *License:* Fair use *Contributors:* http://www.isightpartners.com/wp-content/uploads/2014/05/Newscaster-Blog-Image.jpg *Original artist:* ?

- **File:OPSEC_alert_--_What_is_social_engineering....jpg** *Source:* https://upload.wikimedia.org/wikipedia/commons/0/0e/OPSEC_alert_--_What_is_social_engineering....jpg *License:* Public domain *Contributors:* https://secure.wikimedia.org/wikipedia/commons/w/index.php?title=File%3AThe_Wire_Issue42v12.pdf&page=3 *Original artist:* JTF-GTMO

- **File:OnlineRomanceScamTarget.PNG** *Source:* https://upload.wikimedia.org/wikipedia/commons/f/fe/OnlineRomanceScamTarget.PNG *License:* Public domain *Contributors:* Internet Crime Complaint Center: 2011 Crime Report *Original artist:* Internet Crime Complaint Center

- **File:PhishingTrustedBank.png** *Source:* https://upload.wikimedia.org/wikipedia/commons/d/d0/PhishingTrustedBank.png *License:* Public domain *Contributors:* en:Image:PhishingTrustedBank.png *Original artist:* Andrew Levine

- **File:Phishing_chart_Oct_2004_to_June_2005.svg** *Source:* https://upload.wikimedia.org/wikipedia/commons/5/55/Phishing_chart_Oct_2004_to_June_2005.svg *License:* Public domain *Contributors:* Own work *Original artist:* Offnfopt

- **File:Pranknet.jpg** *Source:* https://upload.wikimedia.org/wikipedia/en/7/7c/Pranknet.jpg *License:* Fair use *Contributors:* http://www.thesmokinggun.com/archive/years/2009/0803091pranknet1.html *Original artist:* ?

- **File:Question_book-new.svg** *Source:* https://upload.wikimedia.org/wikipedia/en/9/99/Question_book-new.svg *License:* Cc-by-sa-3.0 *Contributors:* Created from scratch in Adobe Illustrator. Based on Image:Question book.png created by User:Equazcion *Original artist:* Tkgd2007

- **File:Robin_Sage.png** *Source:* https://upload.wikimedia.org/wikipedia/en/5/55/Robin_Sage.png *License:* Fair use *Contributors:* ThePOC.net *Original artist:* ?

- **File:Scale_of_justice_2.svg** *Source:* https://upload.wikimedia.org/wikipedia/commons/0/0e/Scale_of_justice_2.svg *License:* Public domain *Contributors:* Own work *Original artist:* DTR

- **File:Scam_Watch_1280x720.ogg** *Source:* https://upload.wikimedia.org/wikipedia/commons/1/17/Scam_Watch_1280x720.ogg *License:* Public domain *Contributors:* Federal Trade Commission website *Original artist:* Federal Trade Commission

38.7.3 Content license